Transforming C
Networks to In
Networking

Pieter-Jan Nefkens

Cisco Press

221 River Street

Hoboken, NJ 07030 USA

Transforming Campus Networks to Intent-Based Networking

Pieter-Jan Nefkens

Published by:

Cisco Press
221 River Street
Hoboken, NJ 07030 USA

1 2019

Library of Congress Control Number: 2019914065

ISBN-13: 978-0-13-546633-9

ISBN-10: 0-13-546633-4

Warning and Disclaimer

This book is designed to provide information about Intent-Based Networking. Every effort has been made to make this book as complete and as accurate as possible, but no warranty or fitness is implied.

The information is provided on an "as is" basis. The authors, Cisco Press, and Cisco Systems, Inc., shall have neither liability nor responsibility to any person or entity with respect to any loss or damages arising from the information contained in this book or from the use of the discs or programs that may accompany it.

The opinions expressed in this book belong to the author and are not necessarily those of Cisco Systems, Inc.

Trademark Acknowledgments

All terms mentioned in this book that are known to be trademarks or service marks have been appropriately capitalized. Cisco Press or Cisco Systems, Inc., cannot attest to the accuracy of this information. Use of a term in this book should not be regarded as affecting the validity of any trademark or service mark.

Special Sales

For information about buying this title in bulk quantities, or for special sales opportunities (which may include electronic versions; custom cover designs; and content particular to your business, training goals, marketing focus, or branding interests), please contact our corporate sales department at corpsales@pearsoned.com or (800) 382-3419.

For government sales inquiries, please contact governmentsales@pearsoned.com.

For questions about sales outside the U.S., please contact intlcs@pearson.com.

Feedback Information

At Cisco Press, our goal is to create in-depth technical books of the highest quality and value. Each book is crafted with care and precision, undergoing rigorous development that involves the unique expertise of members from the professional technical community.

Readers' feedback is a natural continuation of this process. If you have any comments regarding how we could improve the quality of this book, or otherwise alter it to better suit your needs, you can contact us through email at feedback@ciscopress.com. Please make sure to include the book title and ISBN in your message.

We greatly appreciate your assistance.

Editor-in-Chief: Mark Taub	**Technical Editors:** Denise Donohue, Shawn Wargo
Alliances Manager, Cisco Press: Arezou Gol	**Editorial Assistant:** Cindy Teeters
Director, Product Management: Brett Bartow	**Designer:** Chuti Prasertsith
Managing Editor: Sandra Schroeder	**Composition:** codeMantra
Development Editor: Christopher A. Cleveland	**Indexer:** Ken Johnson
Project Editor: Mandie Frank	**Proofreader:** Gill Editorial Services
Copy Editor: Geneil Breeze	

Americas Headquarters	Asia Pacific Headquarters	Europe Headquarters
Cisco Systems, Inc.	Cisco Systems (USA) Pte. Ltd.	Cisco Systems International BV
San Jose, CA	Singapore	Amsterdam, The Netherlands

Cisco has more than 200 offices worldwide. Addresses, phone numbers, and fax numbers are listed on the Cisco Website at **www.cisco.com/go/offices**.

Credits

Figure 2-3a   Shutterstock

Figure 2-3b   Shutterstock

Figure 3-1   Courtesy of The Open Group

Figure 6-11   Screenshot of NetBrain Technologies © NetBrain Technologies, Inc

Figure 9-2   Courtesy of Everett M. "Ev" Rogers

Figure 10-2   Screenshot of iPhone app © 2019 Apple Inc.

Contents at a Glance

Contents

About the Author

Pieter-Jan Nefkens is a long-term Dutch-based IT and network consultant. From early on in his career he has been connecting devices and people, even before the Internet era. Pieter-Jan started his career immediately as an entrepreneur in IT with expertise in networking, security, virtualization, and active software development. Throughout his 20+ years of experience as a consultant, he has always been on top of new trends and technologies and applied them through implementation projects and consultancy to solve specific business problems of his customers, varying from small companies to large international operating enterprises. Pieter-Jan firmly believes that you can only consult and apply technologies if you have used them yourself. Pieter-Jan has always had a strong and close relationship with Cisco since the start of his career, resulting in his participation in beta tests and early field trials, often being one of the first to deploy a new network technology.

Sharing and applying new technology is in the DNA of Pieter-Jan, which resulted in his becoming a Cisco Champion since 2017. Besides networking consultancy, Pieter-Jan also participated in standardization processes for inland shipping across Europe.

Over the past years, Pieter-Jan has been working for both the Dutch government as well as his own consultancy company.

About the Technical Reviewers

Denise Donohue has worked with information systems since the mid-1990s, and network architecture since 2004. During that time she has worked with a wide range of networks, private and public, of all sizes, across most industries. Her focus is on aligning business and technology. Denise has authored several Cisco Press books and frequently shares her knowledge in webinars and seminars, and at conferences. She holds CCIE #9566 in Routing and Switching.

Shawn Wargo is a Principal Engineer of Technical Marketing (PTME) for the Cisco Systems Enterprise Product Marketing team. Shawn has been with Cisco since 1999, and worked in both TAC and Engineering, before becoming a TME in 2010. Shawn primarily focuses on Catalyst multi-layer switching products, with special emphasis on next-generation hardware (for example, Catalyst 9000) and software products (for example, Cisco SD-Access).

Dedications

I would like to dedicate this book to my late father, Piet, whose guidance and counsel I still miss, and my lovely and wonderful partner, Renate, who has been a great support for me throughout the complete process from idea to actual writing of this book.

Acknowledgments

I would like to thank and acknowledge several people who have helped me directly or indirectly with the necessary skills that enabled me to write this book.

First of all, I would like to thank my partner, Renate, and our two beautiful daughters for believing in me, accepting me for who I am, and supporting me when things got a bit more challenging.

I would also like to thank my parents for allowing me to follow my dreams and to provide me with the opportunities to learn skills and gain knowledge. I would specifically like to thank my late father, Piet Nefkens; Jos van Splunder; and Lex de Lijster for teaching and coaching me that consultancy in IT is only successful if you first understand the business and then apply technology to solve a specific problem.

A big thank you goes out to Patrick Nefkens for reviewing my rough writing material and providing honest and candid feedback. It helped me stay on track.

I would also like to thank Dick van den Heuvel for providing me the opportunity to start working with DNA Center and help the team along with automation.

A thank you also goes out to Brett Bartow, Chris Cleveland, and everybody else at Cisco Press for believing in this new concept of merging process and organizational aspects with technologies in a single Cisco Press book.

I would also like to thank Brett Shore, Lauren Friedman, and Andrea Fisher Bardeau for running the Cisco Champions program and allowing me into this program, and—via the program and meeting Brett Bartow—making this book possible.

And, well, a very big and warm thank you goes out to all Cisco Champions. I am honored to be part of that warm community of experts on networking for some years now. All feedback, opinions, good recipes, and meetups have always been great and fun.

Also, a special acknowledgment goes out to the Piano Guys. Their music allowed me to get into the necessary flow and focus for writing this book.

Finally, I would like to thank my technical reviewers Shawn Wargo and Denise Donohue for their patience, commitment, and support in the adventure of writing my first book.

Reader Services

Register your copy at www.ciscopress.com/title/9780135466339 for convenient access to downloads, updates, and corrections as they become available. To start the registration process, go to www.ciscopress.com/register and log in or create an account*. Enter the product ISBN 9780135466339 and click **Submit**. When the process is complete, you will find any available bonus content under Registered Products.

*Be sure to check the box that you would like to hear from us to receive exclusive discounts on future editions of this product.

Command Syntax Conventions

The conventions used to present command syntax in this book are the same conventions used in the IOS Command Reference. The Command Reference describes these conventions as follows:

- **Boldface** indicates commands and keywords that are entered literally as shown. In actual configuration examples and output (not general command syntax), boldface indicates commands that are manually input by the user (such as a **show** command).

- *Italic* indicates arguments for which you supply actual values.

- Vertical bars (|) separate alternative, mutually exclusive elements.

- Square brackets ([ ]) indicate an optional element.

- Braces ({ }) indicate a required choice.

- Braces within brackets ([{ }]) indicate a required choice within an optional element.

Introduction

Intent-Based Networking (IBN) is the next revolution in networking that Cisco, Juniper, Gartner, and others are conveying. Cisco explains the concept with the Network Intuitive communication and solutions such as Cisco DNA Center, Software Defined Access, and Cisco SD-WAN. But IBN is much more than just a combination of those technologies and solutions. It is also a concept on how a modern network infrastructure should be designed, managed, and operated, leveraging Cisco Digital Network Architecture as the foundation.

And although the concept of IBN is accepted by the industry as the next generation of network infrastructures, many IT specialists and organizations face the challenge of how to design and transform network infrastructures and network operation teams into IBN, specifically for existing environments. This challenge is mostly seen with questions like "Yes, I do understand about IBN but how do I get started?"; "Now that I installed Cisco DNA Center, what can I do with it?"; or "How can IBN help me in providing services faster to my internal users?"

This book is written as a compendium to that challenge and its related questions, specifically focusing on campus enterprise networks. This book provides a detailed explanation of IBN, specifically related to campus networks. With that background information, this book documents a unique four-phase approach to answer the question of how an organization can get started on the transformation (or journey as some call it) to IBN for existing campus networks.

As IBN requires changes in both technologies (and how they are applied) and organizations (how networks are managed), this book also provides tips on how change can be realized throughout an organization. This book should be of help and support for anybody who wants to transform their network into an Intent-Based Network.

A large part of my career as an engineer and consultant has been focused on enabling change and making change happen. The change always involved technology in one way or the other, primarily with use cases where technology would solve today's or tomorrow's problems, or sometimes the technology would open up new innovative ideas and concepts. As an external specialist, my role was always to help and support the organization with the change of work.

Intent-Based Networking will bring very interesting times of change to the networking industry in general. The network, specifically the campus, will play an important role in the future of any organization. The rate of change is increasing too, which I see in my day-to-day work as well. The ability to deploy intents in this manner is for me only the first step. What would be the next step when you can do this? The opportunities are really unlimited.

I have used my personal experiences and observations throughout this book together with the concepts of Cisco DNA and IBN to support you on your journey to the next generation of networks.

I do hope that reading this book provides you with enough information and background on why and how to transform an existing campus and network operations team to the concept of Intent-Based Networking.

This book also has two appendixes that are used to provide you with conceptual background information on the technologies named throughout this book as well as reference configurations for the underlay of an Intent-Based Network.

Who Should Read This Book?

This book is written for network consultants, network architects (designers), senior network engineers, and IT managers who have any questions related to IBN and how existing campus networks can be transformed to IBN. A background in networking is helpful when reading this book, but a deep technical understanding is not required as each technology is explained at a conceptual level in an appendix.

How This Book Is Organized

This book covers a diverse set of topics related to the successful transformation of an existing network to IBN and is divided into three logical parts that are best read sequentially:

Part I, "**Overview of Intent-Based Networking,**" provides you with background information related to campus networks and the concept of Intent-Based Networking (IBN). This part contains a logical buildup of information, starting from common classic campus network deployments, why change is required through architecture frameworks, to the concept of IBN. If you are already familiar with the specific topic of a chapter, it is possible to skip that chapter. Part I includes the following chapters:

- **Chapter 1, "Classic Campus Network Deployments"**: This chapter provides you with an overview of campus network deployments found in many organizations today at a conceptual level. The chapter does not provide many details on how technologies are configured and used within a campus network but focuses on the conceptual designs and choices for a campus network with the advantages and disadvantages of each choice. The chapter covers concepts such as a hierarchical campus network, a collapsed-core model, different wireless deployment models, and alternatives for typical networking technologies found in the campus network such as the Spanning Tree Protocol (STP).

- **Chapter 2, "Why Change Current Networks? A Need for Change"**: This chapter provides a summary of external trends, drivers (or forces), that require the current campus network design and operation to be changed to cope with these drivers. You will learn about external trends such as wireless/mobility, (Net)DevOps, complexity, cloud, and digitization.

- **Chapter 3, "Enterprise Architecture"**: This chapter describes the concept of enterprise architecture, why that is beneficial to enterprises in general and specific to a network design within the enterprise. You will learn that a network design (or architecture) is part of a larger technology architecture and an architecture for the enterprise or organization as a whole. This chapter uses the TOGAF® standard for enterprise architectures both as an introduction to enterprise architecture as well as an example for the relationship between network infrastructures and enterprise architecture.

- **Chapter 4, "Cisco Digital Network Architecture"**: This chapter provides you with a detailed explanation of Cisco Digital Network Architecture (DNA) that Cisco introduced in May 2016. Cisco DNA is an architecture that is intended to be the foundation for both modern state-of-the-art network infrastructures as well as the concept of Intent-Based Networking. You will learn the different requirements Cisco DNA has, the building blocks of its architecture, and the different design principles.

- **Chapter 5, "Intent-Based Networking"**: In this chapter you will learn the concept of Intent-Based Networking (IBN) via the explanation of what Intent means, how that can be applied to a network infrastructure, and how it relates to Cisco Digital Network Architecture. You will learn how IBN can help the network operations team cope with the changes described in Chapter 2 and be able to remain in control of the network. Chapter 5 also introduces two technical concepts, Software Defined Access and Classic VLANs, that can be used to deploy an Intent-Based Network. Intent-Based Network (or Intent-Enabled Network) is used throughout this book as a network that is configured based on the concept of Intent-Based Networking (IBN)—that is, IBN describes the concept, and Intent-Based Network is an implementation of that concept.

- **Chapter 6, "Tools for Intent"**: This chapter provides a short overview of the tools that are available to enable Intent-Based Networking within the campus network. In this chapter you will learn about important concepts within IBN, such as automation and assurance, and which tools can fulfill those requirements for the concept of IBN.

Part II, "Transforming to an Intent-Based Network," describes a four-phased approach that supports you in a successful transformation to Intent-Based Networking, including tips, tricks, and problems you might face during the transformation. It is best to read this part completely and not skip a chapter as they are built on one another.

- **Chapter 7, "Phase One: Identifying Challenges"**: This chapter describes the first phase of the transformation and is all about identifying the requirements (I used the word *challenges* on purpose, as that is more positive and challenges can be solved) within a campus network and getting the proper support and commitment. You will learn that IBN is a concept that not only involves (new) technologies and sets specific hardware requirements but also sets requirements and expectations on the organization. You will learn which challenges are to be identified on the required hardware and software as well as challenges related to the organization and its processes. The chapter ends with an action plan that contains details on how to approach the transformation to IBN.

- **Chapter 8, "Phase Two: Prepare for Intent"**: This chapter describes phase two of the transformation. Phase two is used to prepare the campus network and the organization for the transformation. It starts with solving all the challenges identified in the previous phase. After these challenges are solved, the remaining steps of the phase focus on preparing the network (and network operations team) for a successful transformation to IBN. You will learn about the standardization of the campus network, the introduction of automation and assurance to the network operations team, and why these steps are important for IBN. These steps also include tips on why and how to execute them. The last section of this chapter contains information about risks that you might encounter during this phase, including some suggestions on how to cope with them.

- **Chapter 9, "Phase Three: Design, Deploy, and Extend"**: This chapter provides all information required to actually transform the campus network to an Intent-Based Network. You will learn two technology concepts (Software Defined Access and classic VLAN) that can be used to deploy your campus network with their pros and cons. You will be executing sequential steps to gradually implement IBN on the campus network. As with the previous phases, a special section on risks for this phase allows you to identify and prepare for potential problems.

- **Chapter 10, "Phase Four: Enable Intent"**: This chapter describes the last phase of the transformation; now that the campus network is transformed to IBN, it is time to fully take advantage of the possibilities created. The chapter involves a strategy on how you can introduce IBN to the rest of the organization, including a special methodology to allow the campus network to deliver services to the business on demand.

Part III, "Organizational Aspects," is quite a different part compared to the first two. Whereas the first two are primarily focused on background information and hands-on for the transformation, this part provides information on the impact that IBN has on the organization. This part's chapters can be read individually and are as follows:

- **Chapter 11, "Architecture Frameworks"**: This chapter provides a quick recap of architecture frameworks and provides an insight to how IBN will impact and change the traditional enterprise architecture frameworks.

- **Chapter 12, "Enabling the Digital Business"**: This chapter provides a more detailed description of the concept of digitalization and digital business. It describes how Intent-Based Networking fits within (and enables) the digital business and what impact this will have on an organizational level.

- **Chapter 13, "IT Operations"**: This chapter describes the relationship between IBN and common IT operations. It provides an introduction to common IT operation models such as ITIL, DevOps, and Lean. It also describes what impact and change IBN will have on these IT operation models.

- **Chapter 14, "Tips to Make Your IBN Journey a Success"**: The transformation to IBN involves quite some change, including technical, organizational, and individual. This chapter provides background information and tips on how change can be achieved at both an individual and an organizational level. It covers information on human change and associated fears, and it provides tips you can use to make the change happen. It also contains some final tips that can be used to make the transformation to IBN last.

Part IV, "Appendixes" This book also has appendixes that provide you with conceptual background information on the technologies named throughout this book as well as reference configurations for the underlay of an Intent-Based Network:

■ **Appendix A, "Campus Network Technologies":** This appendix provides a conceptual overview of the different technologies used in this book that are commonly found on a campus network. This appendix does not provide a detailed technical explanation of the technologies but rather a more conceptual summary of the technology and how it is applied. This appendix is a recommended read for less-technical readers to provide a more common understanding of the technologies;

■ **Appendix B, "Sample Configurations":** This appendix provides a set of sample configurations that can be used on the campus network to implement IBN; this appendix is rather technical as it contains specific configuration elements. It is provided as a head start to Intent-Based Networking for network architects and engineers.

Part I

Overview of Intent-Based Networking

What is Intent-Based Networking (IBN)? Is it a new technology? Is it a concept? Or is it both? And why would you need Intent-Based Networking? This part provides you with an overview of common campus network topologies, why these topologies need to change, and what Intent-Based Networking really is and how it fits within the enterprise.

Chapter 1

Classic Campus Network Deployments

If you look at current campus networks from a design perspective, not much has changed in the past fifteen years of networking. Speeds have of course been increased, and full-duplex is now the default, but almost all campus networks are still about Spanning Tree Protocol (STP), assigning VLANs to ports, and providing connectivity to applications, regardless of whether these applications reside in internal datacenters or in the cloud. Spanning Tree Protocol and VLANs were introduced very early in the history of campus networks for scalability and redundancy purposes. Security has just added an extra layer of complexity for configuration. Actually, the campus network has become so reliable and available that many end users (and also managers) view the campus network the same way they view running water and power—the network is just there.

Cisco provides a validated design for campus networks on its website inside the design zone (https://www.cisco.com/go/designzone/). These Cisco Validated Designs (CVD) are lab-tested and provide detailed explanations of the used technologies, possible design choices, and reference configurations that work for most campus networks. Although the design (and configuration) is validated, it does not automatically mean that the design will fit all campus networks. There are always corner cases or specific requirements from the organization that will require small (or large) changes to the design and the configuration.

This chapter is not a repetition of the most recent CVD for campus networks but provides an overview of commonly found campus network deployments. The chapter covers the following topologies:

- Three-tier campus network topology
- Collapsed-core campus network topology
- Single-switch campus network topology
- Design choices related to campus networks

Campus Design Fundamentals

In general, the campus (area) network is that part of an enterprise network installed in buildings and offices (and more recently also industrial environments). It is used to connect user endpoints, such as computers, laptops, phones, sensors, cameras, and so on to the enterprise network. It's the first step in connecting users to the enterprise network. The campus network consists of both a wired and a wireless local area network.

A campus network design (or topology) is commonly built using three distinct functional layers, as illustrated in Figure 1-1.

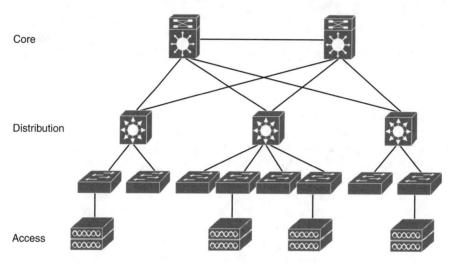

Figure 1-1   *Overview of Campus Functional Layers*

The access layer is where endpoints, both user-specific as well as generic, connect to the enterprise network. The access layer consists of both wired as well as wireless high-speed network access. Because this is the layer where endpoints connect, security services are a critical part of this layer. These security services are implemented using IEEE 802.1X network access control, port-based access lists, IP-based access lists, and possibly Cisco TrustSec. As different types of endpoints connect to the same infrastructure, VLANs are used to isolate different functional devices, and Quality of Service is used to provide control over the available bandwidth for specific applications or services, such as video or voice conversations.

The second functional layer is known as the distribution layer. This layer provides scalability and resilience as they are used to logically aggregate the uplinks of access switches to one or more distribution switches. Scalability is accomplished via the aggregation of those access switches, while the resilience is accomplished because of the logical separation with multiple distribution switches.

If, for example, an access switch has a failure, this failure is contained at the distribution switch to which that access switch is connected. Other distribution switches (and thus other access switches) will not experience problems because of that broken access switch. The same level of resilience would be difficult to accomplish if that misbehaving switch is connected to multiple distribution switches. It would require a more complex configuration on both distribution switches. This added complexity in configuration can be reduced by using advanced technologies where two physical switches are configured in such a way that they act as one. This can be accomplished using Virtual Switching System (VSS) or StackWise Virtual on Cisco Catalyst switches or virtual PortChannel (vPC) for Cisco Nexus switches.

The core layer is the highest level in the hierarchical network. Its function is primarily to route traffic between the different campus network switches and the organization's datacenter, Internet, cloud services, and other connected services. The core layer is required to keep the configuration and operation of the campus network manageable as the number of distribution switches increases in the campus network.

If, for example, an enterprise had six distribution switches and no core layer, each of those six switches would require a connection with all other distribution switches, resulting in a total of 15 (5 + 4 + 3 + 2 + 1) uplinks. If a seventh building were introduced, the number of uplinks needing to be managed would be increased by 6, and so on. Figure 1-2 shows the network diagram for a network without a core layer.

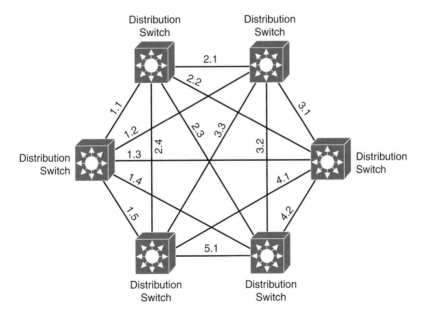

Figure 1-2 *Campus Network Without Core Layer*

With the introduction of a core layer, where each distribution switch is connected to two core routers (or switches), the network and configuration become much more manageable and scalable, as can be seen in Figure 1-3.

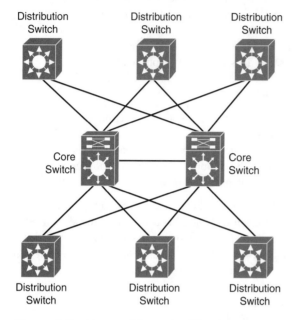

Figure 1-3 *Campus Network with a Core Layer*

In this setup, each distribution switch has two uplinks, one to each core switch. If an extra distribution switch needs to be added to this network, only two extra links on the core switch are required instead of adding six links, as shown previously in Figure 1-2. In case of a failing distribution switch, only two interfaces on the core switch will see that issue instead of having an issue on all distribution switches. The other distribution switches remain active with no errors or failures.

These three layers combined provide for a campus network topology that is scalable, resilient, and manageable. The topology also allows for adding security, quality of service, and other network services that the enterprise could require.

Three-Tier Design

The most extensive campus network topology is called a three-tier network design. In this design, the three functional layers described in the previous section are all executed by separate switches and other network equipment. Figure 1-4 displays a large campus network based on a three-tier hierarchy.

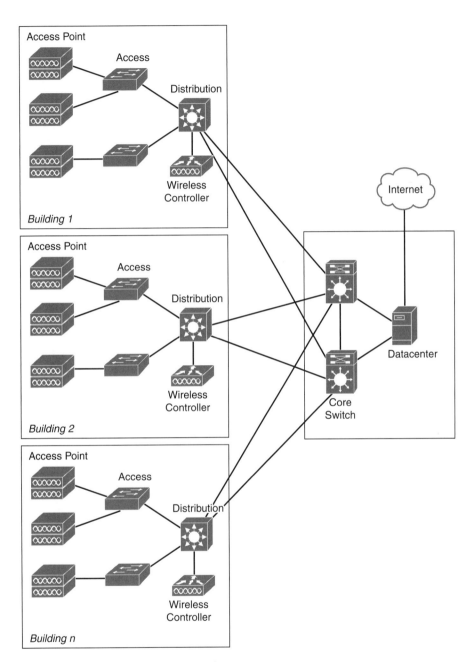

Figure 1-4 *Large Campus Network*

The three-tier campus network is mostly deployed in environments where multiple offices and buildings are located closely together, allowing for high-speed fiber connections to the headquarters owned by the enterprise. Examples could be the campus network at a university, a hospital with multiple buildings, or a large enterprise with multiple buildings on a privately owned campus.

Two-Tier/Collapsed-Core Design

One of the more modern adoptions of the CVD campus design is a collapsed-core campus network. In this design, the function of the distribution switch and core switch is merged into a single switch. Figure 1-5 displays a collapsed-core campus network design.

The key principle behind this design is that there are no loops in the network. Each stack of access switches in a satellite equipment room is connected to the core switch using (usually two) uplinks combined into a single portchannel. The Wireless LAN Controller (WLC) is connected to the core switch, whereas the access points, printers, and workstations are connected to the access switch.

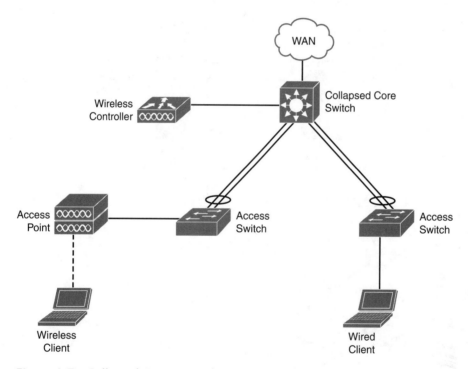

Figure 1-5 *Collapsed-Core Network*

Using local breakout for the wireless network, both wired and wireless clients will share the same functional IP space allocated to this campus network. The different wireless network topologies for campuses are described later in this chapter. It is, of course, possible to have the controller in the datacenter, with its own advantages and disadvantages.

It is common for a collapsed-core network to have the core switch configured in high availability. This is accomplished by having either two switches in a single stack or two core switches in VSS mode. In either design option, the uplinks from the access switches in the satellite equipment rooms are physically separated over the two core switches (that act as one). Even with this high availability, there are physically and logically still no loops in the network. This topology can have the added benefit of removing complexity such as Spanning Tree Protocol.

In general, the access switches act as a Layer 2 switch with a management IP and have all the VLANs defined for the campus network. The core switch provides the Layer 3 functionality for the different VLANs using switch virtual interfaces. The core switch in turn has Layer 3 uplinks to the WAN for connections to the datacenters and the Internet. Depending on requirements, it is possible to use VRF-Lite to logically separate the different IP networks into different VPNs over the WAN to provide isolation of different endpoints.

Collapsed-core campus network designs have become common and typical for a single (large) building.

Single-Switch Design

In smaller environments, such as branch offices or smaller enterprises with fewer endpoints connecting to the network, it is not economically and functionally sound to have separations in the access, distribution, and core layers, so these functions are combined in a single switch. Figure 1-6 displays this network campus design.

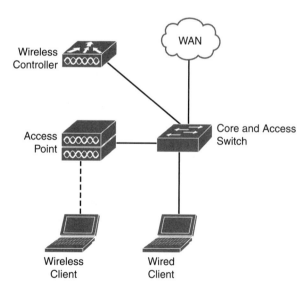

Figure 1-6 *Single-Switch Campus Network*

As the different functions are merged into a single switch, more complex technologies such as Spanning Tree are not required and can be disabled. This is similar to a collapsed-core network where Storm Control can be used to reduce the impact of broadcast storms on the network. The Layer 3 connections are usually configured on the same switch (most modern access switches support Layer 3 switching with static routing), but in very small networks the Layer 3 connections can also be handled by the router that provides connection to the WAN.

High availability in this type of campus network is, if required, accomplished by creating a stack of two switches, which allows the users to "patch over" the connections to the other switch in case of failure.

The wireless network design itself is dependent on the type of organization. If the campus network is a small branch in a larger enterprise, the access points are configured in FlexConnect, and the controller is located in the central datacenter. If the campus network is a small business or small enterprise, usually a small wireless LAN controller is connected to the access switch to provide wireless controller functionality. The controller functionality could also be cloud-based, depending on the chosen solution.

Wireless Networks

Wireless networks have become common in any enterprise network. In the past decade, the wireless network has changed from a nice-to-have feature (for management) to a mature network infrastructure that more often than not is the primary connecting interface for enterprise endpoints. Wireless networks make use of the shared frequencies in the 2.4Ghz and 5Ghz band. These bands, with distinct specifications within the different IEEE 802.11* standards, make the deployment of a wireless network a complex process that requires specialist knowledge. This section provides a conceptual overview of how Cisco wireless networks operate and which kind of wireless deployments are found in campus networks. Many Cisco-based wireless networks are controller-based wireless networks. In this concept, there is a wireless LAN controller (WLC) and access points.

The WLC is the central point of configuration and management for the complete deployment. The wireless networks, security settings, and configuration of IP interfaces for clients are defined within the configuration of the controller. Also, the operational management of the wireless spectrum is executed by the controller.

The access points (APs) have one or more wireless radios (most commonly two radios, one in 2.4Ghz and one in the 5Ghz band) and handle the communication of the wireless network. Commonly in campus networks, the access points are connected and powered from the wired switch. The access point itself does not have any configuration of its own but receives all information and configuration from the controller.

When an AP boots up, it obtains an IP address and attempts to find a controller. Once it finds the controller, it tries to register with that controller and establish a Control and Provisioning of Wireless Access Points (CAPWAP) tunnel. The CAPWAP tunnel is in essence a transport tunnel for both control traffic between the AP and the controller as well as client traffic.

Once the tunnel is established, the controller sends the proper wireless configuration settings to the AP. The radios are enabled and the wireless networks are broadcasted.

In turn, the AP listens for information on the wireless network and shares that information with the controller, so the controller can tune wireless parameters of all the APs in its control to provide as optimal as possible coverage and operation of the wireless network. This latter process of sharing information and managing wireless properties is also known as Radio Resource Management. Figure 1-7 displays a schematic approach of the CAPWAP tunnel and communication flow.

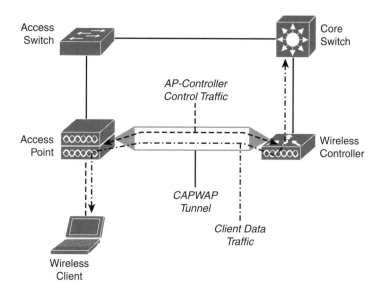

Figure 1-7 *Schematic Approach of a Wireless CAPWAP Tunnel and Communication Flow*

Once a wireless client wants to connect to the network, it tries to associate itself to a specific wireless network. The AP forwards that request to the controller. The controller in turn handles that association request and executes the authentication process for that client. In this process the AP forwards the messages between controller and client. Once the client is successfully authenticated and associated, a Layer 2 connection exists between the wireless client and the controller. The AP is in essence a bridge between the shared half-duplex wireless network and the controller, forwarding ethernet frames back and forth between the client and the controller. This is shown in Figure 1-7 as the open-arrow dash-dotted line marked as Client data traffic.

Based on this general controller principle, there are four common deployments for a Cisco wireless network:

- Central controller with central breakout
- Local controller with local breakout
- Central controller with FlexConnect
- Mobility Express

The following sections describe these deployments in more detail.

Central Controller with Central Breakout

In this deployment, several APs of different campus networks are registered and managed on a central controller inside the datacenter. The client traffic is transported via the CAPWAP tunnel over the WAN toward the central controller, and the wireless client traffic enters the wired network inside the datacenter. Figure 1-8 displays the topology for controller-based central breakout wireless network.

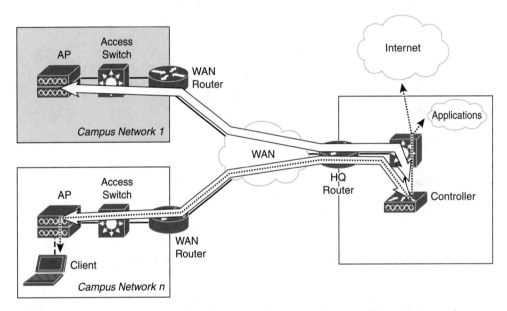

Figure 1-8   *Wireless Network Topology Based on Central Controller with Central Breakout*

The advantages of this setup are as follows:

- Only a single controller needs to be configured and managed for the complete enterprise wireless network.

- Traffic is transported from the different campus locations over the WAN toward the central controller so that client traffic can be inspected and optimally routed through to the enterprise applications or the Internet.

There are some disadvantages for this kind of deployment as well:

- If the controller has a problem, the problem is essentially replicated across all campus networks. This can have severe impact on being able to get maintenance windows for upgrades, as the complete wireless network is updated all at once.

- There is a huge dependency on the WAN. If the WAN is disconnected, the wireless network is down as well.

- Also, communication between clients on two different APs always flows through the controller, which adds extra load to the WAN.

Local Controller with Local Breakout

In this specific deployment, the controller is placed within each campus network. CAPWAP traffic remains onsite (within the campus network), and the breakout for wireless clients is from the location of the WLC. Figure 1-9 displays a wireless topology based on local controller with local breakout.

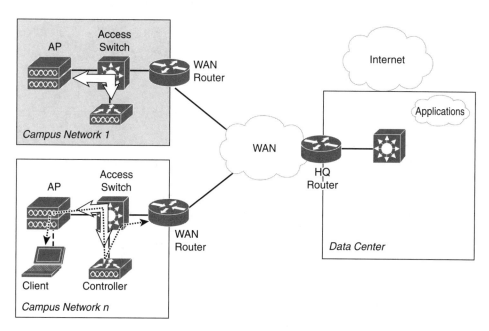

Figure 1-9   *Wireless Topology with Local Controller and Local Breakout*

One of the key benefits of this deployment is that the wireless network of a campus location is not dependent on the availability of the WAN. Another benefit is manageability and the fault domain. If an onsite controller is broken, only that specific location has wireless issues. The drawback, of course, is that each campus location needs to have its own controller, which not only adds cost but also introduces the requirement of a central tool to manage the configuration of the distributed controllers.

Central Controller with FlexConnect

This deployment option uses a central controller for the configuration and management of the APs; however, the traffic of clients is not sent out via the central controller but locally over the Ethernet interface of the AP. Figure 1-10 displays the topology of a central controller with FlexConnect.

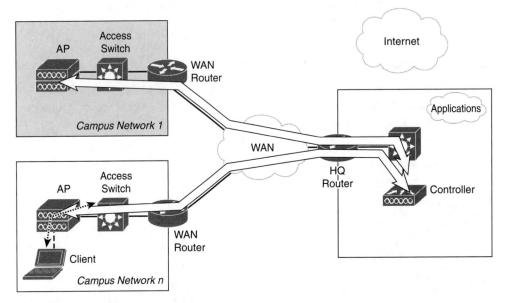

Figure 1-10   *Wireless Topology Based on Central Controller with FlexConnect*

The primary targets for this kind of deployment are smaller branch locations with up to 100 APs inside the campus network. Although this feature works well, clients roaming between two access points will incur a mac-move from one port on the switch to another. If this happens frequently, the switch will log messages that can be interpreted as an error, while it is normal behavior.

Mobility Express

Instead of using a dedicated local controller for radio resource management and configuration management, it is now also possible to use Mobility Express. Mobility Express is available on 802.11ac Wave2 access points. It allows the AP to become a lightweight controller to provide central configuration, radio resource management, and some other features to APs in the local network. Mobility Express is limited up to 50 APs, depending on the type of 802.11ac Wave2 AP that is used as controller. FlexConnect is used for the breakout of client traffic, and failover is realized (and configured automatically) between all 802.11ac Wave2 access points in the network that can become a new master AP.

Functionally, the AP has controller software running besides the AP functions with a separate IP address and management. Figure 1-11 provides a schematic function of a Mobility Express–enabled access point.

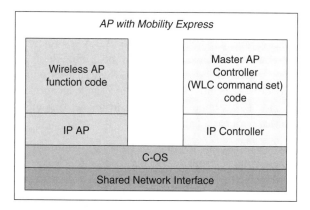

Figure 1-11   *Mobility Express Enabled Access Point*

Within the AP, the network interface is shared via the operating system (C-OS) to both the IP address of the AP as well as the controller software. Each has its own IP address, and the AP is managed by the IP address of the controller software.

Anchor Controller

On top of these four Cisco wireless network deployment options, there is also a special use case for wireless guest services that involves a second controller, called anchor controller. In this case, the specific wireless guest network is not terminated on the normal controller (which also terminates the AP), but the client traffic is forwarded via a second tunnel to the anchor controller. This anchor controller is often placed in a DMZ, to prevent wireless guest users from accessing the internal network.

Each deployment option for wireless has its own advantages and drawbacks. Which choice is valid depends on several factors, including not only technical but also organizational aspects, such as the size of the organization, number of campus sites, availability of the WAN, and security requirements. Cisco provides several design considerations and technical factors in its Wireless Deployment Guide. Of importance for campus networks is that the wireless network has become the primary connection option for many enterprise networks.

Design Choices

As with any design, several choices or options are available within the framework to adapt the concepts to the specific requirements of an enterprise, whether it is a single switch, collapsed core, or a full three-tier campus network. Two design choices genuinely affect the way the campus network behaves and have an impact on scalability and possibly even an impact on the transformation to Intent-Based Networking.

Handling Redundancy

There is one inherited complexity when it comes to local area networks (LANs). This complexity is redundancy in Layer 2 of a LAN. A Layer 2 network is built upon the assumption that all devices within the same Layer 2 domain are directly reachable from one another (for example, a single broadcast domain). Every device in a single broadcast domain can be reached over a single path. Furthermore, single paths in any network guarantee a single point of failure in case that path has a failure.

As a network engineer you want to remove these single points of failure without introducing too many complex problems. Over the years many concepts and protocols have been designed and implemented to overcome this problem in Layer 2. And thus there are some design choices in a hierarchical campus network design model.

The most common option to realize redundancy in a Layer 2 domain without having a loop in the network is Spanning Tree. It is a protocol that uses the shortest path algorithm from Moore-Dijkstra and a root election. Every Layer 2 network has a single root, and every other switch is connected in the most optimal path to that root switch. Every other alternative path is blocked for traffic by Spanning Tree Protocol. Figure 1-12 displays a campus network with Spanning Tree enabled where single uplinks are blocked.

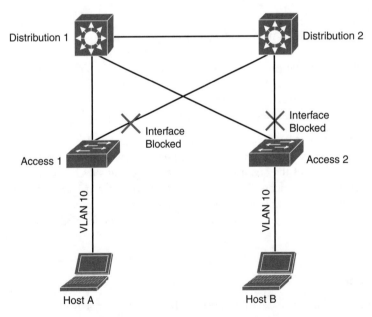

Figure 1-12   *Campus Network with Spanning Tree Blocking Uplinks*

There are a few drawbacks to Spanning Tree Protocol in general. One is that if the switch sees an incoming Bridge Protocol Data Unit (BPDU) packet, Spanning Tree Protocol will kick in and no traffic will flow as long as the shortest path algorithm is running. A second problem is that the root election is primarily based on a MAC address and priority. If you do not configure them, it is possible that the distribution switch is not configured as root, but instead an access switch or a non-manageable switch that is accidentally connected by an end user. Troubleshooting Spanning Tree Protocol is a complex task in large environments. And last but not least, every alternative path is blocked by Spanning Tree Protocol, so only half the available bandwidth is used.

Another option to have redundancy is to make the Layer 2 domains smaller and use Layer 3 on the redundant paths. As opposed to Layer 2, IP (as Layer 3 protocol) is designed with the assumption that multiple paths are available for the destination IP address. So if the uplinks between two layers are based on Layer 3, the problem of loops in the Layer 2 network is mitigated. Figure 1-13 provides a campus network with Layer 3–based connections between distribution and access layer.

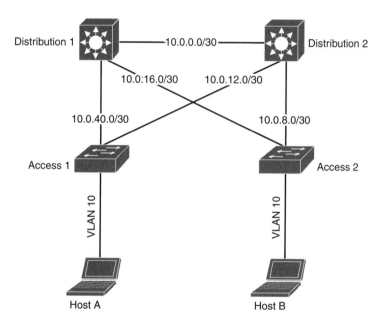

Figure 1-13 *Campus Network with Layer 3 Uplinks Between Access and Distribution Switches*

Unfortunately, using Layer 3, for example, between the access switch and the distribution switch, means that a host in VLAN10 on access switch A cannot talk to another host in the same VLAN10 on access switch B. Although these two VLANs have the same VLAN identifier, they are logically two separate broadcast domains. Another problem is the introduced complexity of configuring point-to-point IP addresses on the uplinks.

A third option to have redundancy in Layer 2 and using all bandwidth is by introducing technologies so that two physical switches act together as one, whether it is via a stack, Virtual Switching Solution (VSS) on Catalyst switches, or Virtual PortChannel (vPC) on Nexus switches. The access switch thinks it is communicating with a single switch over two interfaces bundled in a Portchannel. The technology is proven and is commonly used in campus networks.

Because there are no loops in this network, it is a valid design to either remove Spanning Tree configuration completely or use a single Spanning Tree instance for all VLANs in the campus network. By using technologies such as storm control, it is possible to prevent broadcast storms and loops. BPDU Guard helps in preventing other switches from introducing Spanning Tree in the campus network. You do have to be careful that the BPDU packets are sent over the default member interface of a portchannel and not over the portchannel itself. So you cannot use Spanning Tree Protocol to detect failures of the portchannel. Figure 1-14 displays a Collapsed-core campus topology with VSS.

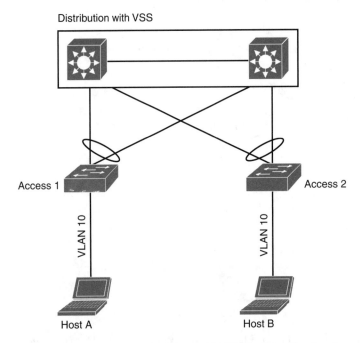

Figure 1-14   *Campus Topology with VSS in Distribution Layer*

Other technologies such as UniDirectional Link Detection (UDLD) can be used for that matter. Removing STP provides the benefit of preserving single path broadcast domains, but introducing VSS can have a (limited) drawback on complexity for operating and troubleshooting the distribution switch. The benefit of not having Spanning Tree often outweighs this disadvantage. In smaller campus networks a stack of Cisco switches can also be used to accomplish similar functional behavior.

In general, all options are used extensively in campus topologies. It is very common nowadays to use VSS or VPC for connecting access switches to the distribution switches. It is a valid design option as long as access switches are not interconnected and loops still exist in access switches. In some environments, such as a campus network for a production facility, VSS or VPC cannot be used because of cabling restrictions (for example, some satellite rooms can be connected only via another satellite equipment room), and Layer 3 can be a good option in such situations. It is up to the network designer to balance out all options in conjunction with the specific requirements and physical constraints of the campus network to create the most optimal campus network design with redundancy.

Cloud-Managed

The cloud is perhaps not immediately thought of as a design choice for campus networks, but actually there are several situations where it does have an effect on your deployment.

With the acquisition of Meraki, Cisco now also has a completely different line of solutions for the design and deployment of campus networks. Meraki networks are based on two key design principles:

■ **Cloud-managed:** Every Meraki device, whether switch, access point, or firewall, is managed through a portal in the cloud. The devices might have a limited interface to do the minimal required configuration to get the device connected to the Internet. The rest of the configuration is managed completely through a cloud portal. If you want to create a new wireless network (SSID), it's done via the cloud portal and pushed to the access points. Creating a new VLAN is done via the portal and again pushed via Internet to the device.

If there is no Internet connection, the switch or access point will continue to work; you just cannot manage the device.

■ **Easy graphical user interface:** The other key design principle is ease of use. As with many cloud-managed services, they are commonly easy to use and configure. (It's part of the business case for cloud-managed services.) A Meraki engineer once said that if a technology or feature cannot be enabled/configured with the flip of a switch in the portal, that feature will not be implemented. Another reason for this key design principle is also that Meraki networks are aimed for small and medium enterprises. These enterprises usually do not have a fully trained network operations staff available but more a general systems operator/manager and external partners that supply extra hands and experience if needed. So configuring a Meraki network (and its devices) needs to be simple and easy.

These design principles are, of course, reflected in their network switches and access points. And although the conceptual structure of a campus network topology (three-tier, collapsed-core, or single-switch) is not dramatically changing, there are some extra design choices that can be made for some (smaller or specific) situations.

Perhaps one of the most visible extra design choices is for wireless networks. With Meraki, it is now possible to use a cloud-based controller instead of having a controller on the campus network. By not having a local controller (for smaller collapsed-core and single-switch enterprise environments), there is a reduction in the number of network devices at a specific site, and by not using a central controller, a possible strain on the

WAN (both bandwidth as well as availability) is also reduced. As long as the site has an Internet connection, there is a wireless connection. Another benefit is that the cloud portal provides an easy overview of connected clients and sites, which can make remote troubleshooting easier.

As with any design choice, there are also drawbacks. Specifically in larger enterprises it can become a problem to implement and operate two distinct and different platforms. It is, for example, more difficult to create a single pane of view for all managed network devices and connected endpoints. Also, it could be that, due to the design principles, certain features are either limited or not available with the Meraki products, and there is a requirement for that specific feature. A good example for this situation is a wireless network that needs to be designed and configured in an office or warehouse with some complex spectrum behaviors.

A similar design choice is applicable for the wired part of a campus design. Although functionally the concept of a collapsed core or single switch is not changing, if the specific campus network does not require advanced routing protocols or complex security mechanisms, a cloud-managed campus network can be a valid choice to have the benefits of ease of use and central management without too many complex tools.

Summary

In general, three types of topologies are deployed in campus networks:

- A three-tier deployment in which each function of a campus network (access, distribution, and core) is placed in dedicated switches. A three-tier deployment is commonly found and used in enterprises where the campus is comprised of several (large) buildings with a high-speed fiber network (LAN) interconnecting those buildings with the main building that contains the datacenter. Inside each building access switches connect to the distribution switch, which in turn is connected via the high-speed LAN between the buildings to the core switch. Quite often in this kind of deployment the connection between the core and distribution is based on Layer 3, so that VLANs are isolated within a building.

- Within a collapsed-core deployment the distribution and core function are merged into a single logical core switch. Access switches still connect to the distribution switch, and the distribution switch is connected to a WAN/MAN for connectivity to the datacenter. This kind of deployment is commonly used in environments where there is either a single building or buildings are connected to the datacenter via external WAN providers.

- The last deployment topology commonly found is a single-switch deployment, where all three functions are merged into a single switch. This is the simplest campus network deployment and is commonly found in branch offices and smaller enterprises.

On top of the wired deployment topology, a wireless network is being deployed. Over the past decade, wireless networks have transitioned from "nice-to-have" to the primary connection method for enterprise endpoints. Most wireless deployments found inside campus networks are controller based, where the access points communicate with a controller. The controller centrally manages both the wireless configuration and the security settings as well as radio resource management and client authentication.

Although wireless has become increasingly more important and the speeds inside the campus have increased over time, the designs and technologies used in campus networks have not changed much. VLANs are still used to logically separate endpoints into different logical fault domains, and the Spanning Tree Protocol is intensively used to prevent loops in the network. Campus networks have become so available, reliable, and trustworthy that many users see the campus network similar to power and running water—it is always there and it just works.

Chapter 2

Why Change Current Networks? A Need for Change

The campus network itself has not changed dramatically over the past decade. Although technologies like Virtual Switching System (VSS) and virtual PortChannel (vPC) have been introduced to eliminate the need for Spanning Tree Protocol (STP), many campus networks still implement Spanning Tree Protocol, just to be safe. A similar statement can be made on the design itself; it has not changed dramatically. Some might even state that the campus network is quite static and not very dynamic. Then why would today's campus network need to transform to Intent-based? There are some drivers that force the campus network to change. This chapter describes some of these major drivers and covers the following topics:

- Wireless/mobility trends

- IoT and non-user connected devices

- Complexity and manageability

- Cloud

- (Net)DevOps

- Digitalization

Wireless/Mobility Trends

Wireless networks were introduced in early 2000. (The first IEEE 802.11 standard was published in 1997; the wireless network standard that really evolved wireless networks was IEEE 802.11b, published in 1999.) Although you needed to have special adapters, the concept of having a wireless Ethernet network with connection to the emerging Internet and corporate infrastructure provided a lot of new concepts and possibilities. New use cases included providing "high speed" access for those users who were relying on the much slower cellular networks (megabits instead of 9600bps) as well as an optimization in logistics, where a wireless infrastructure would send the data to the order picker.

> **Note**   The order picker is the person in the warehouse who "picks" the items of an individual order from the stock in the warehouse and prepares them for shipment.

In the early stages, wireless networks were primarily deployed and researched for these two use cases. A third use case was of course the wireless connection for the executives; the first enterprise campus wireless networks were implemented.

Once wireless adapters were built into laptops by default, more use cases emerged, such as hotel hospitality services and enterprise wireless campus networks. The introduction of mobile handheld devices such as smartphones and tablets helped in the exponential growth of connected wireless devices (see Figure 2-1 and Figure 2-2) to an average of 2.5 wireless devices per capita in 2016 compared to 0.2 wireless devices per employee in the past.

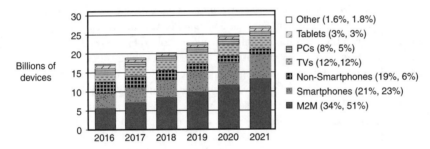

10% CAGR
2016-2021

Figures (n) refer to 2016, 2021 device share.
Source: Cisco VNI Global IP Traffic Forecast, 2016-2021.

Figure 2-1   *Global Devices and Connections Growth (Source: Cisco Systems, VNI 2017)*

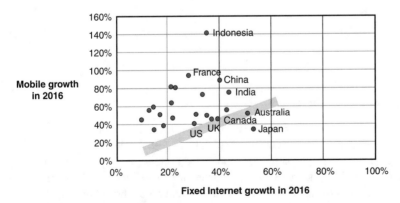

Source: Cisco VNI Global IP Traffic Forecast, 2016-2021.

Figure 2-2   *Fixed and Mobile Internet Traffic Growth Rates 2016 (Source: Cisco Systems, VNI 2017)*

Traditional enterprise campus networks primarily focused on (static) wired access located on fixed workplaces, while wireless access to the network was a nice-to-have but not necessary feature. But focus has been changing over the past five years.

Use Case: FinTech Ltd.

At first, FinTech Ltd. wanted to introduce a wireless network for its visitors as well as for employee-owned devices. Because of media attention about another organization where journalists were able to access the internal network via a wireless access point, the executive board decided that the wireless guest network must be completely separated (both logically and physically) from the corporate network. A pilot project was started with a small controller with five access points at strategic locations (conference rooms, executive wing, and so on) to demonstrate the purpose and effect of the wireless network. The pilot project was successful, and over time the wireless guest network was expanded to the complete office environment, so that wireless guest access could be provided within the whole company with coverage over speed as a requirement, as the service was for guests and simply nice to have.

Recently, FinTech Ltd. executives also decided that they wanted to test using laptops instead of fixed workstations to improve collaboration and use the office space more efficiently. (FinTech Ltd. was growing in employees, and building space was becoming limited.)

Extra access points were placed to provide for more capacity (capacity over coverage), and a site survey was executed to place the access points to accommodate the new laptops being used for Citrix. Of course, the wireless network was still separated from the corporate network, and Citrix was used for connecting the laptop to the desktop.

Access points were properly installed, the pilot was successful, and a large rollout was initiated, using different kinds of laptops than originally piloted.

Shortly after rollout, some of the laptops began having connectivity issues. Troubleshooting was difficult because changes to the wireless network to support troubleshooting were not allowed as it would affect the ability of other users to work. Overnight, the wireless network went from "nice-to-have" to business critical without the proper predesign, a redundant controller, and an awareness at different management levels of what those consequences are.

Eventually, the wireless issues were solved by updating software on the wireless network as well as the laptops (which had client-driver issues compared to the tested pilot laptops), and the wireless network was back to operating as designed.

An example like FinTech Ltd. can be found across almost every enterprise. The wireless network has become the primary connection method for enterprise campus networks. Although perhaps less reliable than wired, the flexibility and ease of use by far outweigh this performance and reliability issue. Results are obvious if you look at an average office building 15 years ago versus a modern enterprise office environment (see Figure 2-3).

Figure 2-3   *Office Area 15 Years Ago and a Modern Office Area*

The strong success of wireless networks is also their weak spot. It's not only that all wireless networks are in a free-to-use frequency band (also known as unlicensed spectrum), and with more devices connecting within the same location, the wireless network needs to be changed because of an increase of usage in both density and capacity. Users will complain if the Wi-Fi service inside the office is not fast and reliable. After all, the selection of hotels and other venues based on the quality of the Wi-Fi service provided is fairly commonplace these days.

In summary, the number of wireless devices is increasing, and thus high-density wireless networks (used to allow many wireless devices in a relatively small area) are not exclusively targeted for conference venues and large stadiums anymore. They have become a must-have requirement for the enterprise.

Connected Devices (IoT/Non-User Operated Devices)

The network infrastructure (Internet) has become a commodity infrastructure just like running water, gas, and electricity. Research by Iconic Displays states that 75% of the people interviewed reported that going without Internet access would leave them grumpier than going one week without coffee. The number of connected devices has already grown exponentially in the past decade due to the introduction of smartphones, tablets, and other IP-enabled devices. The network is clearly evolving, and this growth will not stop.

In the past, every employee used only a single device to connect to the network. During the introduction of Bring Your Own Device (BYOD), the sizing multiplier was 2.5. So every employee would on average use 2.5 devices. This number has only increased over time and will continue to do so. See Table 2-1 for the expected average number of devices per capita.

Table 2-1 *Average Number of Devices and Connections per Capita (Source: Cisco VNI 2017)*

Region	2016	2021	CAGR*
Asia Pacific	1.9	2.9	8.3%
Central and Eastern Europe	2.5	3.8	9.1%
Latin America	2.1	2.9	7.0%
Middle East and Africa	1.1	1.4	5.4%
North America	7.7	12.9	11.0%
Western Europe	5.3	8.9	10.9%
Global	2.3	3.5	8.5%

*Compound Annual Growth Rate

This table is sourced from Cisco's Virtual Networking Index. Although the number might already seem high, it is based on adding up all the different types of connected devices seen at shops, grocery stores, homes, businesses, and so on. The numbers add up. Smartboards such as a Webex Board or videoconferencing system are also connected to the network and increasingly are being used to efficiently collaborate over distance.

The same is applicable for traditionally physical networks as well. More and more security systems, such as those that monitor physical access (such as a badge readers) or cameras, are connected to the network and have their own complexity requirements.

Another big factor in the growth of devices on the campus network is the Internet of Things (IoT). IoT is absolutely not about just industrial solutions anymore. An increasing number of organizations set up smart lighting and provide an IP-telephone in the elevator for emergencies, and even sensors in escalators provide live status feedback to the company servicing them. In general, IoT is coming in all different sorts and sizes to the campus network within an enterprise, more often than not driven by business departments that procure services from others.

Finally, a major reason for the explosive growth of devices is the consumerization of technology in personal devices such as smartwatches, health sensors, and other kinds of devices. Some designers are already working on smart clothing. All these devices will be used by employees and thus need a connection to the commodity service called the Internet.

Based on these developments, it is safe to state that the number of connected devices will increase dramatically in the coming years. And as a consequence, the number of network devices will increase. These network devices, of course, need to be managed by adequate staff.

Complexity

The campus network used to be simple. If required, a network port for a specific VLAN would be configured, and the device would be connected to that port. Every change in the network would require a change in configuration, but within an enterprise network not many changes would occur besides the occasional department move that would result in moving the HR VLAN to a different port. Some engineers or architects still regard today's campus networks as simple; they are statically configured, and changes are predictable and managed by executing commands on-box.

This has not been the case for some time now. Several factors have already increased the complexity of the campus enterprise network. To name a few examples, IP telephony, instant messaging, and videoconferencing (now collectively known as collaboration tools), as well as video surveillance equipment, have all been added to the campus network infrastructure. Each of these types of network devices has its own requirements and dynamics, and all applications running on those devices require their services to work as expected. This has led to the introduction of quality of service in the campus network as a requirement. And the campus network needs to manage that expectation and behavior. The dynamics of the campus network are only increasing as more and more types of devices are connected to and use the campus network. As a result, complexity is increasing.

Use Case: QoS

The default design for the larger branch offices within SharedService Group is based on 1-Gigabit switches in the access layer with two 10 Gigabit uplinks to the distribution switch. As the employees primarily use Citrix, there was an assumption that Quality of Service was not necessary as there is sufficient bandwidth available for every user. Although not entirely correct, the ICA protocol used by Citrix would handle the occasional microburst or delays in the traffic. They could just happen sometimes.

In the past, IP phones were introduced in the network. During both the pilot project as well as the rollout of IP phones, no problems with audio quality or packet drops were found, so another application was introduced to the network, like any other new application.

Recently SharedService Group replaced the access layer made up of Catalyst 3750 switches with Catalyst 3650 switches as part of the lifecycle management. At that time problems started to occur with voice, and in the meantime video was introduced to the network as well. The protocols used for voice are predictable in bandwidth in contrast to video. Video uses compression techniques to reduce the used bandwidth. Because compression results can vary, the used bandwidth varies too, resulting in bursty traffic. Users complained about calls being dropped, having "silent" moments in the call, and other voice-related issues.

Once troubleshooting was started it became clear that there were output queue drops on some of the access switches facing the end users. To validate whether this was normal behavior, similar troubleshooting was executed on the older Catalyst 3750 switches. Although less frequent, they would sometimes occur.

Eventually the reason for the packet drops was found in the default behavior of the Catalyst 3650 switches compared to the older switches. In the older switches the QoS bits would be reset, unless you configured **mls qos trust**, and even if no QoS policies were configured, the bits were used in the egress queue by default.

However, the behavior of QoS on the Catalyst 3650 is very different. The bits are preserved in transiting the switches. But there is no queue-select on the egress port unless a selection policy for QoS has been set on the ingress port. In other words, if you do not "internally mark" the ingress traffic, all traffic is placed in the same default egress queue. And the default configuration for a Catalyst 3650 switch is to only use two of the eight egress queues.

The conclusion for SharedService Group is that in any enterprise campus network, some form of QoS must be implemented to make more queues and buffer space available in the switch, whether in the access or the distribution layer.

Besides the dynamics of adding more diverse devices to the network, security is becoming more important as well, putting even higher requirements on the campus network. The security industry is in a true rat race between offense (cybercriminals) and defense (security staff within the enterprise). The ransomware attacks of the past years emphasize the importance of security. The nPetya attack via Ukrainian Docme software in June 2017 even superseded those attacks in impact. Before the attack was launched, the malware was already distributed via the software update mechanism within Docme. Once the attack was launched, the malware became active, and in some environments had an infection rate of more than 10,000 per second. After cracking the local administrator password, the malware moved laterally through the network infecting and destroying any computer found in its path. It didn't matter if the software was up-to-date or not. This malware software was written by professionals who knew networking.

Increased security requirements (which are necessary) to protect the organization result in an increase in the complexity of the campus enterprise network.

In summary, the campus network is slowly but surely increasing in complexity of configuration, operation, and management. And as this process occurs slowly over time, the configuration of the campus network is becoming much like a plate of spaghetti. Different patches, interconnections, special policies, access lists for specific applications, and other configurations also result in reduced visibility of the network, thus increasing the chance of a security incident as well as increasing the chance of a major failure that could have been prevented.

Manageability

Based on the trends of the previous sections, it is clear that the operations team that manages the campus network is faced with two major challenges: the exponential growth of the number of connected devices and the increased complexity of the network. Furthermore, the exponential growth of the number of connected devices will have a multiplying effect on the increase in complexity.

Often in today's networks, the required changes, installations, and management are done based on a per-device method. In other words, creating a new VLAN requires the network engineer to log in to the device and create the new VLAN via CLI. Similar steps are executed when troubleshooting a possible network-related problem, by logging in to the device and tracing the steps where the problem might occur. Unfortunately, most IT related incidents are initially blamed on the network, so the network engineer also has to "prove" that it is not the network (Common laments are "the network is not performing," or "I can't connect to the network.")

Current statistics (source: Cisco Systems, Network Intuitive launch) show that on average every network engineer can maintain an overview of roughly 200 concurrent devices. This overview includes having a mental picture of where devices are connected, which switches are touched on the network for a specific flow, and so on. In other words, the current network operations index is 200 devices / fte (full-time equivalent) approximately. Of course, this index value is dependent on the complexity of the network combined with the size of the organization and the applicable rules and regulations.

So an IT operations staff of 30 can manage 6,000 concurrent devices, which matches up to approximately 2,500 employees with the current 2.5 devices per employee. But the number of devices is also growing exponentially in the enterprise. The average number of devices per employee is moving toward 3.5 on average, but in certain areas can go up to 12.5. (This number includes all the IoT devices that connect to the same enterprise campus network, such as IP cameras, IP phones, Webex smart boards, light switches, window controls, location sensors, badge readers, and so on.) That means that for the existing 2,500 employees, a staggering 20,000 concurrent devices would be connected (taking a factor of 8). Add the number of smart sensors and smart devices into the count as well, and it is easy to have that same enterprise network handling 50,000 concurrent endpoints.

That would mean that the network operations staff should be increased to ± 300 employees (250 for the devices plus some extra for the added complexity). And that is simply not possible (not only for cost but also finding the resources). In summary, the manageability of the existing campus enterprise networks is in danger and needs to change.

Cloud (Edge)

The principle of using cloud infrastructures (in whichever form) for some or all applications in the enterprise has become part of the strategy for most enterprises. There are, of course, some benefits to the business for this strategy, such as ease of use, application agility, availability, and ease of scalability. However, it also implies some challenges to today's enterprise networks.

Most traditional enterprise networks are designed hierarchically with a central office (HQ) and an internal WAN that connects the several branch offices to the internal network. The Internet access for employees is usually managed via one (large and shared) central Internet connection. At this central Internet connection, the security policies are also managed and enforced. Figure 2-4 illustrates this global design.

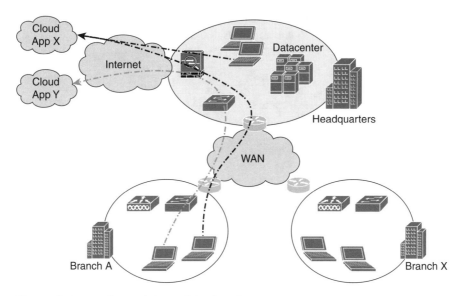

Figure 2-4   *Traditional Central Outbreak*

Traditionally, most applications are hosted inside the enterprise datacenter, which is located in the HQ. With the transition of these applications to the cloud, the burden of these applications on the Internet connection is increasing. In essence, the enterprise's datacenter is, from a data perspective, extended from its own location toward the different clouds that are being used. And the number of cloud services is increasing as an increasing number of companies provide software as a service (SaaS) and label this service as a cloud service. For example, take an enterprise with 3,000 employees with an average mailbox size of 2 Gigabytes moving its email service to Microsoft Office 365. The initial mailbox migration alone would already take 6 Terabytes of data to be transferred. Even with a dedicated 1 Gigabit Internet line and an average of 100 Megabytes per second, this transfer alone would take roughly 70 days.

Even after the initial migration, every time a user logs in to a new workstation, the user's mailbox is going to be downloaded to that workstation as cache. So it is logical that with a move to the cloud, a significant burden is placed on the central Internet connection and its security policies.

In parallel, most enterprises have adopted WAN over Internet besides the traditional dedicated WAN circuits with providers using technologies such as Cisco Intelligent WAN (IWAN) and more recently the Cisco Software-Defined WAN (SD-WAN) based on Viptela. Some enterprises have completely replaced their dedicated WAN circuits with these technologies. As a result, not only the internal WAN capacity is increased, but a local Internet connection becomes available to provide wireless access to guests of the enterprise.

If you combine these two trends—local Internet access at the branch office and an increased use of cloud applications by the enterprise—it is only common sense that a preference starts to emerge for offloading cloud applications access to the local Internet breakout at the branch. Figure 2-5 illustrates this design.

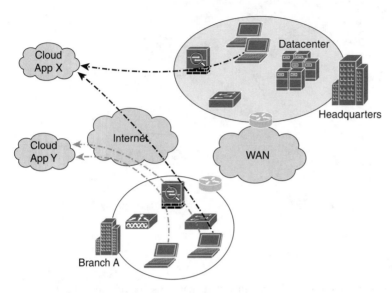

Figure 2-5   *Connecting Cloud Applications via Cloud Edge*

This preference is also known as *cloud edge* and will impose some challenges on enforcing and monitoring security policies, but it will happen. And as a result, the campus network at that branch office will receive extra network functions such as firewalling, anti-malware detection, smart routing solutions, and the correct tooling and technologies to centrally manage and facilitate this trend.

(Net)DevOps

DevOps is a methodology that has emerged from within software engineering. DevOps is fulfilling the increased demand to release new versions and new features within software more rapidly. The DevOps methodology itself was being pushed because of the Agile software development methodology.

Classic software engineering methodologies usually follow a distinct five-step process for software development:

Step 1.   Design

Step 2.   Development

Step 3.   Test

Step 4.   Acceptance

Step 5.   Release in production

Each of these processes was commonly executed by a dedicated team with the process as its specialty. For example, development would start only after the design was completed by the design team. The development team usually had limited to no input into the design process. As a result, the majority of software development projects resulted in products that were delayed, over-specified, over budget, and usually not containing the features the customer really wanted because the design team misunderstood the customer's requirements and the customer's requirements evolved over time.

The Agile software engineering methodology takes a different approach. Instead of having distinct teams of specialists executing the software engineering processes sequentially, multidisciplinary teams were created. In these teams, the design, development and testing engineers work together in smaller iterations to quickly meet the customer's requirements and produce production-ready code that can be demonstrated to the customer. These smaller iterations are called *sprints* and contain mini-processes of design-build-test. The team closely cooperates with the customer on requirements and feature requests, where the primary aspects for prioritization are business value or business outcome in conjunction with development effort required.

This Agile software engineering methodology provides a number of benefits. First, due to the fast iterations, the software is released many times (with increased features over time) instead of a single final release. These releases are also discussed and shared with the customer, so the customer can provide feedback to the product, and as a result the product better matches the request of the customer, thus providing a better product.

Second, by having a team made responsible for the features, a shared team effort and interaction is created between designers, software engineers, and test engineers. That aspect results in better code quality because of the shared responsibility.

Within Agile software engineering teams, it is also common to use so-called *automated build pipelines* that integrate the different steps in building and deploying software in an automated method. Committed source code versions of the software are merged, automatically compiled, and unit tested to bugs. With that automation taking place, the release of a new software version can be deployed much faster.

However, Agile itself is primarily focused on the development of software—the "dev" side, so to speak. Taking the released code from the pipeline into operations usually still took quite some time, as that required change requests, new services, servers, and other aspects. Consequently, the deployment of new software versions within the IT systems of an enterprise took much more time and effort compared to deploying that same version into cloud-enabled services.

This is where DevOps emerged, where development (Dev) and operations (Ops) work closely together in single teams. The automation pipeline for the software engineering is extended with automation within the application-server side, so that the release of software is inside the same automated process. As a result, if an Agile team decides to release and publish software code, the deployment of that code is done automatically.

This completed DevOps pipeline is also known as Continuous Integration/Continuous Delivery (CICD). Large technology organizations use this mechanism all the time to deploy new features or bug fixes in their cloud services.

Toolchains

Automation pipelines used within CI/CD (or CICD) are also referred to as *toolchains*. Instead of relying on a single tool that can do all, the team (and thus the pipeline) relies on a set of best tools of the trade chained together in a single automated method. This toolchain, depending on the way the team is organized, usually consists of the following tools:

1. **Code:** Code development and review tools, including source code version management

2. **Build:** Automated build tools that provide status if the code is compliable and language-error free

3. **Test:** Automated test tools that verify, based on unit tests, automatically if the code functions as expected

4. **Package:** Once accepted, the different sources are packaged and managed in repositories in a logical manner

5. **Release:** Release management code, with approvals, where the code from the different packages are bundled in a single release

6. **Configure:** Infrastructure configuration and management tooling, the process to pull the (latest) release from the repository and deploy it automatically on servers (with automatic configuration)

7. **Monitor:** Application performance monitoring tools to test and measure user experience and generic performance of the solution

There are also other similar toolchain sequences available, such as Plan, Create, Verify, and Package. This is usually dependent on the way the Agile methodology and toolchains are integrated within the team.

With DevOps, the release frequency of new features and bug fixes is increased, and the customer can get access to the new features even faster. But still if a new server needs to be deployed, or a complete new application, well, you do need to create VLANs, load balancer configurations, IP allocations, and firewalls. And all those operations are executed by the network operations team. Because of the potential impact (the network connects everything, usually also without a proper test environment), these changes are prepared carefully with as much detail as possible to minimize impact. Change procedures commonly require approval from a change advisory board, which takes some time. As a result, deploying new applications and servers still takes much more time than strictly necessary.

The term NetDevOps represents the integration of Network operations into the existing DevOps teams to reduce that burden. This integration is possible because of the increased automation and standardization capabilities inside the datacenter with technologies like Cisco Application Centric Infrastructure (ACI).

Although the NetDevOps trend is focused primarily on the datacenter, a parallel can be made into the campus environment. Because of the increased complexity and diversity of devices in the campus, more functional networks need to be created, deleted, and operated. End users within enterprises have difficulty understanding why creating a new network in the campus takes so much time without understanding that adding a new VLAN takes proper preparation to minimize impact to other services. Consequently, NetDevOps as a methodology is moving toward the campus environment as well.

Digitalization

If you ask a CTO of an enterprise what his top priorities are, the chances are that digital transformation (or digitalization) is part of the answer. What is digitalization, and what is its impact for the campus enterprise network?

IT is becoming an integral part of any organization. Without IT, the business comes to a standstill. Applications have become business critical in almost every aspect of a business, regardless of the specific industry. Traditionally, the business specified the requirements and features that an application would need to have to support itself. The business would then use that application and chug along, changing a bit here and there.

With more devices getting connected and entering the digital era, more data (and thus) information is becoming available for the enterprise to use. This data can be collected in data lakes so that smart algorithms (machine intelligence) and smart queries can be used to find patterns or flows that can be optimized in the business process.

This process of digitizing data and using it to optimize business processes is part of the digital transformation. In parallel, Moore's law[1] is causing the effect that technology velocity is ever-accelerating, enabling technology to solve more complex problems in ever-decreasing timeframes. This leads to the fact that technology can suggest or even automatically reorganize and improve business processes by finding the proper patterns in the data of the enterprise and finding ways to overcome those patterns. This process is called *digitalization*. The key for successful digitalization is that IT and business must be aligned with each other. They must understand each other and see that they jointly can bring the organization further. Thus, digitalization requires that the way the campus enterprise network is operated needs to be changed and be more aligned with the business. A more detailed explanation of digitization and its stages is provided in Chapter 12, "Enabling the Digital Business."

---

1   Moore's law is the observation that the number of transistors in a dense integrated circuit doubles about every two years.

Summary

The design and operation of a campus network have not changed much over time. However, the way the campus network is used *has* changed dramatically. Part of that change is that the campus network (whether it is a small consultancy firm or a worldwide enterprise with several production plants) has become critical for every enterprise. If the campus network is down, the business experiences a standstill of operations. That is a fact that not many organizations comprehend and support. The digital transformation (also known as digitalization) is emphasizing that IT and thus the network are becoming more important and that organizations not adapting will experience a fallout.

The complexity of the campus network has slowly but surely increased over time as more applications use the network and with each application having its own requirements. This added complexity results in reduced visibility with an increase in security risks and higher troubleshooting times. The digitization of environments means that more endpoints will be connected to the enterprise networks. These endpoints are often not operated and managed by employees, but they are managed and operated via a gateway; in other words, the campus network will also connect endpoints that are not owned or managed by employees. Both factors result in a complex and unmanageable campus enterprise network.

Faster adoption of new features is the way technology is now being used by organizations all over the world. As a result, IT departments are increasingly organized in multidisciplinary teams using efficient automation and standardization processes to deploy new technologies and features faster and become more aligned with the business processes that have that requirement. This adoption of automation and standardization needs to apply to campus networks as well; otherwise the campus network will not be able to keep up with the changes.

All these aspects combined make it necessary to change the way a campus network is designed, implemented, and operated; otherwise, the campus network will in time become an unmanageable, chaotic, and invisible network environment with frequent downtimes and disruptions as a result. And these disruptions can put any organization at risk for bankruptcy due to the loss of revenue and trust.

The Cisco Digital Network Architecture and Intent-Based Networking Paradigm are the way to cope with these challenges, transform the campus network, and prepare it for the new digital network in the future.

Chapter 3

Enterprise Architecture

It is clear that the design and operation of campus networks need to be changed to facilitate all those forces mentioned as trends in Chapter 2. In the past, creating and adopting for these forces where needed was a common approach, although it often led to increased complexity and decreased manageability. This is not uncommon for other parts of the IT industry or business in general as well. It is better, in the end, to design and operate a network using a structured methodology toward design and integration. This is commonly referred to as *working with architecture frameworks*.

This chapter provides an overview of why architecture frameworks are beneficial and where technology, currently and in the future, is in relation to the enterprise itself. To facilitate this overview, The Open Group Architecture Framework (TOGAF®) standard is used as an example architecture framework.

This chapter covers the following topics:

- Why architecture frameworks and working with architecture frameworks is beneficial
- A brief overview of the TOGAF® architecture framework
- A summary of other enterprise architecture frameworks
- A description of where networking and IT fit in these frameworks

What Is an Architecture Framework?

According to the Oxford dictionary the noun *architect* is defined as a person who designs buildings and in many cases also supervises their construction. A subsection describes the term as a person who is responsible for inventing or realizing a particular idea or project.

The latter definition of the term *architect* is used not only in buildings but has become a very common approach in many industries where design and production require a certain methodology of working.

For example, in car manufacturing the architect role is responsible for translating the design of a car into modular components that can be reused across different models. The Volvo models XC60, V60, V90, XC90, S90, and S60 all use the same SPA chassis. Other car manufacturers use the same principle. The goal of reusing components is twofold: to reduce cost of design and to decrease time to market. Why reinvent the wheel for a second or third time if the first time is right?

Another example using the architectural role is within manufacturing of computers and specifically the combination of standard computers and built-to-order systems. The computer manufacturer has designed the casing, the logic board, possible drive configurations, and other options. The consumer can choose to either order a prefabricated computer (e.g., off stock) or modify some options on the computer, and this computer will be built to order. The production lines where the systems are produced are the same and only vary with easily adjustable options, such as CPU, memory configuration, disk configuration, or keyboards that can be changed.

Many similar examples exist. All environments with an architectural role have a common ground: a layered approach that uses modularization. In other words, a large design is divided up into smaller logical and functional modules. Each function of a module is described, including its interdependencies, input, and output.

Because the modules are small and logically contained, they are easier to understand and implement. These (most often) implementations in technology provide another benefit as well—longevity of the design. If a technological implementation becomes obsolete, only that specific module needs to be implemented with a new technology as long as all functional requirements are met. The larger design remains valid and in place.

These modules are also called architecture building blocks (functional) and solution building blocks (technical), or building blocks in general. Does this sound familiar? It should. Many IT systems are designed in a similar way, whether it is an application, operating system, or even an enterprise network (comprised of components like campus LAN, WAN, datacenter, or cloud).

There are several methodologies to design, implement, and support a system that is built under architecture. These methodologies, including guidelines and principles, are usually combined in architecture frameworks. All frameworks aim to provide the following benefits when used:

- **Flexibility:** As a specific module can be replaced by another module, as long as it meets the requirements, the system as a whole is more flexible. To relate to the computer manufacturing example, the amount of memory in a system is in essence a module, and by implementing three or four different modules, flexibility for the end user is created.

- **Reusability:** Once a module is designed and implemented, it can be reused more than once. This reusability results in lower costs for the module and the complete system. As an example, most car companies use the same engine type across different models. The engine is designed only once and reused in many different models.

- **Faster implementation:** If a system already has an existing set of designed and tested modules, it is easier to design a new system or new approach based on existing modules. As a result, systems can be designed and built faster.

- **Serviceability:** When every system is divided into logical correct modules, it is easier to troubleshoot a specific problem once the module that behaves erroneously is found. Only that module needs to be fixed instead of a complete system.

- **Possibility of change:** If a system needs to behave differently due to changes in organization or business demands, it is now possible to reorder existing modules, reuse them, and (if needed) design and build only the required changed modules. The generic system is still available and applicable.

A common pitfall though is that the creation of the enterprise architecture becomes leading in the process, instead of being supportive and providing concrete results to the enterprise. This results in less performance of the enterprise and thus the lack of support and usability of an enterprise architecture. This pitfall is often part of the discussion whether an enterprise architecture is actually beneficial to the enterprise. The TOGAF® standard (explained in the next section) is one of the generic frameworks that is focused on removing that pitfall.

The TOGAF® Standard

The Open Group Architecture Framework (TOGAF®) standard (currently at version 9.2) describes a generic framework for developing enterprise architectures. It is one of the more common frameworks to facilitate the development of such architectures, and in a sense can also be used to develop other architectures. The TOGAF® standard and its related standards are published and managed by The Open Group.

The TOGAF® standard consists of several components, such as a methodology to develop the enterprise architecture, a method to functionally (abstract) describe an enterprise, its inner relationships at different levels, a process on how to manage and operate an architecture, and many other aspects related to the enterprise architecture. The following paragraphs provide more information about some of these components. More information can be found on the website of The Open Group (https://www.opengroup.com).

As with any standard or framework, it is of utmost importance that both the authors and readers (consumers) have the same understanding of the definitions used in the specific standard. Over time, quite a few meetings ended in very intense discussions, with interventions and possibly even escalations just because members had different understandings or interpretations of the same definition or described process.

In this sense it is important to know which definitions and contexts are used within a specific framework. The TOGAF® standard uses the ISO/IEC 42010:2007 definition of "architecture," which is

The fundamental organization of a system, embodied in its components, their relationships to each other and the environment, and the principles governing its design and evolution.

And although the TOGAF® standard adheres to this definition, it also provides two more specific meanings toward this definition upon which the TOGAF® framework is modeled:

- A formal description of a system, or a detailed plan of the system at component level to guide its implementation

- The structure of components, their interrelationships, and the principles and guidelines governing their design and evolution over time

With these two extra meanings, TOGAF® uses this definition to see an enterprise as a system and therefore as the basis for the TOGAF® standard.

Aspects of the TOGAF®

Three key aspects to the TOGAF® standard make it one of the more common frameworks used to develop architectures in the enterprise as described in the following sections.

Framework, Tool, and Methodology

The TOGAF® standard is not only a generic framework, but a tool that you use to implement an (enterprise) architecture. The TOGAF® standard contains all the elements, methodologies, and sample elements based on best practices to develop a successful enterprise architecture.

Pragmatic Approach

The TOGAF® standard takes a pragmatic approach to the development and maintenance of an enterprise architecture. It's not only based on open standards and best practices, but based upon client requirement. This pragmatic approach is reflected in the fact that one of the targets of the framework is concrete and usable results. And by focusing on usable and concrete results, there is always an added value to the enterprise by describing the use case in the architecture.

Another display of being pragmatic is the "just-enough" architecture approach. The TOGAF® standard states that the architecture must not be over-specified, but just enough to move the enterprise forward.

Iterative

The TOGAF® standard takes an iterative approach to the enterprise architecture. This means that developing and maintaining an enterprise architecture is not a one-time project but is a continual process with repeatable steps to improve and integrate the architecture within the enterprise. This iterative process facilitates the required integration and adoption.

To implement this iterative approach, the Architecture Development Method (ADM) is an integral part of the TOGAF® standard. ADM describes different steps and stages that need to be executed and/or organized for the successful creation of an enterprise architecture. The different ADM steps are described in more detail later in the chapter.

These three aspects underlie every part of the TOGAF® standard. And although these aspects are usually overseen in (large) projects to develop and integrate an (enterprise) architecture, these key aspects can make or break the adoption and usability of any enterprise architecture, or in general any architecture.

Four Types of Architectures

Within the TOGAF® standard, the enterprise (as a system) can be described via four types of architectures:

- Business

- Data

- Application

- Technology

These architectures describe in a functional and abstract way how the enterprise works. Within the TOGAF® standard, these four architectures only provide the functional (and abstract) descriptions and requirements and do not provide solutions or implementations to those descriptions and/or requirements.

These four architecture types are, in the approach, similar to the layered approach within the OSI model. (The OSI model is widely used within the networking industry and is a conceptual model that describes, using a layered approach with distinct functions, how applications can communicate with each other over a computer network.) The technology architecture provides the necessary requirements and capabilities needed to enable the application architecture to successfully be implemented. The application architecture is used to set the requirements to successfully implement the data architecture and in a sense the business architecture.

Business Architecture

In general, the business architecture defines the strategy, governance, organization, and key business processes. The business architecture attempts to describe, without specifying persons, tools, or other implementations, how the business itself is organized and what the enterprise provides to the outside world. The business architecture should also provide the necessary information and support the way to implement the enterprise's vision. In other words, the business architecture is a translation of the enterprise's vision into several components required to accomplish the vision.

For example, the business architecture of a manufacturing company would contain the business processes such as procurement, sales, quality and development, and logistics. These four business processes would be described functionally, for example:

- Procurement is responsible for procuring the necessary ingredients in a just-in-time method with the highest quality standards.

- Sales is responsible for selling the goods with the responsibility to keep the available stock to an absolute minimum.

- Quality and Development is responsible for monitoring current quality standards and developing new products based on feedback from customers.

- Logistics is responsible to ensure proper and timely delivery of the goods sold via Sales.

In this architecture, there is no description of any technology or ingredients specified.

Data Architecture

The data architecture describes which data assets (both physical and logical) are available within the enterprise and how that data is used by the different processes of the enterprise. The data architecture also describes how the data is structured within the enterprise and how data is managed. Although not downplaying the data architecture, it can be seen as a collection of data models of database servers together with the organization and structure of the data inside file servers.

Application Architecture

The application architecture defines the kind of application systems needed to process the data and support the business. It defines the major applications used within the enterprise, the requirements that those applications must meet, as well as the way application lifecycle management is being managed.

Again, this architecture is only functional and would describe applications such as an order and invoice management system to register orders and generate invoices for products sold to customers, a product quality application to monitor and manage the quality process, and so on.

Another example, for the manufacturing company, is that a warehouse management application must be used to keep information about the available stock. This application is also used to provide logistics with sufficient information to pick up products for a sales order and prepare for them shipping. The application also provides the necessary information to the order and invoice system to generate invoices after orders have been shipped and to facilitate the process of order picking by logistics.

Technology Architecture

The technology architecture describes the logical software and hardware capabilities required to support the deployment of the business, data, and application services. The technology architecture is traditionally where IT meets the business and where the primary interaction takes place. It commonly includes the IT infrastructure, required middleware, (application) gateways to external partners, networks, communication, used standards, and processes required to operate the IT to facilitate the business as well.

Again, within the same manufacturing company, the logistics department would have set forth a few requirements for successful operation. This could include the requirement for a wireless technology so that order picking devices can connect directly to the warehouse management system to optimize the order picking and stock management processes. The wireless network availability should meet the operating hours of the warehouse with critical times between 4:00 a.m. and 6:00 a.m. because that is the busiest time for order picking.

ADM

The Architecture Development Method (ADM) is the core of the TOGAF® standard and is a methodology used to develop and implement an enterprise architecture. The ADM is based on an iterative approach and describes the different phases that need to be executed for the development and maintenance of an enterprise architecture.

The ADM is modeled in a circle of eight distinct processes and a single central process. Figure 3-1 displays the phases of the ADM, and the following sections describe the phases in more detail.

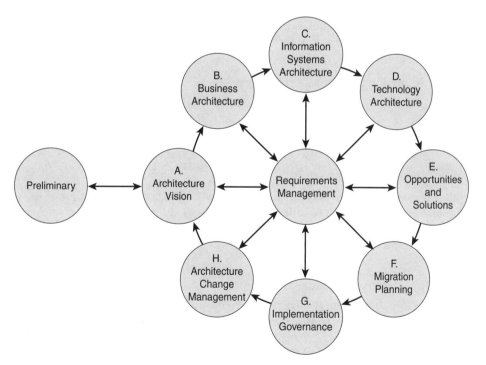

Figure 3-1 *The Architecture Development Method Phases (Courtesy of The Open Group)*

Preliminary Phase

The preliminary phase is the exception of the iterative aspect of ADM. It is executed only once to start all necessary preparations activities, and initiatives to have a directive to implement a new enterprise architecture. This directive is the output of the preliminary phase and is used as the basis for subsequent phases.

Phase A. Architecture Vision

The architecture vision is the first phase of ADM. It describes the initial phase of the architecture development cycle. It also provides the necessary information about stakeholders, scope of the architectural work to be executed, and support (via approvals and mandate) from executive management to define a new or refine the existing enterprise architecture. The products (output) of this phase are stored and managed via the requirements management process.

As in many organizations the only constant is change. The last phase—Architecture Change Management (ACM)—can also be the initiator to restart this phase to define and implement small improvements. This is a key part of the iterative process within TOGAF®.

Phase B. Business Architecture

Business architecture describes the development of a business architecture within the scope set in the Architecture Vision phase. The output contains process descriptions, process models, responsibilities, organizational diagrams, and other business-related artifacts. (An artifact is an element of the enterprise architecture.)

Phase C. Information Systems Architecture

This phase describes the development of an Information Systems Architecture that includes the development (or adjustment) of Data and Application Architectures. The phase can also result in a project required to develop such architectures.

Phase D. Technology Architecture

This phase describes the processes and development of a technology architecture. The output, based on the output of earlier phases as well as existing artifacts, is a technology architecture within the scope of the architecture vision that supports the architectures from phase B and phase C.

Phase E. Opportunities and Solutions

This is the first phase where the functional architectures are to be implemented using products and solutions. This phase encompasses several processes to globally identify opportunities and possible solutions. These opportunities and solutions can also be seen as target architectures, describing the future architecture the enterprise will adopt. The identified opportunities and solutions are grouped into different delivery methods, such as projects or programs. These groups of opportunities are assessed on priority and dependency so the proper priority can be defined.

Phase F. Migration Planning

The output of the previous phase is used to set up a detailed implementation plan as well as an architecture roadmap based on priorities, cost/benefit analysis, and risk assessments. The output of this phase can be seen as the initiation of projects to implement the earlier defined target or solution architectures. The implementation project itself is outside the scope of ADM.

Phase G. Implementation Governance

The ADM including the enterprise architecture needs to be managed and maintained. This phase describes the methods used to develop the governance rules on how the architecture (and its artifacts) is to be managed and changed. This also includes information about its authority structure and the way decisions are made, and it provides answers to responsibility, accountability, and involvement.

Part of this governance is also the way the architects validate and approve the result of the implementation projects. The governance is built upon the mandate and approval of the executive board described in the Architecture Vision phase.

Phase H. Architecture Change Management

This phase describes the methods for continual monitoring of new developments or changes in the enterprise. This phase ensures that all changes made to the architecture are executed in a cohesive and architected way. It is common that new iterations through the ADM are initiated based on triggers from this phase.

Requirements Management

The requirements management process is the central axle in the ADM. It receives and provides all necessary requirements within the enterprise architecture itself. It also provides the necessary steps to take through ADM.

In general, before an enterprise architecture exists, a full cycle around the ADM phases is executed. That first cycle results in an initial enterprise architecture that might not be completely detailed or worked out. But there is a tangible result as an enterprise architecture. In the next iterations of the ADM, only a specific set of phases can be executed, depending on business drivers or specific triggers. An example could be that the governance needs to be changed because of changing rules and regulations, or the data architecture needs to be changed because the regulation on data has changed (GDPR). The ability to specifically select a subset of phases provides the power, flexibility, and possibility to continuously adapt and improve the enterprise architecture.

Guidelines and Principles

Every design is based on requirements and a number of design principles. This is also applicable for an enterprise architecture. Within the TOGAF® standard, these architecture and design principles are managed via the requirements phase of ADM. Architecture principles provide a common set of principles that every aspect of the enterprise architecture must meet. The same is applicable for design guidelines. Although design guidelines are less strict, they also make sure that the different components of the architecture are designed in a consistent way. This consistency increases the transparency and usability of the architecture.

These architecture and design principles must be generic in focus, so that they can be applied to every aspect of the architecture. In general, a design principle commonly consists of a name, the statement, a rationale, and the implications of the principle.

Sometimes external rules and regulations provide the necessary architecture principles upon which the architecture is modeled and designed. This could be an applicable law or specific rules for specific industries.

A few examples of architecture principles common across an enterprise are as follows:

- **Non-proliferation of technology:** Technical diversity will be controlled to reduce complexity in the environment.

- **Compliance with law:** The solution is compliant with all relevant laws and regulations.

- **Business aligned:** Every IT project must be aligned with business goals and strategy.

- **Common use solutions:** Cross-silo solutions are preferred over duplicative silo-specific applications, systems, and tools. This prevents silo solutions as much as possible.

- **Simple solutions:** IT will be as simple as possible. Where complexity is required it will be encapsulated and hidden behind an interface that is as simple as possible.

- **Shared resources:** Solutions will seek to have maximum sharing of resources such as network, computing, storage, and data.

- **Security:** Security should be an integral part of any design to reduce the risk of leaking potential sensitive data to unauthorized devices and persons.

As you can see, these principles are generic and provide a framework within a design is to be implemented. These architecture principles are, of course, also applicable for a network designer or architect when a new network infrastructure is designed.

Building Blocks

Building blocks are common in any methodology to design or develop a framework, whether within a software framework or a campus network design. The TOGAF® standard is no different; the most common artifact is the building block.

In TOGAF®, the building block represents a (potential reusable) component of business, IT, or architectural capability that can be combined with other building blocks to deliver architectures and solutions. The building block describes, in a clear and concise way, its functions and relationship with other building blocks.

A building block can be as large as the description of a complete system (with its relationship to other systems) or as small as a building block describing the way NTP or syslog is configured on all network devices. It is common to model a building block using other building blocks. One of the benefits of reusing building blocks in a larger design is that it eliminates the need to reinvent a solution twice or even more times. A building block improves on standardization, and it also improves the efficiency of the enterprise in case a building block is updated with a new solution. It is therefore very important to define building blocks in a clear and concise method, including a clear description of its relationships to others.

Within TOGAF® there are two kinds of building blocks:

- The Architecture Building Block (ABB) describes on a functional level the requirements and usage of the building block.
- The Solution Building Block (SBB) in turn describes how the requirements and functional description of an ABB is translated into a solution.

An example of an ABB is that an enterprise has the requirement for a wireless network infrastructure in all its warehouses to facilitate the requirement that order-pick equipment can communicate with the warehouse management system. The wireless network needs to be highly available and adhere to the latest industry standards and amendments in wireless networking. The coverage of the wireless network needs to be implemented in such a way that there can be no loss of connectivity.

An example of an SBB that translated the wireless network ABB would be a Cisco Wireless LAN Controller (WLC) setup, using the IEEE 802.11ac amendment in conjunction with wireless site surveys that are designed for balanced capacity and coverage with near-overlapping cells.

Repository

The different artifacts—parts of the enterprise architecture, such as an architecture principle, a building block, a catalogue (list of things), use case specifications, or diagrams—need to have a location where they can easily be stored and retrieved. This is the architecture repository. It is a central location, with versioning, where every aspect of the enterprise architecture is stored. The process of defining versions and releases of the elements inside the repository is defined within the governance phase of ADM.

When the items of this repository are combined and ordered in a specific way, so-called architecture deliverables are created. A deliverable can be a target architecture, a solution architecture, or a solution building block.

The architecture repository can easily be compared with a code repository used by software engineers to share and commit their work to, such as GitHub. Its output in turn is an application. For network designers, the output would be a configuration template for a specific network device type in the enterprise.

In summary, the TOGAF® standard itself contains many more elements, definitions, reference models, stakeholder management, and other information. Different books have been written on the topic of the TOGAF® standard as well as enterprise architecture. As mentioned, more information can be found on the website of The Open Group.

Enterprise Architectures

The TOGAF® standard is not the only enterprise architecture framework. Different frameworks are available—some for specific industries or specific purposes, some more generic. In general they follow a similar pattern of abstracting requirements and processes into layers to create abstractions on design and implementation. They all aim to provide added value to the enterprise in one way or another.

Table 3-1 lists some more enterprise architecture frameworks related to specific industries.

Table 3-1   *Overview of More Enterprise Architecture Frameworks for Specific Purposes*

Type	Name	Description
Generic	ARCON	A reference architecture for collaborative networks, not directly focusing on a single enterprise but on how to collaborate
Generic	GERAM	Generalized Enterprise Reference Architecture and Methodology
Generic	RM-ODP	The reference model for Open Distributed Processing (ITU-T recommendation X.901-X.904, ISO/IEC 10746 standard) defining specifications for open distributed systems
Generic	IDEAS Group	A four-nation effort to develop a common approach for architecture interoperability
Generic	ISO 19439	ISO framework for enterprise modeling
Defense	AGATE	The France DGA Architecture Framework
Defense	DNDAF	The Canadian DND/CF Architecture Framework
Defense	DoDAF	The US Department of Defense Architecture Framework
Defense	MODAF	The UK Ministry of Defense Architecture Framework
Defense	NAF	The NATO Architecture Framework

Type	Name	Description
Government	ESAAF	European Space Agency Architectural Framework
Government	GEA	Government Enterprise Architecture by the Queensland Government
Government	NORA	Dutch Government E-government Architecture
Government	NIST	NIST Enterprise Architecture Framework

Use Case: DIY Architecture

Although FinTech Ltd. did not follow an existing architecture design framework such as TOGAF®, IT noticed a requirement for a more structured approach toward IT, implementation projects, and the network infrastructure. FinTech Ltd. decided to take small steps and to describe several of its processes (besides quality processes) in a technical design as well. The technical principles and designs were based on where the network was going to be in a number of years–in essence a roadmap. They then defined projects to reach that goal.

Within the Windows server environment a similar process was taking place to more easily manage their server environment and optimize the workflow. A separate track was started to model the information flowing over the network, as one of their customers was demanding that such information be made available. Over time, these tracks grew together and started to collaborate on a shared architectural approach upon which projects were also implemented. A shared group was established to share experiences and information about relationships. This group eventually became the architecture board.

Although FinTech Ltd. didn't adopt a formally acknowledged architecture standard, they organically grew into working with architectures, roadmaps, and projects. This method of building and defining your own architecture is not faulty; for some specific situations it might actually be the best solution. The purpose of working with an architecture is to provide a consistent and concise method of describing the environment at both the design and the solutions levels. Its purpose is to improve the enterprise as a whole, and a custom self-designed architecture using a bottom-up approach can be as valid as a top-down approach.

Summary

Although the TOGAF® standard itself is a tool aimed to design and deploy a full enterprise architecture, the components described in this chapter, including the ADM, are common for any IT-related design and implementation process.

The mechanisms described, such as a building block for modularity, reusability, and scalability, are a common practice and the basis for almost any network design. By defining clear distinct principles and following those rules, the network design will increase in visibility and usability as well. When a new network product is to be used, only a new solution building block needs to be developed, instead of a complete new network design.

There are quite a few benefits for network engineers or architects to follow these same principles to also create more understanding of other IT-related architects or the business as a whole.

For a network architect, or network engineer, it is important to be aware that the network design itself is critical for the enterprise, but its design and implementation only play a "smaller" part of the complete enterprise architecture. From that perspective it is important to also be aware that when changing a network infrastructure design, this change can have dire consequences for the rest of the enterprise architecture and even the enterprise itself.

Chapter 4

Cisco Digital Network Architecture

In May 2016 Cisco introduced its Cisco Digital Network Architecture (Cisco DNA). Just like the architecture frameworks described in Chapter 3, "Enterprise Architecture," it is an architecture framework that describes how network infrastructures (not only campus) should be designed and implemented. As with the other frameworks, Cisco DNA in itself is not a product but a collection of design principles, abstract building blocks, and guidelines that, if implemented correctly, will assist (almost) any enterprise or organization in implementing an efficient network infrastructure.

This chapter describes in more detail what Cisco DNA exactly entails. It is important to understand that, just like any other architecture or design within IT, Cisco DNA is not a product on its own but a collection of rules and specifications that can be implemented with specific tools and solutions.

This chapter covers the following topics:

- Requirements upon which Cisco DNA is built
- Guiding design principles of Cisco DNA
- Design concept of Cisco DNA
- Derived design principles
- Overview of Cisco's solution in conjunction with Cisco DNA
- Cisco DNA in relation to enterprise architecture

Requirements

Any design or architecture should be based on a defined set of requirements that match and solve a problem. Cisco DNA is no exception and defines requirements common for the problems today's enterprise networks and corresponding enterprises face.

These requirements are primarily focused on solving the issues and drivers described in Chapter 2, "Why Change Current Networks? A Need for Change."

One of the key drivers for digitalization is faster innovation and development of new services. As a result, a new network architecture must meet the following requirements:

- Faster innovation
  - Flexibility
  - Context
  - Intelligent feedback mechanism
  - Integration and faster deployment
- Reducing complexity and cost
  - Simplicity
  - Increased efficiency
  - Compliancy and technology
  - Security
  - External compliancy rules and regulations
  - High availability
- Cloud-enablement

The following sections describe these requirements in greater detail.

Faster Innovation

One of the key drivers for digitalization is faster innovation and development of new services. As a result a new network architecture must meet the requirements described in the following sections.

Flexibility

The diversity of devices connecting to the enterprise network is rapidly growing. It is a requirement that the enterprise network must be used to facilitate this wide number of endpoints, regardless of how that device needs to be connected. Each set of devices has its own connection and security parameters. This requires flexibility in the connection methods available in the infrastructure.

Besides a diversity of devices, the number and diversity of applications used in the enterprise are changing as well. Studies show that applications have an increased velocity in terms of features and requirements; for example, an application's behavior changes might be more dynamic and use different datasets from the enterprise. Therefore, the network architecture also needs to be flexible in such a way that it supports these applications, which can run anytime and anywhere.

Context

The campus network is the foundation of the enterprise architecture. In essence, the campus network is the principal element within the enterprise that connects devices, its users, and applications to the datacenters, Internet, and/or cloud-based applications to provide and consume data. Without the campus network, the enterprise comes to a standstill. In traditional networks it was sufficient to view statistics based on the IP connectivity and flows that an application was using. Applications were recognized on specific flows and port usage.

With the dynamic behavior, the growing number of devices used by an employee, and an increase in encrypted application flows, there is a need for more context. The network needs to be able to recognize applications and users regardless of whether encryption is used. Based on the recognition, the network needs to be able to adjust policies and prioritize applications if required.

Intelligent Feedback Mechanism

Traditionally campus networks were measured against availability. As both the integration with business processes and the demand for quantifying the network performance increase, the traditional poll-based mechanisms (Simple Network Management Protocol [SNMP]) for monitoring the campus's network state are not meeting that requirement. The traditional monitoring environments (often requiring manual configuration) based on SNMP provide trends on generic availability and capacity. They lack the granularity to define key performance indicators (KPI) or metrics based on applications or processes.

With the tighter integration into business processes with trends such as IoT, physical security over IP, applications as a service (cloud), and wireless/mobility, it is important that the right metrics can be defined and monitored on to provide the required KPIs to the right department within the enterprise as part of a service level agreement.

Cisco DNA must have the necessary analytics to provide this granularity and metrics to support the enterprise.

Integration and Faster Deployment

Rapid application development and deployment has been a growing trend in applications used in the enterprise. The release cycle of applications, existing and new, is increasing (potentially even up to once a month); each change can result in different requirements on the network. With every release of a new application there is a need to consume the enterprise network as a transport service. The network architecture needs to be able to keep up with this release cycle of applications and provide the necessary constructs for facilitating transport services, either individually or grouped with other applications, to the department that consumes or releases the application.

This implies that changes need to be deployed in the network much faster and that the network needs to facilitate a mechanism for application developers to request transport services (semi)automatically.

Reducing Complexity and Cost

Traditionally the increase of diversity in systems and applications also increases the complexity of the network system and its operations, with an increase in cost and loss of efficiency as consequences. The requirements of simplicity and increased efficiency are set within Cisco DNA to counter this effect, as described in the following sections.

Simplicity

Traditionally, networks were designed to facilitate a specific function—for example, a network for office automation, a network for guests, a logistics network in the warehouse, a production network in the plant, and so on. Over time, these networks needed communication between them as well and were interlinked, introducing even more complexity. Operation of these types of networks increases in complexity and results in longer delays to execute a change or troubleshoot a network.

To prevent history from repeating, the Cisco Digital Network Architecture must assume that a diversity of devices and applications will run on the network, where interconnection is possible, based on policies that need to be implemented in the network. Therefore the network must be designed for simplicity where policies, based on software, determine how and in what way specific access is permitted.

The network needs to be set up with a deterministic, flexible, and predictable set of services upon which specific (complex) policies can be implemented via software and predetermined behavior so that complexity in the network infrastructure itself is not increased.

Increased Efficiency

The operation of a business relies on an excellent performing network. However, there will always be an incident or problem that affects the network and thus the business. The tighter integration between the two results in an increased impact on the operation of the business in case of an incident in the network. There have been many instances where issues in IT disrupted network services. For example, in the past within Cisco a misconfigured Active Directory caused an outage to the network access control with loss of service as a consequence.[1]

---

1   This information was shared via several CiscoLive breakout sessions regarding ISE best practices.

Because incidents will happen, Cisco DNA must be designed with increased efficiency in solving such incidents in the most optimum way. The increased efficiency not only provides the benefit of faster recovery from an incident but also reduces the overall operational costs of operating the network.

Compliancy and Technology

Cisco DNA is part of a larger whole, and its design is also based on a more direct interaction with business applications and processes. The interconnectivity with the cloud and a multitude of external managed devices such as IoT sensors facilitate both technology innovation as well as the requirement for a tighter demand for compliancy. The requirements associated with compliance and technology are security, external compliancy rules and regulations, and high availability, as described in the following sections.

Security

Network security is evolving at an even more rapid pace than the dynamic application environment or the endpoint proliferation. Network security has to keep up with the constant threat of users with malicious intent and where malicious software gets more intelligent and professional by the day. From security intelligence centers, such as Talos[2], it is clear that malicious users have started to act as regular enterprises with normal business hours, software targets, quality assurance, software warranties, malware as a service, and other similar activities like normal businesses.

It is therefore important that security policies be set up in line with other requirements described in this chapter, such as simplicity and increased efficiency.

External Compliancy Rules and Regulations

IT is maturing at an ever-increasing pace. Part of this maturity is that data (and meaningful data results in information) is becoming more important for any enterprise. Data has for some businesses even become the new currency and is also critical to the success of the digital transformation of the business.

The collection and handling of more data inside the enterprise also requires the enterprise to be compliant with different external rules and regulations, such as the EU General Data Protection Regulation (GDPR),[3] PCI, HIPAA, or other specific market regulations.

---

2 Talos is the security intelligence organization from Cisco Systems that provides continuous updates on the threat landscape in the field. More information can be found on https:// www.talosintelligence.com/.

3 General Data Protection Regulation, European Union (2016/679) directive that specifically states how businesses need to manage privacy-sensitive data, such as personal information. Not being compliant can result in heavy fines for the business.

Compliance with these rules is becoming increasingly important for enterprises to be successful and to prevent potential fines or loss of business due to lack of compliance, which can result in negative media attention.

Cisco DNA needs to be able to comply with external compliancy rules and regulations, enabling the auditability of the network operations and therefore increasing the maturity of the network architecture. Chapter 12, "Enabling the Digital Business," provides more details on the organization aspects for a digital network architecture and maturity.

High Availability

The enterprise network connects every device in the business. Without the network, almost all businesses run into a standstill. Therefore, the digital network architecture needs to be designed with high availability in mind. The network needs to be resilient and fault-tolerant to prevent single points of failure in the network that can bring an entire business to a standstill.

Cloud-Enablement

The cloud (IT elements as a service) has become a key element of most ICT strategies within enterprises. These strategies can vary from "cloud-only, unless" to "no cloud for corporate data" and include a variety of alterations such as operating and designing internal cloud-like datacenters and a full multicloud strategy. In conclusion, the cloud is a standard component of the IT in the business. As a consequence, not only does the specific cloud need to be transparently connected to the enterprise network, but also the employees should not know or see the difference between a cloud application and an internal application.

Therefore, the enterprise architecture itself needs to be cloud-enabled as well, allowing applications to run in both the cloud and inside the enterprise environment. This means that the network operations for policy, analytics, and change management need to be applied with equal simplicity between cloud-enabled applications and enterprise applications.

Furthermore, Cisco DNA must be able to take full advantage of cloud potential (permitting security policy). This can be, for example, optimizing business processes using open and available data, out-tasking specific processes to the cloud based on a larger software scale, or driving faster innovation by allowing faster adoption of new features and functions.

Cisco DNA Design Concept

To meet and be able to implement the earlier set of requirements, Cisco has translated these requirements into a vision named Digital Network Architecture. Figure 4-1 displays the conceptual overview for the Cisco Digital Network Architecture.

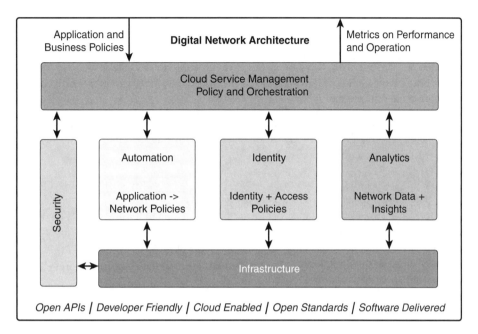

Figure 4-1   *Conceptual Overview of the Cisco Digital Network Architecture*

Figure 4-1 is, for purpose of explanation, slightly different from the figure used within Cisco's white paper about Cisco DNA.[4] Cisco DNA consists of five different functions that collectively meet the requirements. These five different functions result in a number of guiding design principles and derived design principles. These principles are explained in more detail later in this chapter. First each of the five distinct functions of Cisco DNA is explained in the following sections.

Cloud Service Management

Although the title of this function might be a bit misleading, cloud service management is in essence the umbrella function of the network architecture toward the business. The cloud service management function translates the application policies into several policies, such as identity, access, network, and application definitions. The cloud service management is responsible for pushing these policies into the different underlying functions and validating via the analytics that the state of the network is as designed and set forth via the policies.

---

4   *The Cisco Digital Network Architecture Vision—An Overview*, published by Cisco Systems November 2017.

Cisco uses the term *cloud service management* for this function for two distinct requirements:

- That the platform itself fully integrates with different cloud models, such as private clouds, virtual clouds, or public clouds. This means that the platform must be able to run on any of these clouds.

- That the cloud device management platform must also be capable of orchestrating policies and models across a multitude of cloud platforms as well to provide an end-to-end implementation of the policy.

Figure 4-1 displays two directions of information. One is to receive business and application policies from applications or business processes. This capability is presented via a user interface as well as open standard application programmer interfaces (APIs) so that applications can embed the required functions inside the applications. The second arrow provides, also via user interface and APIs, the necessary information toward applications and other business processes about the operational state of the network, its connected devices, and applications being serviced.

Automation

Within Cisco DNA, the automation function fulfills the responsibility of translating network policies received from the cloud services management function into concrete network configurations intended for the appropriate network devices inside the infrastructure function.

The automation function uses APIs to present its own functions toward the cloud service management function as well as leverages APIs and preferably a stateful transaction mechanism to push the configurations in a controlled manner to the network devices.

The section, "Network Automation Tools," in Chapter 6, "Tools for Intent," describes the concept of automation in more detail with network-related examples.

Identity

The identity function defines and is responsible for the identity and access policies within Cisco DNA. Both policies are based on the available policies and resources from the cloud services management function. The identity policy determines who is allowed to access the network infrastructure, and the access policy is used to define which resources (applications and other resources) the user or device is entitled to.

Both policies work in close cooperation; the identity policy is used by the infrastructure to determine which user is connecting to the network. The identity function in return provides the proper mandated access control to the infrastructure function, so that the proper resources can be configured for the connected device.

The identity function is also responsible for facilitating changes in the access control if, for example, malicious activity is found on the network and the device needs to be isolated from the network (or needs to be investigated further).

This function relies heavily on the usage of open and accepted standards, such as the IEEE 802.1X standard (in combination with RADIUS) to provide both functions toward the network devices inside the infrastructure function.

Analytics

Analytics is a key concept function within Cisco DNA. It provides the necessary functions to provide feedback to the monitoring and orchestration tool (inside the cloud services management function) about the operational state of the network, the connected endpoints, its users, and how applications are performing over the network (regardless of whether they run inside the cloud or not).

The analytics function uses APIs to obtain the necessary information from the infrastructure function. These APIs are based on open standards and open mechanisms so that all devices providing network infrastructure functions can provide the necessary information.

Infrastructure

The infrastructure function comprises all network infrastructure–related devices that perform network functions, such as wired access, wireless access, router, WAN, enforcing security policies, and so on. In essence every network device—whether a switch, router, access point, wireless LAN controller, firewall or other security device, physical or virtual—is part of the infrastructure function.

In essence this function is the execution part of Cisco DNA; all network policies, provisioned via automation, are translated into actual network configuration and network operation. Information about the state of the network, the way the network is behaving, and which users attempt to connect are in turn sent to the analytics function.

The receiving of policies or sending analytics of network data in return is preferably executed via open standards and/or APIs. This enables the diversity of network devices to be managed in a single function and in a single manner. Using a single function results in a single view across the complete enterprise network, regardless of where applications and users reside.

Security

Although security is drawn as a vertical column in the image, security itself is not a separate function but must be integrated in every function and implementation of Cisco DNA. It is therefore more a common design principle than a function. The security design principle is covered later in this chapter in the section "Common Design Principles."

Design Principles

Cisco DNA is founded upon four distinct design principles:

- Virtualize network functions

- Design for automation

- Pervasive analytics

- Policy driven and software defined

These design principles govern and support a modern network architecture design for the coming decade. Together, these principles and implicit Cisco DNA design fundamental functionality collaborate to build a modular network concept that can accommodate the radical and rapid changes described in Chapter 2. The following sections describe the four Cisco DNA design principles in more detail.

Virtualize Network Functions (VNF)

Virtualization is common within IT and has been for quite some time now. The introduction of server virtualization consolidated significant server compute power and was one of the enablements for the cloud (as different virtual application functions could be shared on a single server provided by a managed provider). Virtualization within IT means that software (which defines a server or service) runs on top of hardware using an abstraction layer, so that not only multiple services can run on the same hardware, but it is also possible to run different services on that same hardware. In summary, virtualization creates the possibility of running different services on the same hardware instead of using dedicated hardware. It also provides the flexibility that over time different services can be implemented during the lifecycle of the physical server. Besides server virtualization, it is also possible to virtualize applications (known as containers or microservices). It is common for new application development to use application virtualization instead of using monolithic application services.

With Cisco DNA, the virtualization concept is also taken into the network infrastructure. It has been common for network infrastructures to use fit-for-purpose hardware and design the rest of the network around it. Routers are used for running routing protocols and interconnecting several functional routing domains, switches (either campus or data-center) are used to connect network endpoints to the network, utilizing VLANs to logically separate them (if needed), and firewalls (preferably dedicated appliances) are used for securing those networks.

One of the drawbacks of virtualization is that the network functions run on generic purpose hardware, which can result in a decrease in performance as the number of network functions increase. It is therefore important to only set up VNF in network infrastructure devices that are hardware-optimized for these functions in the network.

Use Case: Virtualize Network Functions

Traditionally SharedService Group had the policy to "pull" all traffic from branches to HQ where the central breakout to the Internet was controlled with the necessary security policies. This policy was also applicable to the different branches located worldwide. Although it was accepted by its employees, the employees did have a preference for accessing the local translated web services, such as Google.

At a certain moment the wireless guest services provided at HQ were also to be deployed at the different branch locations. As the design for this new service was being validated, it became clear that it was not desired to have the wireless guest services brought back into the HQ for a central guest Internet connection for a number of reasons. Besides security risks, the risk of requiring extra WAN capacity and providing a less than adequate service at branch locations where English was not the native language were reasons to decide that wireless guest services must use a local Internet connection.

This decision provided the need to procure and implement new hardware at the branch offices so that the central security policies could still be applied. This resulted in a much higher than anticipated investment; therefore, the wireless guest service at branch locations was put on hold until network equipment was to be replaced during a lifecycle management process.

The example of SharedService displays one of the key benefits to Virtualized Network Functions (VNF). The service was requested by the business, but the required investment did not weigh up to the cost of the new service, and the new service was put on hold. With VNF in the branch offices, it would have been possible to deploy virtual firewalls with the same policies and use a VLAN with a router provided by the local Internet Service Provider to implement this new service. With the increased adoption rate of cloud-enabled sensors and applications in the enterprise, the use of VNF allows for deploying new network functions with a much lower investment cost.

An added benefit of VNF is that new services can be deployed much faster. The network devices are already available, and it is only a matter of software to be deployed. This speed increase supports the need for faster service delivery and will drive innovation.

The first design principle of Cisco DNA is that all network functions must be virtualized in order to achieve flexibility in the deployment of network functions.

Design for Automation

The FreeBSD 10.x and 11.x Frequently Asked Questions[5] contains the following question (joke):

"Q: How many FreeBSD hackers does it take to change a lightbulb?"

A: One thousand, one hundred and sixty-nine:

Twenty-three to complain to -CURRENT about the lights being out;

Four to claim that it is a configuration problem, and that such matters really belong on -questions;

Three to submit PRs about it, one of which is misfiled under doc and consists only of "it's dark";

One to commit an untested lightbulb which breaks buildworld, then back it out 5 minutes later;

Eight to flame the PR originators for not including patches in their PRs;

Five to complain about buildworld being broken;

Thirty-one to answer that it works for them, and they must have updated at a bad time;

One to post a patch for a new lightbulb to -hackers;

One to complain that he had patches for this three years ago, but when he sent them to -CURRENT they were just ignored, and he has had bad experiences with the PR system; besides, the proposed new lightbulb is non-reflexive;

Thirty-seven to scream that lightbulbs do not belong in the base system, that committers have no right to do things like this without consulting the Community, and WHAT IS -CORE DOING ABOUT IT!?

Two hundred to complain about the color of the bicycle shed;

Three to point out that the patch breaks style(9);

Seventeen to complain that the proposed new lightbulb is under GPL;

Five hundred and eighty-six to engage in a flame war about the comparative advantages of the GPL, the BSD license, the MIT license, the NPL, and the personal hygiene of unnamed FSF founders;

Seven to move various portions of the thread to -chat and -advocacy;

One to commit the suggested lightbulb, even though it shines dimmer than the old one;

---

5   http://ftp.freebsd.org/pub/FreeBSD/doc/faq/book.pdf

Two to back it out with a furious flame of a commit message, arguing that FreeBSD is better off in the dark than with a dim lightbulb;

Forty-six to argue vociferously about the backing out of the dim lightbulb and demanding a statement from -core;

Eleven to request a smaller lightbulb so it will fit their Tamagotchi if we ever decide to port FreeBSD to that platform;

Seventy-three to complain about the SNR on -hackers and -chat and unsubscribe in protest;

Thirteen to post "unsubscribe", "How do I unsubscribe?", or "Please remove me from the list", followed by the usual footer;

One to commit a working lightbulb while everybody is too busy flaming everybody else to notice;

Thirty-one to point out that the new lightbulb would shine 0.364% brighter if compiled with TenDRA (although it will have to be reshaped into a cube), and that FreeBSD should therefore switch to TenDRA instead of GCC;

One to complain that the new lightbulb lacks fairings;

Nine (including the PR originators) to ask "what is MFC?";

Fifty-seven to complain about the lights being out two weeks after the bulb has been changed.

Nik Clayton <nik@FreeBSD.org> adds:

I was laughing quite hard at this.

And then I thought, "Hang on, shouldn't there be '1 to document it.' in that list somewhere?"

And then I was enlightened :-)"

Although the concept of the joke is applicable to many areas such as technology or large organizations, there's unfortunately a double truth to that answer for operating network infrastructures. Very often many people must be involved for a change based on the processes, validation, alignment with end users, change management, and so on.

It is also, unfortunately, very common that these infrastructures, from small to large, are managed using a per-device approach (using either CLI or on-box management tools). So upgrading IOS on switches, creating or deleting a VLAN, or changing a DHCP helper are all executed by a network engineer typing the required commands onto the box and validating whether the change was successful. This adds an extra layer of complexity, higher risk of error, and extra time requirements to execute a relatively simple change.

Automation allows network operation teams to execute changes automatically in a controlled method instead of executing changes manually per device. The automation tool will execute the mandated change in a very punctual method, repeating the change the same way for each device it is applied to. This reduces the risk of human error greatly, although a mistake in the change can have drastic consequences. Therefore, it is key to test the change before running it through an automation tool.

Use Case: Automation at FinTech Ltd.

FinTech Ltd. has been using network access control for quite a while, changing over time from Cisco Access Control Server (ACS) to Cisco Identity Services Engine (ISE). The same ISE deployment has also been used to introduce central authentication and authorization of the network infrastructure devices as well.

As part of their latest ISE upgrades, the appliances had to be replaced as well as performing a clean install was recommended due to some major internal changes within ISE.

During the migration, a change procedure was documented and crafted. During the preparation of that change procedure it became clear that the RADIUS configuration was not consistent across the sixty-odd access switches; different radius server group names or defaults were used.

As a result, the change procedure itself became more complicated due to these design changes. The lead engineer decided to include a standardized configuration component for the changed RADIUS configuration (using one configuration block for network access control and one for network device management).

The change was further prepared by creating a dedicated application that would execute the necessary changes. This application had the required configuration changes in text (and thus templating the configuration) and used an export of the old ISE environment to know which devices to connect to. A log provided the necessary output to validate whether the changes were executed successfully.

During the change window, the created application was run several times to roll out the necessary configuration changes in small atomic steps. The change itself was faster and more secure, as the tool was executing the changes in a consistent way, leaving the engineer validating if no error occurred. The change was successful as there were no failures or incidents related to network access control on the first day after the change.

This example displays the power of automation. When a campus network is designed for automation, an operation change such as authenticating against a different ISE server can be deployed using templates or other tools instead of copy-pasting changes from notepad into the CLI of sixty-odd devices. The change is in turn executed more efficiently and with no chance of having inconsistencies across the network.

The second design principle of the Cisco Digital Network Architecture mandates that the network infrastructure must be designed with automation in mind.

Pervasive Analytics

There are a few differences between a traditional network and Cisco DNA. One of the primary factors that differentiates both is that Cisco DNA is based on policies (automatically) being pushed to the infrastructure. As these policies can be dynamic and software driven, a feedback mechanism is required to validate the correct state and operation of that infrastructure. This feedback mechanism can be found in the analytics function of Cisco DNA.

Analytics itself can consist of simply checking whether the routing tables and the routing neighbors are set and checking the generic trend on bandwidth utilization and errors found on an interface. This kind of monitoring is traditionally executed via a poll mechanism using SNMP. This traditional method of polling requires some manual configuration per device, is intensive on the CPU of the network device, and is also not capable of providing granular information about the performance of applications or whether a DHCP server is not responding. In summary, the traditional method of only polling the network is not enough for Cisco DNA.

Instead of using polling mechanisms, a more modern approach to obtaining the state and operation of the network is required. Instead of having to poll each device, the infrastructure should provide the analytics function within Cisco DNA the necessary information. Just like how weather sensors provide data to meteorological models, a similar approach is an integral part of Cisco DNA. The infrastructure devices should provide telemetry data (not only including the traditionally available data like interface statistics, but also including client-related data) to the analytics function.

This model-driven telemetry feature allows the analytics function within Cisco DNA to gather more detailed data and perform the proper tasks to determine if the network is operating as expected and therefore provide the proper feedback to cloud service management.

Another requirement for Cisco DNA is to increase efficiency of the network while the diversity and the number of endpoints is increasing. The number of network devices will increase, and the existing network operations team needs to manage and operate the network using different methods. Traditionally the network team would respond to IT-related incidents reported by end users. Most incidents are focused (or blamed) on the network, and it is up to the network team to "prove" that the network is not at fault. The model-driven telemetry already provides a benefit for this task. However, instead of responding to incidents, the intelligence of the network needs to be used to change the network team from responsive to proactive.

In essence, instead of waiting for an incident to happen, Cisco DNA uses programmable network sensors to proactively measure and test the network in a predictive manner. These sensors can be existing network devices, virtual services on these devices, or dedicated test hardware strategically placed in the network.

These sensors will perform the configured tests frequently. The results of these tests are then provided to the analytics function of Cisco DNA so that alerts can be provided to the network team (or other teams) for a possible failure. Using sensors, more intelligence is placed in the network to proactively test several network functions and applications. This provides, in a proactive manner, more information if a client is not receiving an IP address on a site, a DHCP server might be down, or other connectivity-related issues exist. Using network sensors, the network operations team is supported in transforming from reactive to proactive responses.

The data that becomes available from the network infrastructure within Cisco DNA can be used in combination with the evolution of machine intelligence to provide suggested fixes to common problems within the network itself. Machine intelligence is a trend that allows systems within enterprises to use the available (structured) data to provide recommendations on different topics, such as the ordering process, or to determine the cost of an insurance policy. The same principle is to be applied within Cisco DNA. Machine intelligence can use the received telemetry data, information from the identity function, and results from sensors to find relationships to incidents or problems before they might even occur. Based on that "intelligence," recommended actions can be provided to the network operations team, further promoting proactive behavior. The network is intelligently supporting the network operating team to optimize the operation of the network.

The third design principle of Cisco DNA is that pervasive analytics are used in Cisco DNA to fully harness the power of the latent data inside the network to validate the correct state of the network as well as to detect incidents in the network more quickly by using the intelligence of the network.

Policy Driven and Software Defined

A keyword that has been used repeatedly in the previous paragraphs is *policy*. Traditionally the network was configured based on the requirements being translated into a number of configuration lines. There was no abstraction layer as to why a certain set of configuration commands had to be used in a specific way other than there was either a template or another switch with similar functionality available. And this is applicable to many areas of the campus network, including switches, wireless networks, routers, and the WAN. The main disadvantage of this methodology is that it does not provide an easy way to validate whether the configuration is working as expected or to be able to reuse the same configuration. In essence, there is a lack of policy.

Policies provide an abstraction mechanism that can hide the details of a configuration or implementation by using a generic specification of the requested service while being as specific as possible. Although this sounds contradictory, an example might help.

Business application X consists of the client applications installed on tablets communicating with web servers via HTTPS. The web servers in turn communicate with an application server that consumes the required data from a single MySQL database server.

This application description is specific in which communication the application requires, but it does not state which specific IP addresses are used. It does not describe where the database server resides and what IP address those web servers have or that the clients are using. This is a perfect example of a policy description that can be stored/recorded in Cisco DNA.

When this application is implemented, specific implementation IP addresses can be specified and the proper access list rules can be created based on the network topology and implementation. The power of this policy is that it can be reused for other implementations of that same application. Or, if the application is moved to the cloud, only the IP addresses for the web servers need to be changed, and the policy can be reimplemented.

Cisco DNA harnesses the full power of operating based on policies. In the preceding example, if that change needs to be executed, Cisco DNA "knows" that the earlier access list rules need to be changed in the campus network, allowing the clients to communicate to the cloud on those ports.

Policies provide the capacity and power to present complex technical implementations in a more generic form, allowing both the required transparency for visibility in an ever-diversifying network as well as the ability to perform required changes in a consistent manner.

Inherent to a policy-driven methodology is the concept of *software defined*. If a policy is defined by the operations team, the software should translate that policy into a consistent change of specific configurations on the different network devices in the infrastructure. This approach allows the software to keep track of which policy resulted in which change so that when a policy is removed, the necessary specific configuration can be removed from the devices as well.

By using a software-defined approach, it is also possible within Cisco DNA to provide a per-user policy into the network once that user or device is connected to the network. The software-defined approach translates the allowed applications policy to configuration elements specific to that user. This allows for more visibility and control in the diversity of applications used in the enterprise.

The fourth design principle is that Cisco DNA is a policy-driven architecture and uses a software-defined approach to implement and monitor those policies. All communication between the different functions is based on a software-defined approach.

The book *Cross-Domain Segmentation with Intent-Based Networking* by Mark Hazell, Brian Shlisky, Errol Roberts, and David Jansen provides different examples of how a policy-driven and software-defined approach can be applied in end-to-end use cases across the enterprise.

Common Design Principles

The different functions within Cisco DNA and its four design principles rely on a number of common principles. Besides regular common network design principles such as mean time between two failures, fault isolation, and so on, there are four common design principles that make Cisco DNA unique compared to regular (campus) network infrastructures:

- Cisco DNA-ready infrastructure

- Open standards

- Use of API

- Security everywhere

These four common design principles lay the foundation for every solution based on Cisco DNA. The following sections provide an explanation of these design principles.

Cisco DNA-Ready Infrastructure

In the past, network devices were selected based on their primary network functions. (For example, a switch was selected if the primary function was switching, a router for routing purposes such as a WAN, and so on.) The primary cause for this was that the chip (ASIC) that performed the network function in hardware was built for that purpose. In other words, a switch has an ASIC and physical interfaces used primarily used for switching purposes. The ASIC was preprogrammed for that function, and running new technology or network features in hardware was not possible.

Difference Between Switchport and Routed Port

The Ethernet interfaces on a Cisco device are a switchport or a routed port. With the command **no switchport** on a switch, it is possible to make a switchport behave like a routed port. All Layer 2 configurations, such as Spanning Tree, are removed from the interface, and for most switches an internal VLAN (in the extended range) is assigned to that interface, allowing only that interface to have an IP address and respond to ARP requests. As a consequence, that VLAN becomes unavailable for Layer 2 functions. This information can be read in the IOS Command Reference guide under the "Extended-Range VLAN Guidelines" section. Another way that a switchport is different from a routed port is that it is not possible to configure sub-interfaces on a physical switched interface.

Similarly, routed ports do not support Layer 2 protocols unless they are explicitly configured for a Bridge Virtual Interface, which is partially run in hardware and software.

In designing a network based on models and building blocks, it is important to know which type of interface is available as it can have limits on design and function.

With the introduction of the Catalyst 3650/3850 series, Cisco also introduced a new type of ASIC, the programmable ASIC, also known as the Unified Access Data Plane

(UADP) ASIC. The second version of this ASIC was introduced in the Cisco Catalyst 9000[6] series. This ASIC is unique in the sense that it does not know how to handle an Ethernet frame or an IP packet when the switches are booted. The ASIC is literally programmed with the required features when the switch is starting up. This programmable ASIC provides many benefits and has already proven powerful. For example, at the introduction of the Catalyst 3650/3850 switches the technology VXLAN did not exist, and yet with new releases of operating system code, these switches now support this technology. You could even state that if a new network protocol would be designed and adopted, for example IPv11, this ASIC would be able to handle it in hardware.

The programmability of ASICs is discussed in a Cisco TechWise TV episode[7] with Principal Engineer Peter Jones and Distinguished System Engineer Dave Zacks, who both have personally been involved in the development of this ASIC.

Besides the programmable ASIC, the operating system for the more recent Cisco routers (ISR 4000 series, ISR 1100 series) and switches (Catalyst 3650/3850 series and Catalyst 9000 series) run on the same operating system, called Cisco IOS-XE. Cisco IOS-XE is based on Linux and allows the hardware to run other services besides the IOS-daemon that performs the network functions. In essence, running Cisco IOS-XE allows you to run other virtual machines (although limited) on the device, provided that the device has sufficient CPU and memory, like the Catalyst 9000 series has.

Another benefit of running network devices with the same operating system is that features traditionally only available in routers are now becoming available in switches, such as MPLS and routing protocols such as LISP. In summary, technology features are converging and becoming available on other platforms.

The programmability of the ASIC and convergence of features benefit the network devices used in Cisco DNA. These devices become capable of performing new services, technologies, or features as they become available and required in the Cisco DNA without replacing the network device.

Open Standards

Cisco network devices are most often configured via a command-line interface. The engineer, or in some environments the tool, enters the configuration command for command into the device. Besides the chance of locking the tool or the engineer out (by changing an IP address or IP route), the commands are also executed atomically, that is, each single command becomes effective immediately. Transactional changes (committing a set of commands in a single action) are limited to NX-OS (Datacenter) and IOS-XR (Service Provider). Cisco DNA is based on translating policies into pieces of configuration (for example, building blocks) that can be applied and removed from the basic network infrastructure to support the diverse clients and applications on the digital network.

---

6   Cisco has published a book on the capacity of the Catalyst 9000 series at http://cs.co/cat9k-ebook.

7   https://www.cisco.com/c/m/en_us/training-events/events-webinars/webinars/techwise-tv/214-programmable-asics.html

To maintain network integrity it is required to execute these changes (applying and removing policies) in a transactional manner; for example, each policy change should be a single transaction on the network device instead of a sequence of commands executed per device.

Cisco DNA is based on a modern, adaptive approach to the network as a whole, where policies are applied and removed to infrastructure devices. This methodology is required to facilitate network-enabled applications requesting transport over the network via automated processes. This means that application developers (building enterprise applications) must understand how a network operates without the in-depth technical knowledge of commands a network designer or network engineer has. This is accomplished via a model that abstracts the network from specific configuration commands. As Cisco DNA is part of a larger connected environment and this model is intended for third-party developers, the model must be based on open accepted standards.

In conclusion, Cisco DNA prefers the deployment of configurations to be executed in a transactional method to maintain integrity, and a model that abstracts the network from the actual commands is required. Therefore, Cisco DNA requires the usage of internationally accepted open models and standards in its design and implementations. This can be accomplished using NETCONF/YANG models.

Use of API

Cisco DNA consists of five functions (cloud service management, automation, identity, analytics, and infrastructure). These functions represent in a sense their own specific responsibilities and tasks. They also have relationships with other functions, usually as a consumer, provider, or both. For example, the automation function provides methods to the cloud service management function to allow the network to be changed based on policies. Based on the specific change, the automation function translates (or transforms) the policy into distinct, predetermined, and tested configuration changes. These changes are subsequently applied to the network devices inside the infrastructure function.

These methods between two Cisco DNA functions are commonly performed by software without human intervention. It is therefore important that these methods between functions need to be described in such a formal manner that different tools can provide one or more of the Cisco DNA functions. This formal method of describing and enabling functionality between systems is commonly referred to as Application Program Interface (API).

APIs provide software engineers with sufficient documentation and functionality so that software engineers can use the functionality inside their own code without writing that functionality themselves.

Within Cisco these formal methods can exist between two different solutions each performing a Cisco DNA function; therefore, these API calls are to be executed via server-to-server communications. To facilitate a digital network architecture based on a policy-driven, software-defined, and automated approach, the communication between Cisco DNA functions is to be executed via APIs. These open and exposed APIs are also applicable in the communication to and from the cloud service management function.

This common design principle allows external parties, such as enterprise application developers or other software engineers, to programmatically (using a software-defined approach) request the operational state of the network as well as to provide the possibility to request transport services for their application.

RESTful Application Programmer Interface

Within the history of software development, several methodologies and principles have been used in the past to allow server-to-server or client-to-server communication. Concepts varied from Remote Procedure Calls, Remote Method Invocations, Service Oriented Architectures, and Enterprise Messaging Queueing Systems to full Enterprise System Buses. The most recent and widely adopted concept for API-based communication over a network (also known as Web 2.0 services) is called RESTful API. REST is the acronym for Representational State Transfer and has been available since 2000.

The RESTful API is based on the HTTP protocol and uses so-called Create, Read, Update, and Delete (CRUD) methods in combination with URLs. The data being transferred between systems is text encapsulated in specific file formats, such as Hypertext Markup Language (HTML), eXtensible Markup Language (XML), or JavaScript Object Notification (JSON). XML is common, while JSON is gaining more popularity due to its easier-to-read-and-construct syntax.

An example of a REST API call would be a weather app asking the weather for a specific location at a web service. A special GET request would be sent to a weather service, where the response would be the weather forecast in a structured format. That response is parsed by the app and shown to the user.

This example showcases that an app is executing a system-to-system response to a service and receives the response back, which in turn is presented to the end user. More information and examples of APIs are provided in Chapter 10, "Phase Four: Enable Intent."

An increasing number of Cisco products provide an API interface and primarily use a RESTfull API for that. The DevNet[8] website from Cisco provides more details and code examples of APIs.

Security Everywhere

Network security is evolving at an ever-increasing pace. This increase is a direct result of the professionalism that malicious actors apply on their software and approach. In general the malicious actors have near-unlimited funding and time to try to gain access to the data they want. This includes (successful) attempts to compromise software or other elements in the supply chain of the enterprise to achieve their goal.

In classic enterprises security was commonly implemented by a defense-in-depth approach, with several active security perimeters in the network, providing a layered

---

8 https://developer.cisco.com/

approach where the most sensitive data was hidden behind several of these security layers.

However, a negative side effect of the increase in cloud usage, diversity of devices, and other issues is that the possible attack surface available to malicious users increases. Figure 4-2 provides a schematic overview of an enterprise network and shows where different attack points can be used by malicious users. There are many more possible attack vectors compared to the past, where the Internet perimeter was the primary attack surface.

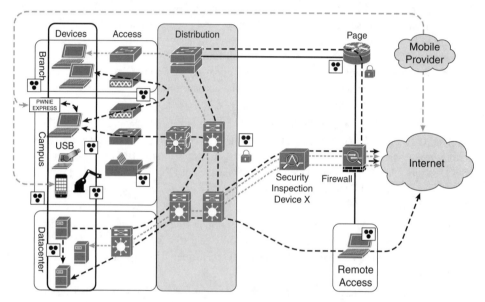

Figure 4-2   *A Conceptual Overview of Potential Threat (Image courtesy of Cisco Live Techtorial on Offensive Cybersecurity)*

To be able to keep up with the pace as well as keep the enterprise manageable and respond to security risks rapidly, there must be a unified security approach to the network infrastructure. This unified security approach must be able to fulfill a minimum set of requirements. These requirements are aimed to improve security across the enterprise network:

- **Visibility and detection:** The network must be able to provide the necessary visibility for devices (and end users) and their communication on the campus network. By having a unified visibility, it is easier to detect if malicious activity is seen within the enterprise.

- **Single consistent security access policy:** With the network being more dynamic, security access policies need to be consistent and created in such a way that the access is defined and determined in a holistic approach, regardless of which device (switch, next generation firewall, or wireless LAN controller) it is applied to. This consistent security access policy increases the visibility and provides an increase in network security.

- **Unified segmentation policy:** With the diversity of types of devices and related access policies, it is necessary to have a unified segmentation policy applied to the (campus) network. A unified segmentation policy improves the visibility and ensures that it is impossible to view the information within flows if not allowed. In other words, using a unified segmentation policy ensures that, for example, IoT traffic is not matched with enterprise traffic so that compromised IoT devices cannot listen to that enterprise traffic.

- **Easy and rapid containment:** The nPetya outbreak in June 2017 resulted in more than 5,000 infections per minute inside an affected enterprise. The cause of this high infection rate was the ability of the malware to move laterally through the network. This real-world example shows that it is key for a modern digital network architecture to enable rapid threat containment. In other words, if malicious activity is seen, the device needs to be isolated from the network as soon as possible to prevent further damage.

In conclusion, network security and visibility must be an integral part of Cisco DNA to maintain the required security policies in the dynamic use of the campus network. Security needs to be everywhere inside a Digital Network Architecture.

Overview of Cisco Solutions

Cisco DNA is in principle a functional architecture design for the enterprise network and fits inside the technology architecture of an enterprise. Cisco's product portfolio provides solutions that can implement the different functions of Cisco DNA. Figure 4-3 provides an overview of the different products and solutions applicable to campus networks with which a Cisco DNA can be implemented.

Tool/product	Design principle							DNA Function				
	Security everywhere	Virtualize network functions	Automation	Cloud Managed	Analytics	Open standards / API	DNA Ready	Infrastructure	Automation	Identity	Analytics	Policy / Orchestration
DNA Center	√	√	√	√	√	√	√		√		√	√
APIC-EM/Prime			√	√	√	√			√		√	√
Software defined access	√		√	√		√	√	√	√			
Network Service Orchestrator		√			√	√			√			
Identity Services Engine	√					√	√	√	√	√	√	
Encrypted Threat Analytics	√				√							
Stealthwatch	√			√	√	√					√	
WLAN Controllers	√				√		√	√			√	
Catalyst 3650/3850	√	√				√		√				
Catalyst 9000 switches	√	√				√	√	√				
Compact switches	√					√	√	√				
Building switches	√					√	√	√				

Figure 4-3 *Overview of Cisco Products and Solutions Matching DNA Criteria*

Figure 4-3 provides a direction in which products and solutions can be used to implement Cisco DNA. As the technology inside products, solutions, and integrations evolves, specific limitations can be applicable for certain devices. At the time of writing, the following limitations are known and should be taken into account:

- The Cisco WLAN Controllers 2504 and 5508 do support AireOS 8.5 code releases; Software Defined Access (SDA) Wireless is supported, but model-driven telemetry (Analytics) is not supported on these devices.

- The Catalyst 3650/3850 is Cisco DNA ready infrastructure but has limitations in number of capacity and sizing in relationship to SDA.

- Certain compact 3560C and industrial switches do support SDA with limitations specified in the release notes.

- Prime Infrastructure and APIC-EM are available solutions for today and have not seen an end-of-life announcement. However, Cisco DNA Center is the successor to these tools, and it is expected that Prime Infrastructure and APIC-EM will get an end-of-life once Cisco DNA Center has a similar set of features. This should, however, not restrict any organization from starting the transformation to Intent-Based Networking.

- Every organization and network is unique. The details in deployment and situation determine which tool fits the purpose best.

The table in Figure 4-3 can be used in the beginning stages to transform existing networks into a Digital Network Architecture, which is described in more detail in Part 2, "Transforming to an Intent-Based Network."

Summary

From the perspective of the TOGAF® standard, the Cisco Digital Network Architecture (Cisco DNA) is part of the technical architecture describing the requirements, principles, and functions of the network infrastructure for the enterprise. Cisco DNA is based on requirements that represent the challenges and drivers described in Chapter 2. These requirements can be summarized as follows:

- Faster innovation through:
  - Increased flexibility
  - Providing more context to allow granular metrics and services
  - Intelligent feedback mechanism
  - Faster deployment through tighter integration
- Reducing complexity and cost via:
  - Simplicity in design
  - Software-driven operations based on policies and automation
  - Increased efficiency of operation

- Tighter integration with compliancy and technology:

  - Security

  - High availability

  - Visibility for external compliancy rules and regulations

- Cloud-enablement by default

Based on these requirements, Cisco DNA is composed of five distinct functions, which can be summarized as

- Cloud service management, to provide business-enabled services

- Automation, to quickly deploy changes in configuration to network infrastructure devices

- Identity, which is used to determine who is accessing the network and what access policy is to be applied

- Analytics, to validate whether the network infrastructure is operating correctly and providing the correct services

- Infrastructure, the actual network infrastructure devices

Cisco DNA also provides a number of design principles and common design principles used to meet the requirements and support a successful implementation of the requirements. These design principles and common design principles are summarized as

- Virtualize network functions

- Design for automation

- Pervasive analytics

- Policy driven and software defined

- Cisco DNA-ready infrastructure

- Open standards

- Use of APIs

- Security everywhere

Cisco DNA provides, on a functional level, an extensive architectural approach to the design of a network infrastructure that is prepared to meet all requirements and the foreseen challenges for a campus network.

Chapter 5

Intent-Based Networking

By and large, Cisco DNA describes the requirements and operations of a network infrastructure of an enterprise on an abstract level. Cisco DNA achieves this description by dividing the requirements of the enterprise network into several functions and design principles. Cisco DNA itself does not describe how to use or implement that network architecture. You can compare it with the design of a large office building. The drawings provide enough guidelines and a viewpoint of how the building will look. But it does not provide details on which materials the contractor needs to create the building or which functionality the building will be used for. Cisco DNA is nothing more than a description of the network in an abstract manner.

Intent-Based Networking (IBN) provides a powerful description and methodology on how you can use that network if it is built using Cisco DNA's specifications and requirements. IBN is essentially a viewpoint or perspective of an implemented network using Cisco DNA's requirements, design functions, and abstraction levels.

But what is Intent Based Networking? What perspective does it provide? This chapter describes IBN in more detail and covers the following topics:

- What is Intent
- Intent-Based Networking paradigm
- IBN designs
- Network as a platform
- Possible IBN implementations
- IBN examples

What Is Intent?

To understand what Intent-Based Networking is, it is important to know more about what *Intent* encompasses. *Purpose* is a synonym and probably makes the definition of intent easier to understand.

Every person, department, or organization has multiple intents or purposes. An organization can have the purpose to provide the best in class of software to schools, or to provide the best phones in the world. A business process can have the intent to fulfill its described task in the most efficient manner. A person can of course have multiple intents or purposes. In general, intent or purpose is a description of a goal to be achieved.

A good example of intent would be that my wife likes me to clear out the garbage cans in the kitchen and put their contents in the containers outside our home. My actions to fulfill her intent would then be: Take out the general-waste trash bag from the can in the kitchen and carry it to the appropriate container outside. Walk back to the kitchen and then take the bag of recyclable waste and put it in its correct container. Clean the kitchen cans if needed and put new trash bags in them.

This example describes intent quite well. My wife has an intent, and I have described steps to fulfill that intent. And once you take this point of view to many common tasks, intent can be seen everywhere. Table 5-1 shows some examples of intent.

Table 5-1   *Overview of Intents*

Intent	Execution Steps
I need the lawn cut.	Take the mower out of the garage, connect it to power, pull cord to start, push onto lawn and mow in lanes until lawn is finished, power off the mower, remove grass from the lawn, disconnect the mower from power cord, clean grass from the mower, and put it back in the garage.
I'm organizing a dinner party.	Invite friends, prepare dinner as much as possible ahead of time, clean up the house, dress up, welcome friends, finish and serve the dinner, clean up the table, and have a great evening.
I want to drive the car.	Check whether enough fuel is in the car; if not, drive to the nearest gas station and fill up the tank; start driving.
This sales order needs to be shipped.	Check the stock for this order, search each item in warehouse, pick the required items of the sales order, place them in a box, print the packing slip and place it in the box, fill the box with bubble wrap and close it, notify shipping organization of shipment, print the shipping label, stick it on the box, and place the box on the outgoing platform.
Next year I need to replace firewalls.	Prepare a budget proposal for the CFO explaining why replacement is required, present the proposal, wait for approval, request quotes, procure hardware, execute project to replace firewalls in production.

Intent	Execution Steps
This car needs to be assembled.	Procure all required parts, components, and implementation details; weld the chassis; place the chassis on the belt; let robots and workers assemble all parts; execute quality and assurance testing; prepare the car for shipment, and ship the car to the dealer.
I need to upgrade the code on the network switch.	Determine the new version of the software, upgrade the test environment with the new version, execute tests to check if the new version works with existing designs, validate results, request a change window for update, notify end users, execute update, validate if the upgrade was successful, update documentation, and close the change.

As you can see, intent is everywhere. An intent is essentially a brief description of the purpose and a concrete predetermined set of steps that need to be executed to (successfully) achieve the intent. This principle can also be applied to the operation of a network infrastructure. The intent and its steps describe very specifically what needs to be done on the network to accomplish a specific task. Table 5-2 provides a number of examples of how intent can be applied on a network infrastructure.

Table 5-2 *Overview of Network-Based Intents*

Intent	Execution Steps
I have a telepresence session at 10:00 a.m.	Create an HD video session to the remote peer, create the required end-to-end Quality of Service parameters for this specific session, reserve the bandwidth, set up audio, validate performance, keep the connection safe and secure during the session, once finished disconnect the HD video session, remove the end-to-end quality of service session, and remove the bandwidth reservation.
This application is migrating to the cloud.	Take the existing access policy for that application from the datacenter policy, transform the policy into an application policy for Internet access, deploy the policy on all perimeter firewalls, and change routing for that application to the cloud.
This new IoT application needs to be enabled.	Create a new logical compartment on the network, create an IP-space, set up Internet access policies, create access policies to recognize the IoT devices, and assign them to the logical compartment.
This application needs access to HR systems during salary runs.	Once the user starts the run, request access to system via the network, open the required ports and IP addresses for the device that user is connected with via an access policy, wait until salary run is finished, remove the temporary access policies, and clear the open connections.
Potential malware has been found on a device.	Reallocate the device to an investigate policy that includes in-depth monitoring of traffic and host isolation, execute a Change-of-Authorization to place the device in the new policy, notify security and administrator of a possible incident, and await investigation.

Table 5-2 provides only a small number of examples, but the possibilities are endless. The most important condition (and restriction) is that the proposed intent must be written in controllable, repeatable execution steps, so that the automation function within Cisco DNA can execute those steps automatically. In summary, Intent-Based Networking is a perspective or viewpoint on how a network infrastructure that meets Cisco DNA's functions, design principles, and requirements is operated. Using this perspective to operate the network will in turn enable the enterprise to embrace digitalization and the digital enterprise.

The following sections describe in more detail how this perspective leverages Cisco DNA's functions and design principles to achieve Intent-Based Networking.

Intent-Based Networking Perspective

IBN can be seen as a perspective on a Cisco DNA-based network infrastructure that describes how the network can be managed, operated, and enable a digital business. It translates an intent within the business into the configuration of the network required for that specific intent. This is achieved by defining the intent as a number of (repetitive) steps that can be deployed. The IBN perspective uses all aspects of Cisco DNA (design principles, concepts, and so on) to accomplish this method of approaching the network.

The IBN perspective is based on a systematic approach where the network infrastructure is seen as a holistic system.

Figure 5-1 shows this systematic approach.

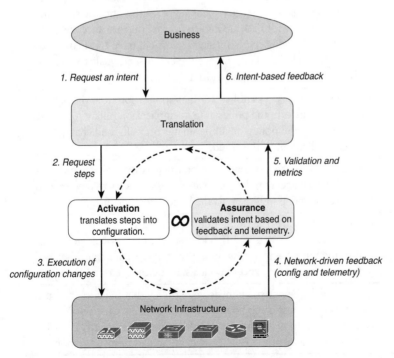

Figure 5-1   *IBN Systematic Approach to the Network*

This approach resembles the functional approach of Cisco DNA a lot. It is, of course, a perspective on how a Cisco DNA-based network infrastructure is operated. This approach is based on six steps in a continuous loop.

1. **Request an intent:** A part of the business, whether a process, front-end application, or operator, specifies a specific Intent request to the network infrastructure. This is of course based on a number of available intents, where the variety of the Intent also depends on the organization and the level of availability.

   The translation process, receiving the request for Intent, translates the specific intent into a number of repetitive executable required steps. This is, for deploying a network Intent, perhaps one of the most important aspects of Intent-Based Networking. These steps need to be designed, tested, and defined within the translation process. Depending on the solution, these steps could be predefined templates or specific pieces of network configuration specific to the enterprise. The implementation of these repetitive executable steps needs to be as predictable as possible and is quite often defined by the network designer.

   For example, if the intent is a new IoT network, the Intent is translated into steps like create a new network, assign an IP-pool to that network, and place this network into a single logically separated compartment.

2. **Request steps:** Once the required steps for the specific intent are defined and created, the requested steps are sent to the Activation process. This process receives the requested steps and translates these steps into device-specific configuration changes that are required on the network infrastructure. The Activation process knows which configuration changes are required on which devices and uses automation to activate the changes on the applicable network devices. In turn the Activation process pushes the required changes to the network infrastructure.

   Based on the earlier example of intent, the Activation process translates the new network into a new VRF on a number of core switches in the network and allocates a new VLAN where the IoT devices are placed. The allocated IP pool is translated into a DHCP scope on the device that provides DHCP services to the network. A security policy can automatically be added to detect and authorize the new IoT devices.

3. **Execution of configuration changes:** This is the step where the Activation process actually connects to the network devices and deploys the changes to the network infrastructure. At this stage the requested Intent has been translated into a specific configuration on the network infrastructure. The requested intent is implemented. Although the Activation process performs pre- and postchecks to validate if the configuration of the network infrastructure devices was successful, the Activation process cannot determine whether the deployed configuration has the desired outcome.

4. **Network-driven feedback:** In this step, the network infrastructure devices provide feedback to the assurance process. The feedback is based on a number of data flows, including the generated network configuration, telemetry on the network, which client is connected, and how clients behave on the network. The network-driven feedback is used to validate if the executed configuration changes from step 3 have resulted in the desired outcome.

Using the same example, the IoT devices are now connected to the network and assigned to the specific VLAN and VRF. Telemetry data on whether the IoT device gets an IP address and which communication flows are seen by the network are sent to the Assurance process.

5. **Validation & metrics:** In this step the Assurance process has analyzed and validated the different data flows received from the network infrastructure devices. The received data is combined and analyzed, and potential issues or correct operation is sent back to the Translation process. This step provides the feedback on whether the requested intent is working as expected, and which IP addresses clients have received, including metrics on the usage, are provided to the Translation process.

Within the same example, the status of the intent, including client-related information is sent to the translation process.

6. **Intent-based feedback:** The translation process receives metrics and the validation of the requested intent operation. The Translation process checks the status of the requested intent continuously and determines whether problems exist with the requested intent. In case of a problem, the operations team is informed of the failed state, and the business can request the status of the requested intent as well. Similarly, statistics on the usage of the requested intent are provided to the business layer using application-based metrics such as number of devices, accumulated data usage, and availability statistics, some of the most often used key performance indicators for the business.

Within the same example, this step provides a positive status back to the business that the requested intent is operating as requested and provides an aggregated overview on availability and bandwidth usage to the business. The new IoT application is running successfully on the network.

These individual steps are executed for every requested intent. A large network can quickly have hundreds of requested intents to be added and run on the network. In addition to the requirement that these steps can run in parallel for different intents, the network must also be able to validate whether the requested intents are still working as expected. Therefore these steps, including the validation, are run in a continuous loop (shown by the dotted arrows in Figure 5-1) to validate whether the network is operating and working as designed. This allows the network to provide intelligent support to the operation teams on the performance and operation of the network.

The first three steps of IBN are common in today's campus networks. They are commonly deployed where automation is gaining momentum using a wide range of automation tools. The key difference between classic networks and an Intent-Based Network is that with IBN there is automated validation of the changes made to the configuration. The testing and validation of a configuration, also in operation, is unique to Intent-Based Networking and raises the quality and capability of the network.

Another key difference is that for IBN all steps and communication are based on APIs and models, conforming to Cisco DNA's design principles. This provides a new unique approach to the network, where applications can now automatically request intent to the network without the network operations team requiring to perform these changes. The feedback, based on the assurance, is also provided via APIs, so the same applications can validate that the requested intent is working as operated.

These two aspects of IBN—automatically validating changes of the network, as well as providing the network as a platform to software engineers—allow the enterprise to use the network in new, intuitive ways and enable the digital business.

Intent-Based Networking Designs

Intent-Based Networking is a perspective to a Cisco Digital Network Architecture. This means that specific designs and technologies are still required to allow a campus network to become Intent-enabled. The following sections describe two common Intent-Based designs (Software-Defined Access or using classic VLANs, known as non-Fabric) that can be used for a campus network to enable IBN.

Before the two Intent-Based designs are described, it is important to be aware that both designs have a certain set of requirements in common:

- **Policy-centric network:** First and foremost is the requirement that an Intent-Based design is based on a policy-centric environment and not a port-centric design. In other words, the network is not configured on a port-by-port basis, but uses a central policy server that pushes the required network port configuration as a policy to a network port.

  All policies for endpoints are pushed from this policy server into the network. This is key to enable intent onto a network, as the intent for an endpoint can change over time based on circumstances.

  For a specific policy to be set to an access port (or wireless network), it is necessary to know which endpoint is connecting to the network. Network Access Control (using IEEE 802.1X standard or MAC Authentication Bypass) is required to identify the endpoint requesting access to the network and to provide it with the proper authorization onto the network (by sending specific policies to the switch using RADIUS). A RADIUS deployment, such as Cisco Identity Services Engine, is thus required for IBN.

- **Microsegmentation:** To greatly enhance the security and tightly integrate it within Cisco DNA (and thus IBN), you should be able to segment a network into smaller bits than an IP subnet based on specific policies. This mechanism, already used in the datacenter, is called *microsegmentation*. Microsegmentation creates the possibility of having a single IP network for all IoT devices and having a policy that only IoT sensors are allowed to communicate with a local storage device where the data for those sensors are stored, while other IoT devices do not have access to that storage device. This microsegmentation must be based on a policy and be able to be programmatically applied to the network. Scalable Group Tags (SGT, formerly known as Security Group Tags) are used within a Software Defined Access (SDA) network (more on SDA in the next section) to provide this microsegmentation. Appendix A, "Campus Network Technologies," describes in more detail how SGTs facilitate the required microsegmentation.

■ **Feedback from network:** One of the true distinctions between a classic campus network as described in Chapter 1, "Classic Campus Network Deployments," and IBN is the feedback of the status of the network back to the controller. In other words, within an IBN the network devices provide feedback to the controller about the network's state. This feedback is used to validate whether the network is accomplishing the intent required. This feedback is of course received programmatically or via telemetry. Several methods and technologies are available to provide this feedback. The technical details for feedback are described in Appendix A, "Campus Network Technologies."

SDA

Software-Defined Access (SDA) is one of the latest technologies introduced in campus networks. It is the most complete technology (or actually a combination of technologies) that can enable Intent-Based Networking on your network.

The key concept of SDA is that there is a single, fixed underlay network and one or more overlay networks (running on top of the underlay). This concept in itself is not new; it is the founding principle for any network where encapsulating and decapsulating data allows the data to be abstracted from the different OSI layers. This principle is also used for VPNs over the Internet, CAPWAP tunnels for wireless communication, and within datacenters.

The principle of an underlay and overlay network can best be described using a common technology in enterprise networks—the Cisco Remote Access VPN solution based on Cisco AnyConnect. This technology allows end users to connect securely to the enterprise network via a less secure network (Internet).

This is realized by creating specific group policies (and pools of IP addresses) on the VPN headend device (a Cisco ASA firewall or Cisco Firepower Threat Defense firewall).

Users use the AnyConnect client to connect to the VPN headend over the Internet. Based on the authentication and authorization, users are allocated a specific internal IP address and the policies determining their access to the enterprise network. The user's endpoint uses the internal IP address to communicate with the enterprise network. This is accomplished by encapsulating the internal IP addresses into an outer packet destined to the VPN headend.

At the VPN headend, the packet is decapsulated and routed into the enterprise network. A similar path is realized for return traffic. The enterprise network only knows that the IP address of that user needs to be sent to the VPN headend. The VPN headend takes the internal traffic and encapsulates it in an outer packet with the destination of the public IP address of the end user.

In this example, the underlay network is the Internet, and the overlay network is the specific VPN group policy that the user is assigned to with the appropriate IP pool. SDA takes the same principle but then applies it internally to the campus network. SDA calls the underlay network a campus network, and it uses virtual networks on top of the underlay to logically separate endpoints. In other words, there are **no VLANs** within an SDA fabric. Figure 5-2 provides an overview of an SDA network.

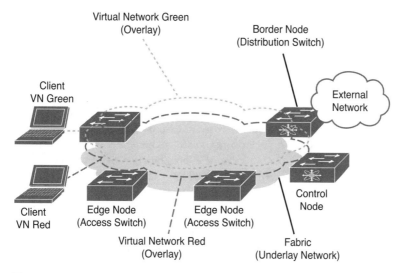

Figure 5-2 *Overview of an SDA Network*

SDA uses its own terminology to describe the roles and functions the switches (or in some cases routers) perform within the SDA fabric:

- **Virtual Network:** A virtual network is used to logically separate devices from each other. It can be compared with the way VLANs are used to logically separate devices on a switched network. A virtual network can be IPv4 or IPv6 based with one or more pools of IP addresses, but it can also be used to create a logical Layer 2 network. Each virtual network has its own routing and forwarding table within the fabric, comparable with VRF-Lite on switches. This principle provides the logical separation of the virtual networks.

- **Fabric:** A fabric is the foundation of the overlay network, which is used to implement the different virtual networks that run within a network. A fabric is a logically defined grouping of a set of switches within the campus network, for example, a single location. The fabric encompasses the protocols and technologies to transport data from the different virtual networks over an underlay network. Because the underlay network is IP based, it is relatively easy to stretch the underlay network across fiber connections on the campus (connecting multiple buildings into a single fabric) or even across a WAN (such as MPLS or an SD-WAN), factoring in specific requirements for SDA. These requirements are explained in Appendix A, "Campus Network Technologies."

- **The underlay network:** The underlay network is an IPv4 network that connects all nodes within the fabric. An internal routing protocol (within an SDA-campus IS-IS is commonly used, although OSPF is also possible) exchanges route information within the fabric between the nodes. The underlay network is used to transport the data from the different virtual networks to the different nodes.

- **Edge node:** The edge node is used to allow endpoints to connect to the fabric. It essentially provides the same function as the access switch layer in a classic campus network topology. From an SDA perspective, the edge node is responsible for encapsulating and decapsulating the traffic for that endpoint in the appropriate virtual network. It also provides the primary role of forwarding traffic from the endpoint to the rest of the network.

- **Border node:** A fabric is always connected with external networks. The border node is used to connect the different virtual networks to external networks. It is essentially the default gateway of the virtual network to external networks. As each virtual network is logically separated, the border node maintains a connection to the external network for each individual virtual network. All traffic from the external network is encapsulated and decapsulated to a specific virtual network, so that the underlay network can be used to transport that data to the correct edge node.

- **Control node:** The control node is a function that cannot be related to a function within an existing classic campus network topology. The control node is responsible for maintaining a database of all endpoints connected to the fabric. The database contains information on which endpoint is connected to which edge node and within which virtual network. It is the glue that connects the different roles. Edge nodes and border nodes use the control node to look up the destination of a packet on the underlay network to forward the inner packet to the right edge node.

How SDA Works

Now that the roles, functions, and concept of an underlay/overlay network are known, how does SDA operate? What does an SDA network look like? The following paragraphs describe the way endpoints within a virtual network communicate with each other. Figure 5-3 provides an example topology of an SDA network.

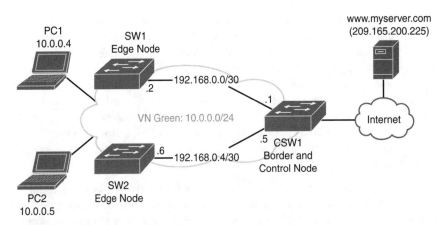

Figure 5-3   *Sample SDA Network*

In this SDA fabric there are three switches. The CSW1 switch provides the Border and Control functionality, while SW1 and SW2 are edge node devices in this fabric. Both SW1 and SW2 have an IP link to the CSW switch, using 192.168.0.0/30 and 192.168.0.4/30 subnets. There is a virtual network (VN) named green on top of the underlay network, which uses the IP network 10.0.0.0/24 for clients. PC1 has IP address 10.0.0.4, and PC2 has IP address 10.0.0.5. The default gateway for VN Green is 10.0.0.1.

CSW1 maintains a table of endpoints connected to the fabric and how to reach them. To explain the concept and operations, Table 5-3 describes the required contents for this example.

Table 5-3 *Overview of Fabric-Connected Devices in CSW1*

Endpoint Name	IP	Network	SGT	VN ID	Reachable Via
PC1	10.0.0.4		Employee	Green	192.168.0.2
PC2	10.0.0.5		Guest	Green	192.168.0.6
Internet		0.0.0.0	Any	Green	192.168.0.1, 192.168.0.5

In this network, if PC1 wants to communicate with www.myserver.com (IP 209.165.200.225), the following would happen:

1. After DNS resolution, the PC sends a TCP SYN packet to the default gateway (10.0.0.1) for destination 209.165.200.225.

2. SW1 as edge switch receives this packet and, as it is an anycast gateway (see Appendix A, "Campus Network Technologies" for more details), the packet is analyzed.

3. SW1 performs a lookup on the CSW1 (as control node) for the destination 209.165.200.225.

4. CSW1 returns a response for the lookup ip-address 192.168.0.1 (IP address of border node).

5. SW1 then encapsulates the *complete* TCP SYN packet in an SDA underlay network packet with source IP address 192.168.0.2 and destination address 192.168.0.1 and uses the global routing table to forward this new packet.

6. CSW1 receives the encapsulated underlay packet from SW1 and decapsulates it. It then, as border router, uses the routing table of VN Green to forward the traffic to the Internet.

7. The server www.myserver.com receives the TCP-SYN packet and generates a response with a SYN-ACK packet back to 10.0.0.4.

8. The incoming SYN-ACK packet is received by CSW1 in the VN Green network. The destination of the packet is 10.0.0.4.

9. CSW1 performs a lookup to the control node for VN Green and IP address 10.0.0.4 and gets 192.168.0.2 as the underlay destination.

10. CSW encapsulates the SYN-ACK packet for 10.0.0.4 into an underlay packet with destination 192.168.0.2.

11. The underlay packet is routed to SW1.

12. SW1 decapsulates the packet, recognizes it is for PC1 (IP 10.0.0.4) on VN Green, and forwards, based on a local table, the packet to the proper access port.

13. PC1 receives the SYN-ACK packet and responds with an ACK to further establish the TCP flow. The principle of lookup is repeated by SW1 for each packet received from or sent to PC1.

The preceding steps provide a conceptual overview of how communication is established and packets are encapsulated/decapsulated onto the underlay network. The same mechanism is used for communication within the VN Green itself. The control node is used as lookup to ask where a specific IP address is located, and then the original packet is encapsulated in an underlay packet destined for the specific node in the fabric. If microsegmentation policy would not allow communication from SGT Employee to SGT Guest, an access list on the edge node would prevent that communication.

An SDA-based topology is very powerful and capable in enabling IBN. The underlay network is set up only once, when the SDA network is created. In addition, there is increased flexibility in adding or removing edge nodes when required (as it is essentially a router in the underlay); all the endpoints are connected to one or more virtual networks. These virtual networks can easily be added or removed from the SDA network, without ever impacting the underlying network. This process of addition or removal can easily be programmed in small building blocks that automation can use. The Cisco DNA center solution is used to deploy and manage an SDA-based network.

Classic VLAN

Although SDA was designed and built for Cisco DNA and is meant to solve some problems on classic campus networks, not all enterprises can readily implement SDA in their network. One of the main reasons is that there are some requirements on the network hardware and topology to enable SDA. This is not only Cisco DNA Center but also a full Identity Services Engine deployment as well as specific hardware such as the Cisco Catalyst 9000 series access switches. Although the Catalyst 3650/3850 are capable of running an SDA network, there are some limitations to that platform, such as an IP services license and a limited number of virtual networks.

However, if you look at an SDA through a conceptual looking glass, it is possible to replicate, with some limitations, the same concepts of SDA using classic VLANs and VRF-Lite. It allows an organization to transform to IBN while also preparing the infrastructure for SDA to take advantage of the concepts within SDA. Table 5-4 provides an overview of the concepts used in SDA compared to the technologies that can be used for IBN within a classic VLAN-based campus network.

Table 5-4 *Overview of Design Choices for SDA and Campus Alternative*

SDA Network	Classic Campus Network
Endpoints are, based on identity, assigned to a virtual network and an SGT.	Endpoints are assigned to a VLAN and SGT.
Each virtual network has its own routing table and IP space.	VRF-Lite can be used to logically separate IP networks and have each VRF instance its own routing table.
The provisioning of virtual networks is easy because the underlay is created only once and virtual networks can be added and removed without interrupting the underlay.	With automation tools, it is easy to programmatically add and remove VLANs on uplinks as well as SVIs on the distribution switch.
Routed links in the underlay are used to remove Spanning Tree and Layer 2 complexities.	In a collapsed-core campus network, there is no need for Spanning Tree, or a single Spanning Tree instance can be run to prevent loops.
An underlay network is used to stretch a fabric over multiple physical locations.	This is not possible without an encapsulation protocol in classic networks.
A control node is used for lookup of endpoints.	This is not required as existing protocols like ARP can be used.

With some limitations (specific conditions) it is possible to enable an IBN design using classic VLAN technologies. Limitations for such a design are a collapsed-core design, ability to assign SGT, and VLANs using a policy server as well as preferably no Spanning Tree or a single Spanning Tree instance. If you take these limitations, Figure 5-4 provides an intent-based design based on a classic collapsed-core campus network topology and VRF-lite.

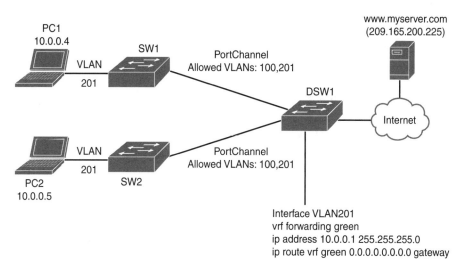

Figure 5-4 *Intent Design Based on Classic Campus Collapsed-Core Topology*

In this design PC1 and PC2 still have the same IP address but are now assigned into VLAN 201 instead of virtual network green. VLAN 201 is configured on the DSW1 with IP network 10.0.0.0/24 and a default gateway of 10.0.0.1 for the endpoints. The SGTs have remained the same: Employee for PC1 and Guest for PC2.

Just as in the previous example, if PC1 would communicate with www.myserver.com on 209.165.200.225, it would send its TCP SYN packet to the default gateway on DSW1, which in turn would forward it to the Internet, while return traffic would be sent via Ethernet to PC1. ARP is used to map IP addresses into MAC addresses.

The principle of SGT ACLs to restrict traffic within a VRF is the same. In both SDA as well as classic, the SGT ACL is pushed from the policy server to the access switch where the endpoint is connected.

Although the end goal is logically separating traffic between endpoints, using SGT for microsegmentation, there are some limitations and restrictions on a classic VLAN over an SDA topology.

- **Spanning Tree:** It is not preferred to run Spanning Tree on the network, as each change in a VLAN can trigger a Spanning Tree recalculation, resulting in blocked traffic for a period of time. If it is required to run Spanning Tree, then run a single instance of Spanning Tree in MST mode, so that adding a VLAN does not trigger a new STP topology as with per-VLAN Spanning Tree.

- **Management VLAN and VRF:** It is required to have a dedicated VLAN and management VRF to be able to create or remove new VLANs. This VLAN may never be removed from trunks and networks, as this is essentially the underlay network. The automation tool that generates and provides the configuration communicates with all devices in this management VLAN.

- **Configuration via automation tool only:** The configuration of the campus network can *only* be executed via the automation tool. This is generally true for any environment that there should only be a single truth for the provisioning of a network. In an IBN based on classic VLANs, this is more important as the automation tool will generate the VLAN identifiers automatically based on the virtual networks to be deployed. Although it is common in enterprises to statically define and assign VLANs, in this design that concept needs to be removed for automation to work.

- **Standardized building blocks only:** It is important to only allow standardized building blocks, defined via the automation tool, on the campus network, where the policy is assigned policy-centric using IEEE 802.1x and RADIUS. The building block can then be standardized in such a way that small pieces of configuration code can be generated on-the-fly to create or remove the required compartments on the network. This is realized by creating small repetitive code blocks of command line configuration to be executed, for example, for the creation of a new compartment on the access switch:

```
vlan $vlanid
name $vrfname
interface $PortChannelUplink
switchport trunk allowed vlan add $vlanid
```

If the campus network configuration cannot be standardized, it will not be possible to enable an Intent-Based Network using VLANs.

■ **Build your own automation:** With SDA, a lot of automation and configuration is executed by Cisco DNA Center in the background. With this design, an automation tool needs to be installed and configured by the network team to provide similar functionality. This can require some custom coding and testing before running the solution in production. This could be Cisco DNA Center with templates or another tool that provides automation functionality.

In summary, both mechanisms (SDA and classic VLAN) work quite similarly, and when you take certain precautions and keep the limitations in mind, it is feasible to start with IBN based on a classic collapsed-core topology. Part 2, "Transforming to an Intent-Based Network," provides more details on limitations, drawbacks, and when which technology fits best for transforming a campus network to IBN.

Summary

Cisco Digital Network Architecture describes the requirements and operations of a network infrastructure of an enterprise at a functional or abstract level. Cisco DNA achieves this abstract description by dividing the requirements of the enterprise network into several functions and design principles. It does not describe how to use or implement that network architecture.

Intent-Based Networking (IBN) describes, using a powerful methodology, how a campus network can be built and operated using Cisco DNA as network architecture. IBN is based on the premise that every endpoint that connects to the network consumes a predefined set of services (that include access, connectivity, security policies, and other network functions). In essence, every endpoint has a specific intent (or purpose) when connecting to the network, and each intent is defined as a set of services to be delivered to that endpoint.

This set of intents (that are deployed on the network) are defined dynamically based on which endpoints are connected to the network. As soon as an intent is not required anymore, its configuration is removed automatically from the network infrastructure.

Although IBN itself is not based on Cisco Digital Network Architecture, its description and methodology are so similar to Cisco DNA that you can state it is a perspective of Cisco DNA. IBN describes how a network based on Cisco DNA can be configured and operated by the network operations team. Figure 5-5 describes the systematic approach IBN describes in providing intents to the network (by defining Intents as repetitive pieces of configuration).

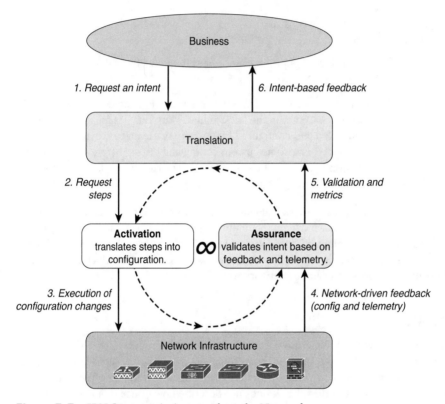

Figure 5-5   *IBN Systematic Approach to the Network*

Figure 5-5 is similar to Cisco DNA, and IBN is based on six steps in a continuous loop:

1. Request intent; business or network operations request a specific intent.

2. Request steps; the intent is translated into a set of configuration changes to be executed.

3. Execution of configuration changes; network configuration changes are executed via automation.

4. Network-driven feedback; the network infrastructure provides feedback on its operation.

5. Validation & metrics; the analytics component validates the received network-driven feedback with the requested intents to validate that the requested intents are operating as requested and designed.

6. Intent-Based feedback; business-outcome based values are used to report on the status of the requested intent and its operation.

Two Designs

Two network designs are available to implement IBN:

- Cisco Software Defined Access (SDA) is based on Cisco DNA and is the most complete technology that can enable IBN on the campus network, but Cisco SDA does have specific requirements on the network infrastructure devices (and Cisco DNA Center).

- Classic VLANs with VRF-Lite can be used, with limitations, as an alternative to SDA for those organizations that are not (yet) able to meet the requirements of SDA.

IBN itself, and therefore both designs, relies on three key requirements on the campus network to be successful:

- **Policy-centric network:** The campus network is not configured port-by-port but uses a policy-centric identity server so that based on the identity of the endpoint the specific network policies (and thus the intents) can be pushed to the appropriate network infrastructure device.

- **Microsegmentation:** Microsegmentation is used within IBN to allow for more granular security policies than those based solely on IP addresses.

- **Feedback from network:** IBN relies heavily on the feedback that network infrastructure devices provide back to the analytics component; it is used to validate whether the requested intents are operating as designed and requested.

In conclusion, IBN is a perspective on Cisco Digital Network Architecture, and it describes a powerful methodology of how a Cisco DNA-based network infrastructure can be operated and managed. IBN can be used to provide the network operations team with the tools and methods to cope with the exponential growth of devices connecting to the campus network.

Chapter 6

Tools for Intent

Enterprise frameworks, Cisco DNA, Intent-Based Networking—they all provide descriptions and context on how network infrastructures are designed and operated and how they should work and interoperate with applications, users, and other "external" sources. It is all abstract and concept-based.

Without the proper tools and technologies, these concepts cannot be implemented and brought into practice. One of the key responsibilities for a network architect or network engineer is to know which tool or technology can meet the specific requirements set by the business.

A significant number of tools and technologies exist that can be used. It is impossible to provide a full compendium of all tools and include an in-depth explanation of them. This chapter provides you with an overview of some of the tools available for campus networks that can be used to enable Intent. Chances are that you are using some of these tools already, and this will help in enabling Intent-Based on your network infrastructure.

This chapter covers the following topics:

- Description of what automation entails in networking
- Overview of automation tools for Intent
- Network visibility in Intent
- Overview of network visibility tools for Intent

What Is Network Automation?

Network automation is one of the key concepts used to enable an Intent-Based Network. There is no Intent-Based Network without a process for network automation. The word *automation* is defined in the Oxford dictionary as "the use or introduction of automatic equipment in manufacturing or other process or facility." This definition is clearly related to automation processes in industrial environments like factories. The definition can be applied to a network infrastructure as well. In general, the operation of a campus network consists of creating the network and operating it by performing software updates and changes to its configuration.

Network automation is thus the process (or methodology) where software can automatically provision, configure, test, and manage network devices.

Several examples for network automation already exist, such as a Cisco Application-Centric Infrastructure-based Datacenter, where the Application Policy Infrastructure Controller (APIC) is configuring the network devices (and firewalls) automatically. The concept of network automation also exists in the campus network, where access points are configured and managed automatically by the wireless LAN Controller (WLC).

Network operations are in general responsible for the full lifecycle of the network infra-structure. This lifecycle management is based on executing a number of tasks, whether on an individual device or on a group of devices. Although several methodologies are available that can logically group these different tasks, within network automation, the most common methodology is based on the time when the tasks are commonly executed. Figure 6-1 provides an overview of this grouping.

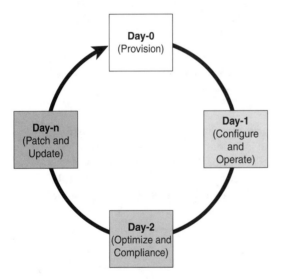

Figure 6-1 *Grouping of Network Lifecycle Management Tasks Over Time*

In essence, the life of the network device (or system as a whole) is looped through a number of stages. These stages are grouped around the tasks that network operations normally perform on the network device (or system).

The tasks related to the installation and provisioning of a new network device (or net-work) are grouped into day-0 operations. In other words, the network device is racked and stacked into the equipment room, supplied with the appropriate operating system version and proper configuration.

The tasks related to configuration and operation management (monitoring) are grouped in day-1 operations. In other words, if a device requires a change in configuration, the change procedure is grouped under day-1 operations.

Troubleshooting tasks, such as responding to an incident or problem resolution, are grouped in day-2 operations. Day-2 operation tasks can be seen as those tasks required to bring the network (device) back into the normal operating state.

Other common operational tasks, such as patching and updating the software on network devices, are grouped into day-n operations. These operations are not performed sequentially from a day-2 operation but can be executed on any day in the lifecycle of the network device (or network as a whole). Therefore, these operations are named day-n.

Unfortunately, no real group is defined for the decommissioning of a network device or network. If it is the removal of a virtual network, it would logically be grouped under day-1 operations, as it is a configuration change.

Network device removal would occur either when the network device is replaced, which would result in day-0 operations, or when the complete network is removed, which basically ends the lifecycle as a whole.

It is, of course, possible to execute the different tasks related to the lifecycle individually on a box-by-box basis. Network automation tools, however, can execute these tasks automatically on all related and required network devices, reducing the risk of human error often at a higher speed. Network automation tools typically provide services and solutions in day-0, day-1, and day-n operations. The focus for automation within an IBN is primarily on day-0 operation (provisioning a base network infrastructure) and day-1 operations (creating or removing networks or policies based on the requested intent). That explains the importance of network automation for Intent-enabled networks.

Network Automation Tools

A vast number of network automation tools are available on the market. It would be near impossible to provide a complete list of available network automation tools that can be used to transform existing networks into an Intent-Based Network infrastructure. A complete book could be written for an extensive list of network automation tools, including a detailed overview of their configuration and inner workings. It is not the author's intent to provide a full detailed overview of all tools available, but rather to provide a brief overview of commonly found and available tools that can be used to transform existing networks into Intent-Based Networks.

Cisco DNA Center

Cisco announced DNA Center (DNAC) in June 2017 together with Intent-Based Networking. Cisco DNA Center is developed for a Cisco DNA-based network infrastructure and integrates the automation, analytics, and cloud service management functions into a single solution. Cisco DNA Center is an evolution of Cisco's APIC-EM software architecture with many internal and external improvements. Cisco DNA Center's solution combines several applications, such as LAN automation, assurance, and policy-generation, into a single unified platform and experience. It is Cisco's targeted platform for any Intent-Based Network.

Cisco DNA Center's first public release was version 1.1, primarily targeting Software-Defined Access (SDA) solutions and a public beta of analytics. Cisco DNA Center version 1.2 introduced new features into the solution focusing on non-SDA-based networks, a plug-and-play application (day-0 operations), and improvements for the assurance and analytics component.

Within Cisco DNAC, the configuration and operation of the campus network is based on a three-step approach. Some steps are more focused on SDA-based networks than others. But these three general steps are used to configure and deploy campus networks:

Step 1.   Design: In this step, the campus network is designed. This design is based on a hierarchical view of the campus network consisting of areas, buildings, and floors. An area could be a geographical area or a single city. The hierarchical design itself is up to the administrator. Each level of the hierarchical view can be used to set specific network settings, such as IP address pools, DHCP and DNS settings, software image versions, as well as network profiles. Network profiles are template-based configurations applied to each network device assigned up to that level in the network hierarchy. The network profile mechanism is used primarily for non-SDA-based networks. Figure 6-2 provides an example view of the network hierarchy and the different settings available within the design step.

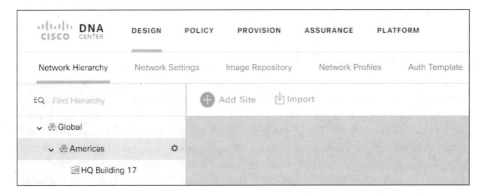

Figure 6-2   *Hierarchical Design Within Cisco DNA Center*

Step 2.   Policy: The specific network policies are defined in the policy step. Although this step primarily focuses on SDA-based networks, allowing you to create virtual networks, access-group policies, and one or more fabrics, it is also used to define specific QoS settings on the network.

Step 3.   **Provision:** In the last step, the information specified in the design and policy step are provisioned onto the network devices. This step is executed for both non-SDA-based networks (where network devices are provisioned to a specific location in the network hierarchy) or SDA-based networks (where multiple fabrics can be defined and deployed). Figure 6-3 provides a screenshot of the provision step within DNAC for a non-fabric network.

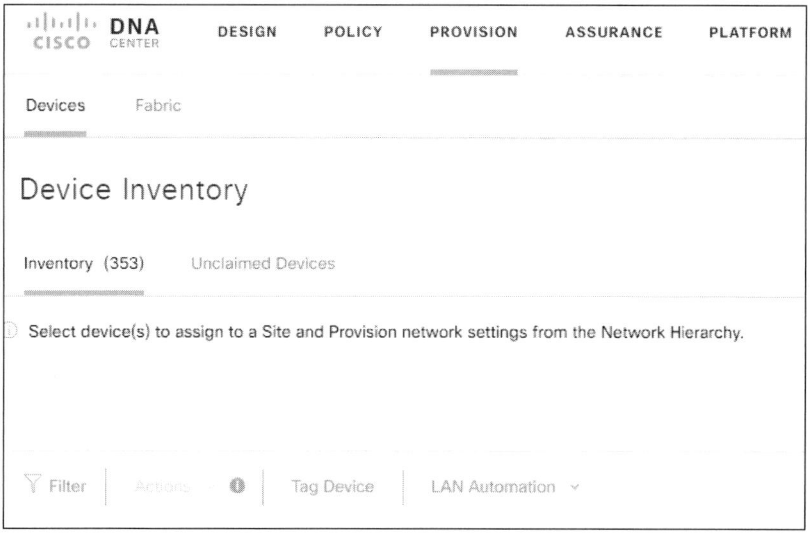

Figure 6-3   *Screenshot of Provision Step Within DNA Center*

These three steps together form the basis for any network managed and operated within DNAC.

From a network automation perspective, several tasks are tightly integrated into different tools and steps within DNAC. DNAC can perform the following tasks from the single pane of view:

■ **Day-0—Provision:** Usin0067 LAN Automation for SDA-based networks or network Plug-and-Play (PnP) makes it possible to provision new network devices with ease of use.

■ **Day-1—Change and operate:** Using the policy and design steps, changes to the network can be prepared and documented. The provision step allows the changes to be executed on the devices that require change.

■ **Day-n—Patch and update:** DNAC includes a software image management application, called SWIM. This application is based on image management within Prime Infrastructure and allows the administrator to define golden images for network device families and for specific locations in the network hierarchy. If devices do not have this software image, a workflow can be used to update those devices to the new golden image.

As DNAC is designed and built for a Cisco Digital Network Architecture, DNAC provides APIs both for network devices (including third-party network device support) as well as APIs that third-party software developers can use to communicate with DNAC. This allows DNAC to be integrated with a wide range of other applications, for example, IT Service Management (ITSM) tools.

These integrations combined with a single solution to design, provision, and operate a campus network allow DNAC to provide a unique holistic view of the complete campus enterprise network. And as DNAC matures, more and more features and applications will be integrated within DNAC.

Prime Infrastructure and APIC-EM

Although Cisco DNA Center is developed for Intent-Based Networking based on SDA, DNAC is still early in its features and possibilities compared to mainstream network management solutions such as Cisco Prime Infrastructure and Cisco Application Policy Infrastructure Controller Enterprise Module (APIC-EM). These two software solutions, tightly integrated, have been around for a while and have matured over time. Although it is not possible to compare both solutions feature-wise as they were developed for different purposes, the combination of Prime Infrastructure and Cisco APIC-EM can be used to transform existing networks to Intent-Based Networks.

Cisco Prime Infrastructure has been the primary campus network management system from Cisco for a number of years. Cisco Prime Infrastructure has evolved over the past years into a stable product. The strong features on wireless (such as the configuration of wireless networks, providing wireless client statistics, extensive reporting capabilities, and generating heat maps) demonstrate the origins of Prime Infrastructure from the earlier Cisco Wireless Control System. Over the past years, an increasing number of features have been integrated into Prime Infrastructure for the management of LAN and WAN solutions. Prime Infrastructure's design principle is that you first design and prepare the network within Prime Infrastructure and then provision (deploy) the configuration or image to the devices. For a campus network to transform into IBN, the most powerful features of Prime are the command-line template deployment, image management, and its API capabilities.

The Cisco APIC-EM solution was introduced in 2015. Its initial launch was intended as an SDN controller for enterprise networks. The architecture of APIC-EM is quite different from Prime Infrastructure. Where Prime Infrastructure is a single monolithic database that contains all data, APIC-EM uses an application-centric architecture. On top of a common infrastructure (within the appliance and operating system), different applications can be installed and deployed to perform network-related functions. The most common and known applications are Network Plug and Play (for day-0 operations), Path Trace (how does a specific packet flow through the network?), and EasyQoS (enable Quality of Service based on best practices and application definitions where the app will generate the proper configuration based on the network device's role). Other applications are available as well. The architecture of APIC-EM has been the basis for the development of DNAC.

One of the true strengths of APIC-EM is its Network PnP application. This application allows a network operator to predefine a configuration (static or template) and attach that template to a switch. As the switch is booted (from factory default configuration), it connects to APIC-EM, and once the template is assigned to the device by the operator, the configuration deployment is executed by APIC-EM. This device configuration can include a specific operating system (IOS or IOS-XE) version that is approved for the specific enterprise. Network Plug-and-Play is explained in Appendix A, "Campus Network Technologies", as it is used by both APIC-EM and DNA Center.

The combination of these two tools can be used to get started transforming existing campus networks to IBN. APIC-EM is used for day-0 operations (provisioning of new devices), and Prime is used to provision templates. If you use APIC-EM for day-0 operations, the CLI templates of Prime Infrastructure are used to deploy and remove services on the network. The APIs available within Prime Infrastructure and APIC-EM are used to enable programmability.

Network Services Orchestrator

One of the probably lesser known products from Cisco for automation is Network Services Orchestrator (NSO). As the name implies, it is a service orchestration tool primarily targeted for service provider networks. But as enterprise networks and service provider networks are merging more and more together (virtualization of network functions, harmonizing software running on devices), NSO makes it quite capable for the automation function within IBN.

NSO takes a model and transactional driven approach to the network. NSO collects the configuration from network devices and stores that configuration in the configuration database called CDB. The data stored in the CDB is not the actual (text) version of the configuration, like the inventory in Prime, but it is translated into an abstracted model of the configuration. This network model is based on the common available YANG models. And as YANG has become the de facto standard, NSO can support a wide number of network devices. In this aspect, Network Elements Drivers (NED) translate the configuration stored in the YANG model into the actual configuration commands required for a specific network device. A huge list of NEDs are available that can be used. Also, sample code for models and configuration has become available on a special GitHub repository (https://github.com/NSO-developer) since NSO has become free for development purposes.

> **Note**   YANG itself is a modeling language and has become an industry standard to model the configuration of a network device.

Besides the CDB for configuration, NSO uses a YANG model to define the services that run on the network. As mentioned, NSO was originally written for Service Providers. A service description is similar to an intent description and thus has similar behavior.

Instead of service descriptions, NSO can be used to describe available intents and allow NSO to provision those intents to the campus network. As the network is abstracted into models, NSO also provides the possibility to manage network functions, or specifically virtual network functions. A package manager is used in combination with a VNF management module to deploy and manage the full lifecycle of virtual network functions. Besides having a CLI and web interface, NSO also provides API support to have self-service systems request automated changes to the network. Figure 6-4 displays a schematic overview of the different elements of NSO.

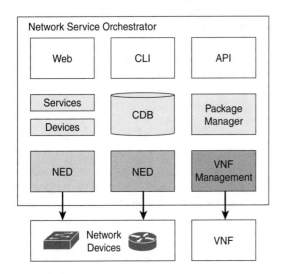

Figure 6-4 *Schematic Overview of NSO*

One of the advantages of NSO is its transactional behavior. If a change is required on the network, the change is prepared in the CDB, and once committed, the change is executed on the network devices using the translations by the NEDs. If the commit fails on one of the required network devices, the complete change is rolled back. So the configuration of the network devices remains consistent with the model defined in CDB and the services applied.

Another advantage of NSO is that the network itself is (if no other access to devices is allowed) represented in the CDB. This allows network engineers or operators to check the applied configuration of all network devices using the CDB instead of having to log in to each device to validate the configuration.

Changes to common items, such as SNMP or Syslog, can be executed easily, using a single transaction. Example 6-1 represents a common template applied to all devices in a single transaction.

Example 6-1 *NTP Configuration via NSO*

```
admin@ncs(config)# devices template "Common parameters" config
admin@ncs(config-config)# ios:ip domain name company.org
admin@ncs(config-config)# ios:ntp server server-list 172.16.1.3
admin@ncs(config-server-list-172.16.1.3)# exit
admin@ncs(config-config)# ios:logging host 172.16.1.3
admin@ncs(config-host-172.16.1.3)# exit
admin@ncs(config-config)# exit
admin@ncs(config-template-Common parameters)# commit
Commit complete.
admin@ncs(config-template-Common parameters)# exit
admin@ncs(config)# devices device-group all apply-template template-name ?
admin@ncs(config)# devices device-group all apply-template template-name
  Common\ parameters
admin@ncs(config)#
```

From an IBN perspective, NSO as an automation tool provides the features required for all automation tasks. For day-0 operations, Zero Touch Provisioning (ZTP) is used, where TFTP and DHCP are combined to provide the initial configuration to a device. Once the device is bootstrapped with the initial configuration, it can be linked to a device group and services applied.

Puppet Enterprise

Puppet Enterprise (from Puppet Labs) is a software automation tool originally developed for server (and application) automation in the datacenter and cloud. Puppet Enterprise takes a unique approach to automation and is truly developed from a DevOps perspective.

The Puppet Enterprise architecture is based on the principle that automation is a method to provide a node into a specific state and keep that node in that specific state. Puppet Enterprise accomplishes this by using a platform-independent language that describes the state a specific file, directory, or server needs to be in. This language is used to create specific Puppet Enterprise modules. (See this as a way to logically group specific states.) These modules are imported (uploaded) to a puppet master server where puppet agents talk. Periodically, by default every 30 minutes, the puppet agent checks which modules are applicable for its host and checks whether its host is compliant with the state. If it is not, the module, together with the language and attributes, provides mechanisms for the agent to place that node into the requested state.

A common example used to illustrate the power of this state-matching methodology is the provisioning of a new server or container. From the puppet master, a new server deployment is requested with a specific number of tags. Puppet communicates with the virtualization platform (or cloud) to request that the new server be created based on a specific template. Once that server is booted, the agent registers itself with the puppet master and requests what state it needs to be in. Based on the provided modules, the agent installs the proper server software, such as mail-server, application server. The agent also installs the correct configuration files and makes sure common things such as NTP and Syslog are configured properly. The expected state is confirmed back to the puppet master. In turn, the load balancer is informed that a new server is ready and is in the correct state, and the server is added into the server pool to execute the work.

This short example demonstrates the power that Puppet harnesses. One of the benefits is that troubleshooting a server problem has become less frequent. The code on the application server has been tested and approved from a test environment. In case of a problem, the problematic server can just be thrown away and a new server provisioned automatically. Besides that new install, the Puppet system itself takes care of the rest.

Puppet provides a few advantages. First, the puppet language is not comparable with any programming language. It is truly a descriptive state language, so no iterations are available; you just describe what you want the server to have. Although the learning curve for developers is steep, this is eventually a powerful advantage. Example 6-2 displays a small piece of a puppet module for the NTP configuration on a Linux server.

Example 6-2 *Puppet Class Definition for NTP Configuration*

```
# @summary
#  This class handles the configuration file for NTP
# @api private
#
class ntp::config {
      file {      $ntp::config:
             ensure => file,
             owner => 0,
             group => 0,
             mode => $::ntp::config_filemode,
             content => $step_ticker_content,
      }
      # remove dhclient ntpscript which modifies ntp.conf on RHEL and Amazon Linux
      file {
             '/etc/dhcp/dhcpclient.d/ntp.sh',
             ensure => absent
      }
}
```

This code example describes that there must be a config file, with owner root (userid 0), and that the content is provided in a specific variable (which is defined earlier in the code). The file ntp.sh must not be present to resolve a conflict with specific Linux versions. This is where the power of Puppet really comes into play. Every 30 minutes the puppet agent checks whether that file is there, and if this is the case, it removes the file automatically.

The other advantage is platform independence. Puppet agents are available for many modern operating systems, such as Windows, Linux, and MacOSX. For example, Google, Inc. has used Puppet to automate workstation management (including Apple MacBookPros) in the past. With funding of Cisco Investments, Puppet support for Nexus and IOS-XE switches was introduced. The requirement was that a puppet agent had to be installed on the specific switch. However, in June 2018 Puppet also launched a module that provides support for IOS switches without requiring an agent on that switch. That puppet module allows you to configure Cisco Catalyst switches running IOS with specific configuration sets. Example 6-3 displays the puppet file for configuration of NTP on that switch.

Example 6-3   *Puppet Code for NTP Configuration on a Switch*

```
ntp_server { '10.141.1.1':
   ensure => 'present',
   key => 94,
   prefer => true,
   minpoll => 4,
   maxpoll => 14,
   source_interface => 'vlan 42',
}
```

This code describes the state the switch must have, including an NTP server configured with IP address **10.141.1.1** and that the source interface is **vlan42**. The puppet agent takes care of the rest. If in time the NTP server needs to be changed, then you just need to change the value in this file, and the automation tool takes care of the rest automatically.

Puppet Enterprise is available as open source (with some feature limitations) as well as a free version for up to ten nodes. Above these ten nodes, a paid subscription model is required. Quite a few resources are available for Puppet Enterprise, including a ready-to-use virtual machine appliance as well as a website called PuppetForge where modules are shared.

Ansible

Ansible is a similar automation solution to Puppet Enterprise. Both Puppet and Ansible originate from server and application automation environments to facilitate the DevOps methodology. Ansible itself is completely open source, and as an automation engine it allows for provisioning and configuration management. In contrast to Puppet, Ansible is an agent-less solution. In other words, instead of an agent polling a master for the state the managed node should be in, an Ansible server connects to the managed nodes and executes the different automation tasks.

The Ansible solution consists of a number of components that work together. Figure 6-5 provides an overview of the components that make up a typical Ansible deployment.

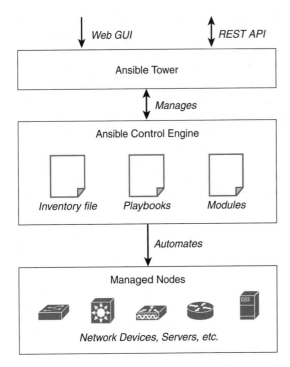

Figure 6-5   *A Component Overview of an Ansible Solution*

Control Engine

At the heart of the solution is the Ansible control engine. As Ansible is written on Linux, you do need a UNIX-based platform to run the control engine. The control engine is configured using a combination of inventory files, modules, and playbooks.

The inventory files define which nodes the control engine needs to manage and how to connect and authenticate to these devices. Within an Ansible deployment, it is common to use asymmetric SSH keys for the authentication of the control engine on the managed node. Ansible modules for Cisco provide support for both username/password and asymmetric keys for authentication.

Asymmetric SSH Key Authentication

It is common for network operators to connect to network devices using SSH. SSH allows a remote user to connect to the shell (or CLI) via a secure communication channel. For Cisco devices, the authentication is commonly based on username and password (local or centralized using TACACS or RADIUS); however, it is also possible to perform authentication using asymmetric keys. The private key is stored on the remote terminal (commonly the user's home directory), and the public key is stored on the remote terminal server. Instead of using username/passwords, data is encrypted with the user's private key. The remote server uses the user's public key to decrypt that data. And as these two keys are uniquely and mathematically tied together, it is used as authentication of the user. This mechanism does not require interactive input of a password, so scripts can use this mechanism to perform tasks on other servers.

Ansible extensively uses this mechanism to execute the different tasks on the nodes it manages.

Playbooks are text files in the YAML Ain't Markup Language (YAML) format. These playbooks define the tasks with the specific configuration that needs to be applied to the managed nodes. YAML is a common format for configuration files and is human readable. Example 6-4 provides a code excerpt of an Ansible playbook to perform two commands on the managed devices.

Example 6-4 *Code Excerpt for an Ansible Playbook*

```
tasks:
- name: run commands on remote devices
 ios_command:
  commands:
      - show version
      - show ip int brief
```

The playbook file (or files) can be seen as a combination of configuration and scripted steps to be executed on the managed nodes.

Modules are used within Ansible to define which tasks or configurations can be executed on a managed node. The contents of playbook files are essentially defined by which modules are used for which device. From a network perspective, network modules are available for almost all Cisco operating systems, including Cisco AireOS (Classic Wireless LAN Controllers), Cisco IOS-XE (Catalyst 3650/3850 and Catalyst 9000 series), as well as Cisco Meraki. By using a modular approach Ansible is flexible and allows for a multitude of supported devices and environments. Already more than 750 modules are available. And because Ansible is open source, it is possible to write your own module if required.

Control Tower

Although Ansible is an automation tool, the tool itself does not execute playbooks (and thus configuration changes) automatically. A command needs to be executed by a user to define which playbook needs to be executed with a number of variables on a number of managed nodes. Only then is the automation started and executed. The success of Ansible is also based on the quality and contents of the playbooks. They essentially contain all the steps that need to be executed automatically. Learning YAML and defining these playbooks does require a steep learning curve, and editing text files from a command prompt is not exactly user friendly.

That is one of the reasons why in 2016 an Ansible Tower was introduced in the solution by RedHat. An Ansible Tower provides a graphical user interface for defining workflows, tasks, and the ability to schedule tasks on the control engine to be executed. The Ansible Tower also provides a RESTful API so that developers can leverage those APIs to request changes (playbooks) to be executed from within applications, which could be web-based frontend servers to customers. Ansible Tower itself is a commercial product, but the development is executed in the AWX project, which is an open source version of Ansible Tower.

In conclusion, the network operator uses the Ansible Tower to configure workflows and playbooks and schedules the different automation tasks. The Ansible Tower in turn pushes the configuration files and playbooks to the control engine. The control engine executes the playbooks onto the different managed nodes. As the playbooks can also be used to execute tests, it is possible to implement a complete CI/CD toolchain within Ansible. Figure 6-6 provides the flow for a network automated via Ansible. The complete Ansible solution is, of course, scalable and redundant, so it is possible to scale out to multiple towers and control engines for redundancy and scale.

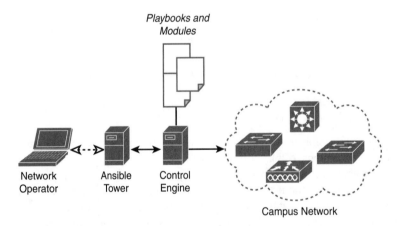

Figure 6-6   *Overview of Ansible Components*

From a network automation perspective, there are a few disadvantages to Ansible. One of the foremost disadvantages is that the network devices need to have a minimum configuration for management access (for example, a reachable management IP address and user credentials) before Ansible can be used. So complete day-0 automation is not possible without using other tools, such as APIC-EM. Another disadvantage is that Ansible is in general trigger-based automation. In other words, a trigger is needed to set the Ansible control engine to execute playbooks. There is no periodic control or validation if the managed devices are still configured as they should. To enable that kind of continuous validation, it is required to develop custom playbooks and schedule these via an Ansible Tower or other mechanisms.

Build Your Own Tool

Not all organizations are the same, and thus not all campus networks are implemented in the same way. In some situations, commercially available software cannot be used for a number of reasons. One could be the size of the campus network in correlation to the available tools. (This could be because the campus network is too large or too small for the cost of the tool.) Other reasons could be related to rules and regulations that apply to a specific industry or a specific organization. For example, the management network is not allowed to connect to the Internet for security reasons, cloud-based applications are not allowed at all, or the network supporting the business processes is too complex for the existing tools.

In those cases, where the requirements cannot be met by the commercially available tools, the alternative is to build an automation tool dedicated for that specific organization.

This option, to build your own automation tool, has become a popular alternative over the past few years. This is not only due to the Cisco DNA design principle to use open standards and APIs within the network architecture, but over the past years the Cisco DevNet community (http://developer.cisco.com), the resource for developers who want to use the APIs available within Cisco, has become very successful. DevNet has evolved from a semirestricted community for third-party integrators to an open and active community.

The community has grown largely because of the tremendous amount of effort Cisco has put into DevNet by providing free video training, sample codes, and software development kits (SDK) to get you started on network programmability.

And for that start on network programmability, the Python programming language was selected for several code samples and libraries. Python is an open source programming language that runs both interpreted as well as compiled. Just as with the Java programming language, the compiled output of Python code is an optimized byte-coded binary file, and a special virtual machine is used to run that byte-code upon execution. The DevNet website from Cisco provides several free video trainings to learn Python.

Type of Programming Languages

Code to write software applications is written in programming languages. Each programming language has its own structure and grammar, just as English and Spanish are languages with their own specific spelling and grammar. In general, there are two types of programming languages: compiled and interpreted. With compiled programming languages, such as C, Obj-C, and C#, the source code is run through a compiler. The compiler translates and optimizes the source code into binary machine code, usually optimized for a specific hardware platform. This byte-code is commonly known as an application or executable. The binary code is not readable by humans anymore, but it runs efficiently on the target computer. Interpreted programming languages are not translated by a compiler. At runtime, an interpreter reads the source code line by line, interprets the code, and executes the statements of that code. JavaScript is such an interpreted code. The advantage of interpreted code is that the code remains readable. The disadvantage is that the code is not optimized and generally runs slower than compiled code.

As DevNet has grown over the years, the available code for network programmability in Python has grown as well. Besides a huge repository on DevNet (The DevNet Code Exchange) a number of open source libraries are available that can be used to create a custom-built automation tool. Open source libraries like Nornir (https://nornir. readthedocs.io/en/latest/) and eNMS (https://enms.readthedocs.io/en/latest/) can already provide a head-start in creating an IBN-enabled automation tool. Open configuration standards such as Netconf also support the ability to develop a common approach to deploying configurations onto the network devices without the difficulties of sending and interpreting specific CLI commands. Also, open standards like Zero Touch Provisioning (ZTP) and Plug and Play (PnP) enable the possibility to include day-0 operations.

In conclusion, a custom-built automation tool can be a valid alternative in situations where commercially available tools do not fit in with the enterprise's specific requirements or limitations.

Use Case: Shared Service Group Datacenter Automation

SharedServices Group provides shared services to a large number of locations and end users. SharedServices Group (SSG) also provides services from its own datacenter. The enterprise has grown via mergers and acquisitions where the services inside the datacenter needed to be consolidated at a rapid pace. Because each merger or acquisition had its own datacenter, the merged datacenter consequently became a large but diverse mix of networks, applications, and services. Essentially SSG has become a service provider (multitenancy) from a service offering perspective but with a collection enterprise–based datacenter design.

Consequently, the datacenter network itself, including the routes—connectivity links between tenants—had become complex and possibly too large. Changes for one tenant on the datacenter network frequently caused failures for other tenants as changes were executed manually device by device. The datacenter network became too large and complex to manage. To reduce the number of failures, the datacenter network had to be standardized to reduce the risk of human error.

But because of the size, the complexity, and the large number of specials (special configurations for non-standard services), it was not possible to use standard automation tools. They were not fit either for the size or for the high number of diversities. Besides these restrictions, network consultants and architects who have the expertise required to implement tools at such a scale were difficult to find. And external tools would require a drastic change in the internal datacenter team and a gaining of trust.

So instead of using and heavily adopting off-the-shelf software for automation, SSG decided to build its own automation tool focused on the specific design and requirements for its datacenter and services.

SSG used open source tooling in conjunction with custom software to develop an automation pipeline that generated and deployed the configuration of a new tenant automatically within four hours instead of four months. And each network service was created in the same manner.

Section Summary

Of course, many more automation tools are available, and the description of tools in the previous paragraphs only provides a limited overview. For an IBN, an automation tool is essential. As such, the maturity and number of automation tools will increase over time. If an automation tool is not yet available, it is important to select the right automation tool. This should be based not only on the requirements set in Cisco DNA and IBN, but also on budget, platform, and features required for the specific organization. In case of a committed strategy toward Software Defined Access, DNA Center would be the most logical choice. However, if Prime Infrastructure is already in use, it is common sense to start the journey toward IBN based on Prime and APIC-EM.

Network Analytics

The other key aspect of Intent-Based Networking is that the intents being pushed onto the network are validated using the analytics function of Cisco DNA. For an Intent-Based Network, the analytics function receives (or obtains) data from the network infrastructure and validates if the Intent is configured correctly. However, the information received also contains other information, such as the operation of the network in general, connected clients, operation of network functions, and other contextual data such as applications running on the network. In general, the analytics component allows the network visibility to be increased. To accomplish that, the analytics component is essentially composed of a number of functions as described in the following sections.

Validation of Intent

For IBN, the most important function of the analytics component is the validation of Intent. Once a piece of configuration has been deployed to the network, the analytics component can use the retrieved data, such as running configuration, but also ARP entries and routing tables to validate whether the specified Intent is working as expected. If an Intent is not behaving as expected, the function can and will report that.

Network Function Analytics

A campus network consists of a number of technologies and network functions that combined form the network. The list of technologies is extensive and includes common technologies like Spanning Tree Protocol, VLANs, wired interfaces, wireless communications, interface statistics, IP interfaces, routing protocols, and so on.

Traditionally, these technologies are monitored individually, or in in other words, without context. If a specific element of a single technology fails, an alert is generated, and the operations team responds to that. But what if that technology is combined with other technology and the network is still functioning? The operations team would still need to respond of course, but perhaps with a lower urgency. The network function itself is still operating.

This type of intelligently combining data collected by the analytics component is used within IBN to analyze and monitor network functions.

An example for this intelligent combination would be that a distribution switch of an IP address is connected to a VLAN interface but no access switches have that VLAN configured. It might not be a direct failure of a network function, but this possible fault could not be detected by monitoring technologies individually. Context is created by combining the two technologies and can conclude that the combination is not as normally expected.

Network Services Availability

Besides network functions, other services are also required to enable a campus network. Services that are critical to network availability would be DHCP and DNS. These servers are usually managed by departments other than the team responsible for the campus network. However, the campus operations team will receive the call that a specific location on the network is not working. The network services availability function, within the analytics component, uses the collected data to analyze whether required network services are available and working as expected. If a DHCP server is responding with an error like the scope is full, or another error, this data can be collected and responded on.

Another example of network services would be a RADIUS check to the central policy server, to check that RADIUS (and thus IEEE 802.1x) is still working.

Trend Analysis

As data about intent, network functions, and services is already collected, enough data becomes available to perform trend analysis. This trend analysis can be used to determine whether, for example, uplinks need to be upgraded. Although this is already common in most managed networks, the function must also exist within IBN.

Application Behavior Analytics

Network devices, such as switches, routers, and wireless controllers, have become more intelligent over the years. With technologies, such as Network-Based Application Recognition (NBAR), Application Visibility and Control (AVC), and more recently Encrypted Threat Analytics (ETA), the network can recognize applications that run over the network. This information can, smartly, be combined with the other data that the network provides to analyze how applications behave on the network. This function is used within IBN to provide business-based feedback on how applications are performing. It is possible to deduce that Microsoft Outlook is slow because the response from the

Microsoft Exchange Server took too long and Outlook has re-sent the request. This kind of analytics provides more insight into the ever-increasing number of applications that run on the network.

These functions are all using data obtained from the campus network infrastructure component within Cisco DNA–essentially the network infrastructure devices. It would be nearly impossible to obtain this kind of information with traditional data collection methods such as command line, SNMP, and Syslog. Although these protocols are used as well, they do have issues in terms of scalability, standardization, and obtaining the proper data. A new concept, called *model-driven telemetry*, is also used to get the required data from the network infrastructure. Model-Driven Telemetry (MDT) is explained in more detail in Appendix A, "Campus Network Technologies," but in general, a collector subscribes to a number of information elements on the network devices. And the network devices send updates on a regular basis. And as MDT is part of Cisco DNA and IBN, the model itself, including the transport, is open and available.

The analytics component is probably for most enterprises currently an underestimated function as most first steps to Intent-Based Networking are focused on automation. However, data combined with machine intelligence does provide big promises in actively supporting network operation teams to manage the network.

Network Analytics Tools

A number of tools are available for analytics and network visibility; however, not all can be applied to Cisco DNA to enable IBN. The following sections provide an overview of network tools that can be used for IBN. Just like with automation, composing a complete list of visibility tools would result in an entire book. This overview is intended to explain the concepts and how certain tools can be used within analytics to enable IBN.

DNA Center Assurance

The most obvious tool available for network visibility is part of the Cisco DNA Center (DNAC) solution. Within DNAC there is an application available called Assurance. This big data analysis platform makes use of Tesseract and a number of big data lake technologies to analyze the data it collects from the managed devices.

DNAC Assurance leverages the data available within the DNAC solution (such as the network topology and type of devices) as well as the required data received from the network infrastructure. DNAC Assurance processes and analyzes the data and tries to determine the overall health of the network. DNAC presents the data using dashboards, with overall health, network health, and client health. All kinds of found issues, such as sticky wireless clients and sudden packet drops in the wired infrastructure, have a place in these dashboards and have an impact on the health.

For example, if the connection to a specific campus location is down or unreachable, the total health of the network will go down and the health of that site will go to 0%. DNAC leverages the information, such as network topology, to provide more context. If in the same example the wireless controller is down, or a number of APs, then the health score of the site will go down, but when the operator views the details, it immediately sees that the wireless health is low while wired is still working. Figure 6-7 shows a screenshot for the health of the connected clients within DNAC Assurance.

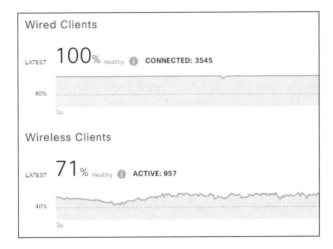

Figure 6-7　*Overview of the Client Health Within DNAC*

Cisco DNAC Assurance is written with the primary use cases of the network operator in mind. DNAC Assurance attempts to prioritize incidents or issues found within the network by showing the top issues first. Also, all information is drilled down, and features like client 360 and device 360 are available as well. A key feature within DNAC Assurance is the ability to go back in time. As the data DNAC Assurance collects is stored in a big data lake, it is possible to reconstruct the state of the network around the time that an issue occurred. This is powerful for troubleshooting incidents such as the wireless network was not working last Friday. Figure 6-8 displays an example of an AP whose health was dropped for a short period of time. By hovering over the moment, the reasons for the reduced health can be seen.

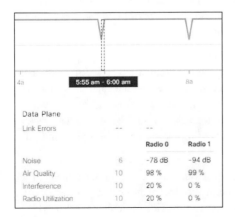

Figure 6-8　*DNAC Assurance Health History of an AP*

From an application or client perspective, DNAC has the capability to analyze a number of behaviors automatically. For example, in DNA Center 1.2, there are more than 77 issues defined related to wireless client behavior, such as sticky client behavior, client not authenticating, or the client onboarding time (how long it takes to connect to the network). Figure 6-9 shows a dashboard example on the client onboarding times.

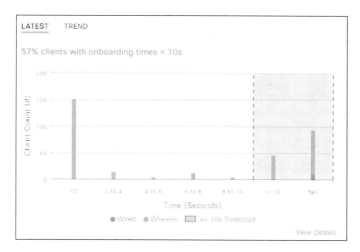

Figure 6-9 *DNAC Assurance Dashboard of Client Onboarding Times*

In conclusion, DNAC Assurance is built for Intent-Based Networking and comes with all necessary functions for the analytics component. Over time, more features are added into DNAC Assurance, providing an even more complete view of the network.

Prime Infrastructure

The Cisco Prime Infrastructure is perhaps not designed and built for the purpose of network analytics in an Intent-Based Network as Cisco DNA Center. But it can provide some functionality required within IBN for network analytics. Prime Infrastructure is a network management and operations tool. It is built around existing protocols like NetFlow, Syslog, and SNMP to proactively monitor the network infrastructure. In that mind-set, it is possible, although perhaps a bit more restricted compared to DNA Center, to use Prime Infrastructure for the network analytics functions described previously.

Although SNMP and Syslog do not provide the same level of network function analysis as MDT, Prime Infrastructure can proactively monitor the network on some basic network functions like the availability of wireless networks, VLAN interfaces up and down, and whether there are errors with ARP.

The reporting in Prime is extensive and provides a number of reports that can be used for availability and trend analysis and thus provides the necessary features for the IBN network assurance functions, such as network service availability and trend analysis.

Prime Infrastructure uses NetFlow to analyze and collect data on application performance and usage of the network by applications. Several screens and reports can be used to view the application performance and therefore create a limited use of the Application Behavior Analytics function.

One of the key features of network analytics is to validate if the network is performing correctly according to the requested intents. Prime Infrastructure does not provide an off-the-shelf feature to check this continuously, but it is possible to create compliance templates and use those templates to validate the deployed intents against these compliance templates and provide a report. This does require quite a bit of manual work, however.

Prime Infrastructure does provide an extensive list of possibilities to proactively report on failures and alerts, including email, Syslog, alerts, and SNMP alerts. These possibilities can be used in combination with reporting and other functions to proactively support the network operations teams in case of a failure or when a device is not compliant to the deployed templates.

Also, from an API perspective, Prime Infrastructure already provides a rather extensive set of REST APIs to obtain data from Prime Infrastructure from other applications. These APIs can also be used to obtain data from Prime that is not available from a screen or report.

API Usage

One of my fellow Cisco Champions asked if there was a report within Prime Infrastructure to view which channel assignments were applied on the radios of each wireless access point. It is cumbersome to check each individual access point as opposed to having a single, easier-to-digest overview, specifically for large deployments where hundreds of access points are deployed. A report is available within Prime, but it would show the number of access points assigned to each channel and not which AP has which channel. An export to CSV of that same report would show the history of channel assignments but not the actual status.

Although there is no report to get the actual information, there is an API call that can be used to get actual information about access points, including radio channel assignments. Using that API (and authentication), a quick program has been written that connects to Prime Infrastructure, fetches the information, and exports it in a CSV format so that the data can be analyzed or processed in a different tool. This example showcases that the APIs within Prime Infrastructure are powerful and can be leveraged to obtain information otherwise not directly available within the Prime Infrastructure user interface.

Prime Infrastructure does not have the same feature velocity as Cisco DNA Center for network analytics. Over time DNA Center will likely replace Prime Infrastructure as a network management tool; however, Prime Infrastructure can certainly be used to start transforming existing networks to Intent-Based Networking as long as the restrictions such as machine intelligence and detailed network function analysis are known and accepted.

NetBrain

NetBrain is a tool that provides network visibility. One of its main powers is that it dynamically can create a map of the enterprise network using the running configuration and live status of the network. NetBrain also offers advanced features like documentation generation, Microsoft Visio document generation, comparison of configurations, and doing path-traces based on the network configuration and how the configuration is run in hardware.

NetBrain features QApps and Runbooks to automate and support troubleshooting. QApps are small apps that operators can write themselves within NetBrain to stream-line a number of troubleshooting steps with a single click. In other words, the QApp defines the steps that need to be executed for a specific troubleshooting step (or test), and NetBrain executes the steps. The development of a QApp is via the GUI within NetBrain. Figure 6-10 displays the general workflow of a QApp within NetBrain.

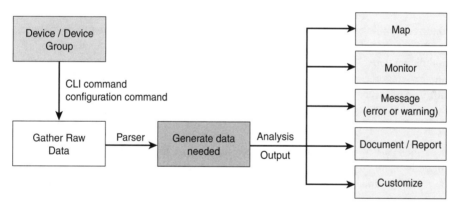

Figure 6-10   *Generic Workflow of a QApp*

Runbooks are similar to playbooks in Ansible. They can be used within NetBrain to execute several actions, including checks and rollbacks. This can be used not only for change management but also to validate enabled intents on the network. Figure 6-11 shows a screenshot of a runbook creation.

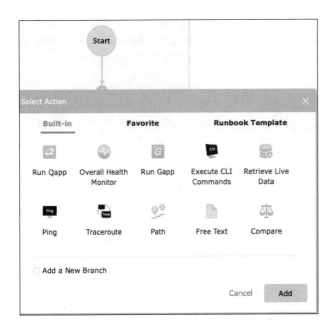

Figure 6-11   *Screenshot of Runbook Creation Within NetBrain*

NetBrain is capable of performing some of the functions related to the network analytics component with an Intent-Based Network, specifically the validation of enabled intents and validating network functions and services. As NetBrain's primary purpose is to operate and maintain the network, functions such as application analysis and trend analysis are not its core strengths.

Ansible

As described earlier in this chapter, Ansible is in principle an automation engine and not directly related to network analytics functions. However, Ansible is used in CI/CD automation pipelines, and that should include automated tests as well. This testing functionality could be used to deploy some form of network analytics functions via Ansible. And although Ansible itself is trigger-based, the Ansible Tower can be used to set up a schedule to periodically execute a set of playbooks.

These playbooks would primarily focus on testing the validity of the network, for example, by checking BGP neighbor status, specific routes, or interface status. The code in Example 6-5 could be used to check if a VLAN is up on the distribution switch.

Example 6-5   *Ansible Configuration to Check if a VLAN Is Up*

```
tasks:
- name: test interface status
 net_interface:
   name: vlan100
   state: up
```

Although this example is straightforward, it does demonstrate that it is possible to check some elements of the campus network using Ansible playbooks. Ansible (in combination with an Ansible Tower) can be used to perform the following network analytics functions within an Intent-Based Network:

- Validation of Intent
- Network function analytics
- Network service availability

By writing extra code in Python it would be possible to generate the required test playbooks based on the Intents that are deployed onto the network.

The other two functions, trend analysis and application behavior analytics, cannot be implemented via Ansible. These functions could be implemented via other software solutions focusing on data collection and analysis.

Ansible cannot perform all network analytics functions. However, if Ansible is used as an automation tool for an intent-based network, it can be used to continuously check for the requested intents. It would require some custom coding around Ansible, though, to generalize the playbooks and validate them toward the dynamic intents.

In conclusion, the functions and features for network analytics within Cisco DNA are still in development. Although Cisco DNA Center is built for an IBN and it does provide all functions, DNA Center itself is not yet applicable to all campus networks for a number of reasons. Also, competitors provide similar functions with other tools, and they also introduce new features and functions over time, as well as probably adopting the open MDT standard as well in conjunction with NetFlow, Syslog, and SNMP.

And as the transition to IBN will most probably take a considerable amount of time as well, it is important to know whether existing tools within the enterprise already provide a number of network analytics functions instead of introducing another new tool to the suite of network management tools.

Summary

An enterprise framework, a technology architecture, and IBN alone all provide descriptions and context on how network infrastructures are designed and operated and should work and operate with applications, end users, and other "external" sources. It is all abstract and not directly implemented. Tools and technologies are required to implement these abstract architectures and designs. Two key areas that make an Intent-Based Network unique are automation and network analytics. Tools should implement these two key areas.

Network Automation

Within an Intent-Based Network, the network automation function translates the network intent requests to pieces of configuration and deploys them onto the devices within the infrastructure. Network automation is a key component of Cisco DNA and must be implemented for a successful Intent-Based Network. Several automation tools described in this chapter are capable of implementing this automation role within Cisco DNA (and thus enable IBN). Table 6-1 provides a schematic overview of the different tools and how they are related to the automation function within Cisco DNA.

Table 6-1   *Overview of Automation Tools and Their Capabilities*

Tool	Day-0	Day-1	Day-2	Day-n
Cisco DNA Center	√	√	√	√
Cisco Prime Infrastructure and APIC-EM	√	√	√	√
Cisco Network Service Orchestrator		√	√	√
Puppet Enterprise		√	√	√
RedHat Ansible		√	√	√
Build your own	√	√	√	√

Almost all tools are capable of performing automation on the different tasks in network management. However, only Cisco DNA Center and the combination Prime Infrastructure with APIC-EM provide an off-the-shelf solution for the provisioning of network devices. It is, of course, possible to perform day-0 operations with a custom-built tool as well.

From an intent-based network perspective, Cisco DNA Center is the preferred tool with Prime Infrastructure and APIC-EM as second best. However, if there is familiarity with RedHat Ansible or Puppet Enterprise in the organization, they could be used as well.

Network Analytics

The other key area within IBN is network analytics. For an Intent-Based Network, the analytics function receives (or obtains) data from the network infrastructure and validates whether the intent is configured correctly. However, the information received also contains data on the operation of the network in general, operation of network functions, connected clients, and other contextual data. In general, the network analytics component allows the network visibility to be increased. This increase in visibility is effectively established by adding extra functions and features in the analytics component of Cisco DNA. These extra features are

- Validation of intent

- Network function analytics

- Network services availability

- Trend analysis

- Application behavior analytics

Leveraging big data and analytics within networking is rather new. A limited set of tools are available on the market, where specific tools are focusing on a specific part of the network, such as Cisco Tetration for the datacenter. This chapter described a number of tools known for their analytics component. It is expected that over time more tools will become available for the analytics function within IBN. Table 6-2 provides an overview of the tools described in this chapter and the features they support.

Table 6-2   *Overview of Tools That Can Perform the Analytics Features of Cisco DNA*

Tool	Intent Validation	Network Function Analysis	Network Service Availability	Trend Analysis	Application Behavior Analysis
Cisco DNA Center	√	√	√	√	√
Cisco Prime Infrastructure		√	√	√	
NetBrain		√	√	√	√
RedHat Ansible	√	√	√		

Part II

Transforming to an Intent-Based Network

As is made clear in the chapters in Part I, the way campus networks are traditionally designed and managed need to change. Cisco DNA as an architecture with IBN as a viewpoint will be the end goal of any campus enterprise network in order to manage and cope with all the changes and dynamics. And for new network infrastructures, it is "relatively" easy to set up the network using new equipment and a DNA Center solution. This allows the enterprise to slowly adopt SDA and IBN.

But the reality is often much harsher than the ideal world. The reality is that often there is already an existing production network, which cannot be removed and replaced with a brand new network infrastructure while the enterprise is put on hold for a number of months (or years). It's like in the ideal world you would rebuild the factory while keeping production at the highest optimum. That is also impossible.

Also, most probably, the network operations team is already faced with demands from business to deliver faster, business not allowing downtime for scheduled updates (because then the business is interrupted), other challenges such as security incidents, being understaffed, and still keeping the network running and getting pushes from upper management to transition to the cloud as if it is a silver bullet for all IT-related problems.

But you realize that IBN is a new method of how to manage the campus network in a smarter way, reducing the strain on network design, changes, and operations. It is the way to move forward. But how do you take the first steps onto that journey, as Cisco describes it with the Network Intuitive, or in other words, a path toward IBN? And while IBN is a viewpoint and DNA is a future-ready generic network architecture, it still has to match with the uniqueness of the network you are responsible for. While each network (and its corresponding enterprise and operations team) is unique, the generic design principles, functions, and building blocks of DNA and IBN can be applied to that network while retaining its own requirements, specials, and specifications.

Consequently, each network infrastructure will transition and transform into a network based on IBN with its own unique path and way.

Chapter 5, "Intent-Based Networking," described IBN as a perspective in detail. It also explained the functions and processes of IBN and how it is being operated. If you translate these functions and methods to an actual campus network infrastructure, then the core of IBN is that there is a basic fixed (static) campus network that does not change too frequently. Intents are defined as small but repetitive steps that are deployed on the network, and a central policy server is used to determine which policy (and thus configuration) is to be applied onto that network port.

Figure P-1 shows a minimalistic IBN-enabled campus network consisting of a distribution switch and one access switch.

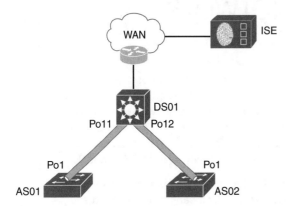

Figure P-1   *A Minimalistic IBN-Enabled Campus Network*

Initially there is no Intent available, and no endpoint can therefore connect. The fixed (static) basic configuration of the switches would be similar to the code examples P-1, P-2, and P-3.

Example P-1   *DS01 Configuration*

```
vlan 900
  name management
vlan 100
  name uplink-management
hostname DS01
domain-name mycompany.com
interface vlan 900
  ip address 10.1.1.1 255.255.255.0
interface vlan 100
  ip address 10.255.255.2 255.255.255.252
interface port-channel11
  switchport mode trunk
  switchport trunk allowed vlan 900
access-list 23 permit 10.0.2.0 0.0.0.255
line vty 0 15
  access-class 23 in
ip route 0.0.0.0 0.0.0.0 10.255.255.1
```

Example P-2 *AS01 Configuration*

```
vlan 900
  name management
hostname AS01
domain-name mycompany.com
interface vlan 900
  ip address 10.1.1.2 255.255.255.0
interface port-channel11
  switchport mode trunk
  switchport trunk allowed vlan 900
access-list 23 permit 10.0.2.0 0.0.0.255
line vty 0 15
  access-class 23 in
ip route 0.0.0.0 0.0.0.0 10.1.1.1
```

Example P-3 *AS02 Configuration*

```
vlan 900
  name management
hostname AS02
domain-name mycompany.com
interface vlan 900
  ip address 10.1.1.3 255.255.255.0
interface port-channel11
  switchport mode trunk
  switchport trunk allowed vlan 900
access-list 23 permit 10.0.2.0 0.0.0.255
line vty 0 15
  access-class 23 in
ip route 0.0.0.0 0.0.0.0 10.1.1.1
```

In the preceding examples, the access port configuration is omitted in the AS01 and AS02 configurations. All the access ports would be configured in the same way, implementing the 802.1X protocol and MAC Authentication Bypass for network access control.

At this stage no endpoint can connect to the network. If an Intent would need to be created and applied to this network, for example an Intent to allow employees on the network, then the automation function would be able to generate configuration snippets, such as shown in Example P-4 for DS01 and Example P-5 for the access switches.

Example P-4 *Employee Intent Configuration for DS01*

```
vlan 10
  name employees
vlan 101
  name handoff-employees
vrf forwarding definition IBN-01
  description employees
  address-family ipv4
interface vlan 101
  vrf forwarding IBN-01
  ip address 10.255.255.6 255.255.255.252
interface vlan 10
  vrf forwarding IBN-01
  ip address 10.2.1.1 255.255.255.0
  ip helper-address 172.16.1.10
ip route vrf IBN-01 0.0.0.0 0.0.0.0 10.255.255.5
!
```

Example P-5 *Employee Intent Configuration for Access Switches*

```
vlan 10
  name employees
interface PortChannel1
  switchport trunk allowed vlan add 10
!
```

Once these code snippets have been deployed to the network, the Intent for employees has become available. If at this stage an endpoint is connected to the network and authenticated as an employee, the access port is assigned to VLAN 10 using an authorization policy within ISE, and the employee is connected in an IP network and virtual network.

If the Intent needs to be removed, the only thing that needs to be done by the automation engine is to remove VLAN10 and the appropriate interfaces. The part of the configuration for the employee's Intent is then removed.

This is essentially what happens within the automation part of an Intent-Based Network. A similar process occurs for SDA-based deployments with, of course, different technologies and commands.

The transformation of an existing campus network essentially has the goal to achieve this functionality for existing networks and existing policies. The transformation also includes the required tools, processes, and methods.

This part contains a description of a four-phased approach to achieve that goal for transformation from a technical or design perspective. It is focused on how the network infrastructure can be changed, in its configuration or used technology, while remaining generic enough to be applicable for most campus networks. Each chapter describes a phase in detail, including why certain steps, actions, or changes are required before moving toward the next phase. The four phases describe several elements or items that are needed to achieve that goal on the existing network. And as each network is unique, it could be that not all information is applicable to the network that is to be changed or implemented.

The transformation on any existing network toward IBN will take much more time in comparison with a brand new installation. The primary cause for this is that the changes need to be made in small steps, carefully considering several stakeholders and aspects normal in running a production campus network. Therefore, the phases in this part can be seen as steps in the strategy to move toward IBN.The chapters in this part of the book are as follows:

Chapter 7   Phase One: Identifying Challenges

Chapter 8   Phase Two: Prepare for Intent

Chapter 9   Phase Three: Design, Deploy, and Extend

Chapter 10   Phase Four: Enable Intent

Phase One: Identifying Challenges

The first phase in the transformation to Intent-Based Networking (IBN) is to determine the state of the campus network and the organization. Because an *Intent-enabled* network, and thus a network based on Cisco DNA, has a number of requirements that must be met, it is important to determine whether it is possible to transform the existing network to IBN at all. Because the transformation has an impact on the organization, some changes need to be executed within the organization as well.

The first phase begins with performing an inventory on the state of the campus network and identifying the challenges that can either block or provide resistance to the transformation to IBN. The word *challenges* is chosen on purpose. Challenges can be solved; however, problems can remain problems for a lengthier period of time.

This chapter describes a number of steps that you need to execute to obtain information and identify challenges that need to be resolved. These challenges are prioritized and summarized in an action plan that will be used in the next phase. The following steps are described in this chapter:

- Challenges in day-to-day network operations
- Inventory of campus network
- Level of standardization
- Maturity level of the organization
- Stakeholders

Challenges in Day-to-Day Operations

IBN primarily describes how a campus network should be operated to meet the ever-increasing number of connected devices and complexity. IBN can therefore also be seen as a new method of running network operations in the (campus) network. However, a number of challenges related to day-to-day operations can affect the success of a transformation to IBN.

Of course, all network engineers are familiar with the OSI layers of abstraction with the process of encapsulation and decapsulation that essentially form the basis of any network infrastructure. However, users and managers just view the network as a single element that is just as common as running water or electricity. Because users and managers only see a single network (users, for example, don't know the difference between 4G and WiFi connections), an analogy can be used to explain that the network is actually a foundation for the applications.

Every organization can be seen as a building or a house, each uniquely built and designed. On the top of the building we see all the applications required for the business to be able to run. This could be Office 365, Google Mail, an ERP system like SAP, but also your office applications and a fileserver to store all your documents. It doesn't matter whether these applications run on-premises, in the cloud, or a combination. It's just the collection of applications that the organization uses in day-to-day operations. Figure 7-1 displays this enterprise building.

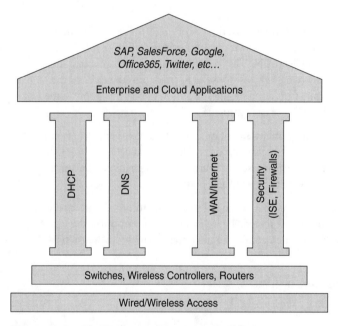

Figure 7-1   *The Enterprise Seen as a Building*

At the first layer of the building, where the employee or contractor resides who wants to get access to the enterprise applications, the physical connection to the corporate network is described. It is literally the physical cable (or wireless network) that is used to connect the endpoint to the corporate network. The second layer is the equipment to which the physical cable (or wireless connection) is connected. These are the network switches, wireless controllers, access points, and routers that comprise a campus location network. Although an endpoint can be connected to the network, there is still no access to the application. That is because four pillars are required to be able to access the applications.

The first required pillar is the Dynamic Host Configuration Protocol (DHCP). DHCP is used to dynamically assign IP addresses to connected endpoints. If DHCP is not working, there is no IP assigned to the endpoint and thus no connection to the applications. Often, DHCP is managed by the server team and not the network operations team.

Note   Although it is possible to statically assign IP addresses to endpoints, this is not a scalable solution, and many enterprises rely on DHCP to provide IP addresses to endpoints (which is also recommended for wireless endpoints).

The second pillar is the Domain Name System (DNS). This service translates domain names into the appropriate IP addresses, like a phone book. DNS is a service that runs on top of the IP network, but if DNS is not working, it is often blamed on the network. While the IP network is functioning and traffic can flow, it's just that the phonebook is not working.

The third pillar is the WAN connection or Internet connectivity in the case of a cloud application. If the WAN or Internet is down, there is again no connection to the applications.

The last pillar is security, which should be integrated everywhere. Cisco Identity Services Engine (ISE), as network access control, or a firewall could block access to an application for any number of reasons. If these services are not available, again there is no connection to the network.

This explains, in a simplified way, that for users to connect so easily to the enterprise applications, many elements need to be in order. Today's enterprise networks, however, despite their complexity, are so reliable (and invisible), most incidents are initially blamed on the network and specifically the campus network. Some examples of frequently reported incidents are

- "I cannot access application X, but I could access it yesterday. It is definitely the network."
- "Application Y is slow; must be the network. It's that uplink again that you mentioned three years ago."
- "I cannot connect to the wireless network, and it's not my computer because everything works at home."
- "I can't log on to the computer; it is the network's fault."
- "The wireless service is terrible. I only see 2 bars for 4G on my phone in the office. Please fix this."

These and similar examples are quite common for many network operations teams. They face these types of issues frequently and probably spend quite a bit of time proving that not all incidents are network-related other teams should address the incidents related to application performance instead of the network operations team.

Besides the fact that the operations team spends quite some time disproving "it's the network," another aspect might play a role in the day-to-day operations. There has been a shortage of qualified staff for a long period of time (decades in the case of Europe). Besides a shortage of staff, the campus network has gradually grown in size and the connected devices. As the network is very invisible for many users and managers, chances are that the network operations team has not been growing in line with the growth of the network. The consequence is that the operations team is understaffed and trying to keep the network operational with too limited resources.

These two aspects together might indicate that the network operations team is under a lot of pressure and do not have time to look at alternatives, as they can be seen as firefighters continuously putting out fires in the foundation of the enterprise (refer back to Figure 7-1). They are too busy solving incidents and executing changes on the network (that take too long) and often must work overtime to update the switches because they are not allowed to do that during the day.

To determine whether IBN is a viable solution for a specific campus network, it is important to determine whether the preceding scenarios are applicable for the network operations team. If that is the case, then the network operations team will not have time available to perform extra changes or even consider changing the way they operate the network. This challenge (of being too busy) needs to be identified early on in the process so that appropriate actions can be taken to free up time within the operations team; otherwise, the network operations team will remain busy while the campus network continues to grow.

It is important to note that the network operations team should be engaged in the process of transformation to IBN as much as possible because most of IBN relates to their responsibilities.

Inventory

In most organizations the campus network is not being replaced very often. It is common to install the network equipment and keep it running for at least five years and for some network equipment even longer. Some enterprises, in fact, still operate with a wireless network that has not been changed since its initial operation, while the wireless access points have been superseded by three new versions. Other examples describe situations where switches were run in the default configuration. Determining the current state of the campus network requires performing a detailed inventory of the network infrastructure components within the campus network.

This inventory should be detailed and extensive and should also include information related to the capabilities for IBN. The output of this inventory should be registered with the help of the examples in Tables 7-1 and 7-2.

Table 7-1 *Overview of Installed Hardware and Software*

Device Family	Device Type	Device Name	SW Version	Update SW Required?	Install Date	Replacement Required?	Replacement Moment
Routers	C2951	C1-RT01	15.2	No	Jan 2016	Yes	Jan 2021
Switches	WS-C3650-24PS-S	C1-AS01	3.7	Yes	Mar 2017	No	
Switches	WS-C6509-E	C1-DS01	12.2	N/A	Oct 2014	Yes	ASAP
Wireless	AIR-CT5508	C1-WS01	8.5	N/A	Jan 2017	Yes	ASAP
...							

Table 7-1 is used to create a complete inventory of all campus network equipment and is validated against Cisco DNA and IBN readiness on both the software version as well as the hardware. For each device, an entry should be made and determined (in case of non-ready hardware) when the hardware is scheduled to be replaced. If there is no active lifecycle management (LCM) within the organization, that lack of LCM is a risk for the transformation, and a mitigation should be defined in cooperation with the appropriate stakeholders. If the campus network has multiple locations it can be convenient to add a column for the location name, as to be able to create an inventory impact overview per location.

Depending on the size of the campus network it is optional to aggregate the available data from Table 7-1 into an overview such as shown in Table 7-2.

Table 7-2 *Aggregated Overview of Campus Network Hardware*

Device Family	Device Type	Total Switches	IBN Ready	Remarks
Switches	WS-C3650-24PS-S	40	Conditional	Max 3 VNs[*]
Routers	C2951	2	No	
Switches	WS-C6509-E	3	No	End of life
Wireless	AIR-CAP2602I	200	No	End of life
Wireless	AIR-CT5508	2	No	End of life
...				

[*] IP Base of the Catalyst 3650/380 provides maximal 3 virtual networks (or VRFs); switches running IP Services (ending with E in the SKU) can have maximal 64 virtual networks.

The aggregated overview in Table 7-2 can be used to determine the impact of creating an IBN-ready infrastructure. Because some switches might have to be replaced, it is possible that some steps of the transformation to IBN will be delayed. The primary cause for this is that financial administrations dictate that investments need to be depreciated over multiple years. It means that an investment last year needs to last for at least two or often four years. It is possible to replace sooner, but it means that the organization is willing to accept a financial disinvestment of the previously made investment.

The inventory should be a "living" document, so as soon as a network device is replaced with other hardware, the inventory should be updated. Also, based on this inventory, it is recommended to get a strategic decision from stakeholders that if hardware is to be replaced, whether due to failure or in normal lifecycle management, the new hardware must be IBN ready.

Level of Standardization

Another element that needs to be identified is the level of standardization. One of the principles behind IBN is that the specifics for an application or policy are pushed onto the network when it is required using predefined blocks of configuration (either CLI or model-based). There is a direct relationship between the level of standardization in the existing campus network and the success factor for IBN. In other words, when there is no standardization, it is not possible to automate changes on the network and thus enable IBN, whereas if there is a high level of standardization using standardized components, these components can easily be configured using automation.

As such, the level of standardization needs to be determined for several aspects of the campus network. Only those elements of a network that are standardized can be automated and thus be deployed onto the network when the intent is required. As a campus network design and its implementation consist of several components, the identification of automation level should occur for those different components as well. The following sections briefly describe each component.

Existing and Up-to-Date Wired Campus Design

If a generic campus network design exists that is applied to all campus locations, that in itself is a huge level of standardization. This means that the design (and thus the configuration) of each campus location is similar with the exception of location- or device-specific elements, such as management of IP settings, hostnames, and possibly local network function services such as DHCP and DNS. It is, of course, important to validate not only the availability of a campus design, but also whether the design has been kept up-to-date and implementations are consistent with the design.

Wireless Design

The same principle is applicable for the wireless design as well. Is a wireless network design available? Are the SSIDs used in the campus network consistent and preferably the same? Are the wireless parameters, such as guest network services, corporate wireless access, and possibly other wireless networks such as IoT and BYOD incorporated in the design? Is the design up-to-date and is the wireless network implemented accordingly? Are there specifics, like a deployment with FlexConnect or special VLAN use cases?

Shared Switch Configuration

Based on the common campus network topology, the switches on a campus have distinct roles and functions, such as access switches, distribution switches, and possibly core switches. Regardless of the role of the specific switches in a campus network, the configuration itself can be divided into three types of configuration:

■ **Specific port configuration:** This can be unique per switch but is commonly different between access, distribution, and core switches.

■ **Layer 3 configuration:** Contains all IP configuration for VLANs and the required routing to the core or the WAN router. This configuration is typically found on the distribution and core switch.

■ **Generic (or global) configuration:** Contains the hostname, Spanning Tree configuration (if applicable), other Layer 2 technologies such as CDP or VTP, management access control, Syslog, NTP, enabled services, control plane policing, and so on. This should all be in a highly standardized configuration similar across all types of switches. A standardized generic switch configuration can benefit in composing templates for the automation within the campus network.

It is important to identify what level of standardization has been applied to these types of configuration across all switches. A high level of standardization will greatly benefit a transformation to IBN because IBN relies heavily on standardized configurations.

Access Port Configuration

Traditionally, the campus network is configured per access port. Some companies adhere to a strategy of shutting down unused ports completely and only configure a port when needed, while others configure the port in a default VLAN with a default policy. The port can be enabled or disabled in the latter case. For the transition to IBN, all access ports will have the same port configuration, as the specifics are configured only when the connected device is known and the proper policy (or Intent) can be applied. A standard port configuration, applicable to all ports, is therefore recommended as a high level of standardization.

Uplink Standardization

Although this could be part of the generic switch configuration, are the uplinks from the access switch to the distribution switch standardized to a single port channel? Is a default port channel used for the communication to a local wireless controller, if applicable? The standardization of uplinks provides a metric of how standardized the current campus network is. The benefit of standardizing the uplink to, for example, PortChannel1, whether it consists of 1, 2, or 4 links, makes troubleshooting and configuring technologies like IP-Device Tracking much easier.

VLAN Configuration Consistent and Identical Across Locations

VLANs are used to logically isolate different types of devices on a physical network. If the VLAN numbering is unique per location, this would mean that there is a limited level of automation for VLAN assignment, and it would be nearly impossible to standardize for an Intent-enabled network. If the VLAN numbering is consistent and identical across all locations, however, whether for endpoints connecting to the network, native VLANs, or management traffic, this would be a huge benefit in the transformation to an Intent-Based Network.

Use Case: VLAN Standardization Across Branch Locations

SharedService Group has deployed a single SSID for all employees to use. Based on the identity of the endpoint, the VLAN override function is used to place that specific endpoint in the correct VLAN.

The choice for a single SSID was not only for configuration simplicity, but also to keep the number of broadcasted SSIDs to an absolute minimum.

As a single SSID is used with certificate authentication, it is possible for SharedService Group to centrally push the wireless settings via an Active Directory group policy. This means that the managed workstations are, once correctly imaged and bound to the Active Directory, automatically connected to the wireless network when the workstation detects the wireless SSID.

This central policy was highly standardized, and the different employees could work without problem. However, when employees started to move more frequently between offices and an employee visited a foreign office, the device could not connect to the network. The employee could manually override the wireless connection to the available guest services, but after a short period of time the connection was lost.

The cause of this problem was related to the VLAN assignment in combination with the group policy. The workstation assumed that as the SSID was available, it was at one of the corporate locations and thus the required connection. However, when that employee was visiting a location and the specific compartment for his business unit (VPN) was not configured at that location, the endpoint was successfully authenticated and placed into a VLAN that did not exist and was not connected. Therefore, the workstation could not connect to the network. The employee could manually select the guest network, but once the enterprise SSID was seen again, the workstation automatically attempted to connect to the corporate SSID and again was unable to receive an IP address, which created the assumption it was DHCP-related.

Eventually, SharedService Group decided to deliver all VPNs to all locations to solve this problem and allow employees to truly be mobile and work from any office.

This use case showcases the power of standardization of VLANs and how to use them. It allowed for a standardized configuration of the wireless network and made for easier changes. However, if the workstation that uses the network acts differently than expected, there could be two solutions. One is to override the VLAN numbering for each location, creating a less-standardized approach and thus a more complex environment. The second solution is to extend the VPNs to all locations, so that the wireless network remains standardized. The organization wisely chose the latter. The first option is valid but has consequences and can become a greater challenge when transforming to an IBN-enabled network.

Standardized Configuration Across Locations

The last task is used to determine whether the configuration of the wired and wireless network components is consistent across all locations of the campus network. In other words, does the configuration between two campus locations only differ in hostnames and IP addressing, or are there more differences?

These components can individually be scored on a level of automation, with a score of 1 for no standardization (or no answer) but up to 5 for full standardization (or confirmation). Table 7-3 provides an overview of the components and a method to note the score of the component.

Table 7-3 *Inventory Table for Level of Standardization*

Component	Level of Automation (1–5)
Existing campus network design	
Campus network design up-to-date	
Campus implemented according to design	
Existing and consistent wireless design	
Wireless design up-to-date	
Wireless implemented according to design	
Generic switch configuration	
Access port configuration	
Uplink standardization	
VLAN configuration consistent and identical across locations	
Standardized configuration across locations (factor 2)	

Although the scoring is not scientifically or statistically approved, it does provide a quick insight into which component could pose a challenge to transform the campus network toward IBN. A score of 4 or higher means that the component is standardized, and it is relatively easy to transform the network for IBN.

Maturity Level of an Organization

It might sound strange, but the maturity level of an organization can tell a lot about how successful any change will be. The maturity level has nothing to do with the age of an organization but is measured along aspects such as people, process, technology, and documentation. The maturity level of an organization provides insights into whether and how a network can be transformed to IBN. The maturity level namely provides information, at an abstract level, about how the organization is documented, whether it is working with or without procedures, how it embraces a vision, and other insights.

A number of frameworks are available that describe the level of maturity of an organization. Control Objectives for Information and related Technologies (COBIT) by ISACA is an extensive framework that provides control objectives for IT governance and IT management. The COBIT 4.1 version of the framework has a maturity model that is useful in this phase. Within this model are five levels of maturity defined that are used and referred to throughout the control framework. Without going into the details of this framework, these levels do provide a good view of how mature the IT within an organization can be. The following sections describe these levels.

Level 1: Ad Hoc

At this level, every IT-related action is executed on an ad hoc basis. If a new computer or switch is required, the computer that best fits the purpose for that task at that moment will suffice—usually procured at the local computer store around the corner. In general, level 1 organizations have a wide diversity of devices and no standardization within the entire IT infrastructure.

Level 2: Repetitive But Intuitive

At level 2, things start to improve. IT departments do not just arbitrarily select a switch or computer, but standardize on vendors and specific switch types, and start to repeat a number of IT operations. As an example, each switch is configured consistently with a proper hostname, IP address, and consistent VLAN(s). So if a switch is to be replaced, the IT department procures a switch in the same series and configures it based on the configuration of another switch. In general, the IT department is doing the repetitive tasks in the right way, but they know they're doing it the right way with limited to no documentation. Responsibilities within the IT department are also unclear.

Level 3: Defined

At level 3, the intuitive controls from level 2 have been documented. There is a level of documentation in relation to design and operation of the IT infrastructure. The organization starts to identify risks and document them, although not completely in a managed methodology and taking a measurable approach. The organization has defined and documented its processes and responsibilities.

Level 4: Managed and Measurable

At level 4, the IT processes are not only defined, but include version control and have specific checkpoints within those procedures to allow external auditors to check that the processes and procedures have been executed correctly. Also risks to the operation of the business, from an IT perspective, are identified, documented, and possibly mitigated.

For example, a change procedure for the network infrastructure contains a quality check and needs approval from the change advisory board before the change can be executed. It is common for organizations that have ISO9001/9002 standards to have these kinds of procedures in place. Also, at this level, there is a vision and strategy related to the IT department, including vendor strategy and lifecycle management.

Level 5: Optimized

Although level 4 provides the identification of risks and controls to mitigate them, there might still be a way to bypass those procedures or controls. At level 5, there are alerts if controls are being bypassed, and management programs are established to continuously improve the risks, mitigations, and procedures. The IT organization actively practices internal control and risk management.

COBIT Framework Summary

In summary, the COBIT framework contains a huge number of controls and questions on a number of aspects within IT (such as procurement, backup, operation, and so on) that assist professionals to determine the maturity level of an organization and how that level can be raised if required. It is, of course, not required to perform a full COBIT audit for the transformation to IBN.

However, the IBN perspective (inherently) assumes a certain level of maturity of an enterprise. As an example, using design documents and having a technical architecture (or even being in the process of having or setting up an enterprise architecture) quickly moves an organization to a level 3 or level 4 of maturity.

If an enterprise is on level 1 or level 2 with regards to anything network-related, the chances of successfully transforming to IBN are slim to none. The risk of starting on the journey and having to change that journey every month because there is no consistent vision or strategy is just too high.

Therefore, part of this phase is to objectively determine the maturity level of the organization and decide whether an increase is required before moving toward technological change. Table 7-4 provides an overview of sample questions and the maturity level they correspond to if the answer is affirmative.

Table 7-4   *Questions and Related Maturity Level*

Question	Maturity Level
Does the enterprise embrace a single vendor strategy for procurement of IT?	3
If so, is there a single vendor strategy for hardware and software for campus networks, such as Cisco Systems?	4
Is there a form of lifecycle management of network devices and software (other than replace if broken) available?	2–3
Is this lifecycle management documented?	3–4
Is documentation of the campus network available?	3
Is the documentation up-to-date and being kept up-to-date?	4
Are change procedures documented?	3
Are changes documented?	4
Have there been discussions on availability?	2–3
Did the discussions result in requirements and procedures?	3–4
Does the organization hold ISO 9001/ISO 9002 certification?	4
Is there an IT architecture available?	4
And is it followed?	4–5
Does the enterprise use IT management processes, such as ITL, PRINCE2, or others?	3–4
Does each network administrator have its own account, or is a shared account used?	2–3
Is role-based access control implemented, or is every IT staff member administrator?	3–4
Does the enterprise have a strategy and vision in relation to how IT can service and benefit the business?	4

Based on the answers of the questions in Table 7-4, it is relatively safe to guess at which maturity level the organization is. If most, if not all, questions are answered with yes, then the organization is between level 3 and level 4. If an organization is at level 1 or 2, it is important to first bring the organization to at least maturity level 3 before transforming the campus network to IBN because the chance of a successful transformation will be slim.

Stakeholders

The transformation to an IBN-enabled campus network is a strategic decision. Chances are that the transformation to an IBN-enabled campus network will not only take a considerable amount of time but will probably also bring extra costs and downtime as required changes are implemented. Although the desire to transform might be initiated from a network operations or network design team, or an IT manager, it is important to identify the stakeholders who can and will support such a long-term strategy in transformation.

Stakeholders are all responsible persons (or departments) within an organization that have either an interest in this strategy or are affected by the execution of this transformation. As the campus network touches many aspects of the organization, it is important to identify stakeholders for business operations, technical, architectural (if applicable), and financial level.

It is important not only to identify those stakeholders but also involve them in the decisions that you need to make for the transformation. They should be informed, and preferably the key stakeholders should also support you in the process of this transformation of the campus network.

A method to register and document the identified stakeholders within the organization is the RACI (Responsible, Accountable, Consultative, Informed) matrix. A RACI matrix is commonly used to visualize for specific tasks (or business processes) who is responsible for executing the task, who is accountable (only one is accountable), who provides support to the task (Consultative), and who needs to be notified of the output of the task (Informed). The same principles can be used within this step to document the identified stakeholders, both formally and informally. Use the Consultative and Informative columns for identified influencers. Table 7-5 provides a sample matrix that can be used.

Table 7-5 *Sample Matrix of RACI Model*

Task/ Process	Responsible	Accountable	Consultative	Informative	Remarks
IT department	IT team	CTO	CSO, CFO		
Security	SOC team	CSO	CTO		
Budget					
Procurement of hardware					Important to know if specific stakeholders influence hardware selection and procurement.
...					
Primary business process	...	...			

Besides identifying these stakeholders, it is important to communicate why the transformation to IBN is needed and how you want to achieve that transformation. Explain why a big-bang transformation might fail and inform them of your balanced choices.

You should not just inform them once, but inform them periodically about progress and decisions. Keep those decisions at the level of the stakeholders, so that they will feel that you understand their concerns, and they will appreciate the effort and will more likely become part of the process. Their involvement is important to getting and keeping support during the journey. The chances are that at some moment in time an unforeseen disruption might happen or extra funding might be required for a big step.

In conclusion, identifying and involvement of stakeholders will assist in a smoother journey and keep commitment and involvement as to why the transformation is required.

Prioritize

As Rome wasn't built in a day, the same is applicable for this phase. At this stage all kinds of information and challenges have been identified, whether they are organizational, lack of IBN-ready hardware, or resource issues. It will be impossible to fix all challenges at the same time, so there is a need to prioritize the identified challenges.

Prioritizing the solutions for identified challenges can be very difficult as the priorities might also change over time. However, a valid strategy can be applied in the prioritization of identified challenges, when the challenges are measured over the hierarchical aspects: chance of success, time, commitment, and budget.

The *chance of success* aspect is used to determine how successfully the existing network can be transformed to IBN. If the chance of success is greatly reduced by the identified challenge, then those challenges should be solved first.

Commitment is the second aspect that can be used to prioritize the challenges. If the organization lacks commitment for a transformation to IBN, then no resources, time, or budget can be made available. Lack of commitment also decreases the chance for support in executing mandatory changes that could impact the business.

The factor *time* is another aspect. This aspect is not intended for the time required to solve a challenge, but the available time to solve any challenge. If no time or resources are available, then it will be impossible to solve any other identified challenge.

The last but not least aspect is that of *budget*. Budget can determine whether certain challenges can be solved quickly or not at all—for example, a premature replacement of hardware or hiring extra staff to relieve the workload on the network operations team.

These aspects can then be used to prioritize the identified challenges of the previous paragraphs. Table 7-6 provides an example of how this can be applied.

Table 7-6 *Prioritized List of Identified Challenges*

Priority	Identified Challenge	Arguments
1	Low maturity level of organization	The organization has too low a maturity level. Too much is executed on an ad hoc basis; therefore, the enterprise first needs to mature and work via documented procedures. Risk of failure for IBN is too high.
2	Stakeholders	Not all stakeholders see the benefit of IBN; this will be a risk to get commitment on changes and other decisions to be made.
3	Too high workload in network operations team	The network operations team is too busy solving incidents, the software on the switches is not up-to-date, and changes are executed at the last minute.
4	Hardware in network needs to be updated	End of life hardware is found in the network. With a lack of commitment and lack of budget these devices will not be replaced.
5	Level of standardization	As much is executed ad hoc, there is no central design and guidelines. Each campus location turns out to be unique.

Action Plan

The last step of phase one is to bundle all collected information into an action plan. The information obtained from the previous paragraphs is not only the identified challenges; the information also is implicitly a readiness scan of the campus network infrastructure and the enterprise. The action plan is used as a guidebook for getting support and approval of actions to be executed in phase two of the process. The action plan is a deliverable for this phase. Therefore, it is recommended to use a fixed format for that action plan that will contain at least the following sections.

Management Summary

The action plan should contain a management summary that describes briefly why the transformation to IBN is needed and how ready the organization is for the journey to Intent-Based Networking. A short, prioritized list of identified challenges for that journey is provided in the management summary with a proposal on the first actions to be taken.

If, based on the identified challenges, decisions are to be made by management, a decision list would need to be included in the management summary as well, to allow management to provide enough information to make the appropriate decisions. A management summary is typically one page—a maximum of two pages—long and contains the call for action (decision) for management to take. It is a great method to maximize the time available by executives for them to make validated decisions.

Analysis

In this section, the collected information from the different aspects, such as maturity level of the organization, identified stakeholders, and level of standardization is provided. At the end of each aspect, the identified challenges are described in a table and a recommendation on how to solve those identified challenges is included.

Action List

The prioritization of the identified challenges is used as input for this section. The prioritized list is amended with proposed solutions and a planned date for when that solution could be implemented. For example, if some hardware is not IBN ready, the solution could be to wait until lifecycle management has replaced the equipment and automatically the network becomes IBN ready. This could be a valid choice if other identified challenges require effort as well and could be executed in parallel.

Table 7-7 provides an example of such an action list. The action list should be as detailed as possible, including all items that need to be solved.

Table 7-7 *Example of Action List Format*

Identified Challenge	Ready	Remediation Is	Planned Date
Maturity level of organization	No	Document procedures and define a vendor strategy.	2 months after approval
Network designs available	No	Write design documents. Change network to follow design.	3 months
IBN-ready equipment	No	Replace wireless infrastructure.	1 year

Decision List

If, based on the collected information, specific decisions are to be made by management, these should be collected and bundled in a decision list. The decision list should provide enough information to allow management to make decisions that enable the transformation to IBN with the appropriate business case. For example, if a decision that needs to be made is in case of campus network hardware replacement, the organization needs to select IBN-ready equipment.

Estimated Timeline

This section of the action plan contains an estimated timeline for when the identified challenges could be solved.

The action plan is the final step of the phase and, once signed and approved by management, is the end of this phase. The action plan is used as masterplan or guidebook for some of the actions to be executed in phase two of the journey toward Intent-Based Networking.

Summary

The first phase in the transformation to IBN is all about getting information about the state of the campus network and the organization. IBN places a number of requirements on the campus network as well as the organization, because IBN is based on the Cisco Digital Network Architecture. To be able to successfully transform, it is important to know how the current network relates to IBN and what challenges might need to be solved to successfully move toward IBN.

To achieve this, a number of steps need to be executed and challenges related to these steps need to be determined:

- **Challenges in day-to-day operations:** IBN is primarily a method for how a campus network can be operated. This is primarily a responsibility for the network operations team. Although it is common to have project teams execute changes on an infrastructure and at project delivery hand the changed situation over to operations, this does introduce the risk that the project will not be accepted by operations because the team is too busy or just will not accept that new tool or solution. IBN must become a true part of network operations, and to do so, the operations team needs to have time and resources available to make steps on the journey. It is therefore important to identify challenges in the day-to-day operations that can hinder that transformation.

- **Inventory:** An inventory needs to be executed on all existing network devices used in the campus network. It is important to know whether both the hardware and the software are capable of running an Intent-enabled network.

- **Level of standardization:** IBN is based on a high level of automation. Automation can only occur if the design and configuration of the campus network, both wired and wireless, are standardized. In this step, the level of standardization is determined.

- **Maturity level of an organization:** Although it might sound odd for a phase within a technical transformation, the maturity level of an organization can be used to determine whether a transformation to IBN is possible from an organizational perspective. It also provides insight into how mature the organization is in relation to processes, documentation, and quality in general. IBN is a perspective on the Cisco Digital Network Architecture, and that poses a certain expectation on the maturity of the organization.

- **Stakeholders:** Last but not least, it is important to identify the stakeholders. As the transformation to IBN will incur changes in configuration, potentially replacing hardware, there will be business-impacting changes. Identifying the correct stakeholders beforehand and obtaining their support are critical for the success of transformation.

Once all steps are executed, a number of challenges have been identified. It is impossible to solve all challenges at once; therefore, a prioritization process is used to determine the order in which these challenges need to be solved. The prioritization is based on aspects like chance of success, commitment, time, and budget.

All collected data will be bundled in an *action plan*. The action plan contains the collected data, the identified challenges with recommended solutions, a detailed action list, a planning of those actions, possibly a list for decisions to be made on the management level, and a management summary. The action plan is essentially the deliverable of this phase and provides insights into the current state of the campus network and which challenges need to be solved to transform the campus network into an Intent-Based Network. Once the action plan is adopted and approved by management, the action plan is used in the next phase.

Chapter 8

Phase Two: Prepare for Intent

Chapter 7, "Phase One: Identifying Challenges," described how phase one is used to identify and organize challenges for a successful transformation to Intent-Based Networking (IBN). This chapter describes phase two of the transformation.

It is assumed that phase one has been completed successfully and management has signed off on the action plan from the first phase. This approval is important for this phase because new technologies or tools can be introduced, and some common workflows might need to change as well. It is also assumed that the operations team is deeply involved in all tasks in phase two. This is critical for the acceptance of new workflows or tools within the operations team and to enable change.

The main focuses of this phase are to meet all requirements, solve identified challenges from phase one, and prepare the network (including the network operations team) for the transformation to IBN.

Phase two accomplishes these focuses by executing the following steps, which are covered in detail in this chapter:

- Matching requirements
- Standardization of configuration
- Implementation of assurance
- Introduction of automation

It is not necessary to execute these tasks sequentially, although some tasks might have preference or priority over another. Elaboration to why a task might have preference over another will be explained at the specific task.

Matching Requirements

One of the most important steps in this phase is making sure that not only the network infrastructure but also the organization matches the requirements for an intent-enabled campus network. As described in Part I, "Overview of Intent-Based Networking," IBN is a perspective on Cisco DNA. It describes how the network should be designed and operated to face the changes that will happen (or are already happening). IBN assumes with this perspective a number of requirements to be met. This task is used to make sure all requirements for IBN as well as the transformation to IBN are met. These are grouped around the organization (process) and networking (hardware and software).

This step is probably the most complex within this phase as it can take a long time for changes to settle in. Although it is possible to perform the next task in parallel, it is strongly recommended to keep the primary focus on this task as it also enables a smoother implementation of subsequent tasks.

Organizational Requirements

Although it might sound strange at first, matching the organizational requirements is one of the most important tasks within this phase. An Intent-Based Network is much more about how to operate and manage the campus network than the technologies. Also, based on the output of the first phase, hardware and software might need to be replaced to be able to run an Intent-Based Network, which can take multiple years to accomplish within a large enterprise. The transition to an Intent-Based Network can be compared with the transition to the cloud in the past. Enterprises had to be ready for that transition too. The following requirements should be met within this phase to enable a successful transformation to an intent-based network.

Maturity Level of an Organization

Chapter 7 described the concept for the maturity level of an organization. For any transformation to be successful, the organization needs to have a certain level of maturity. If not, there is a high risk that a transformation will start with a lot of optimism and energy, but as soon as pressure occurs for the transformation, often the enterprise and/or staff fall back into the old ways and the transformation fails. Part III, "Organizational Aspects," provides more details on this behavior. If an enterprise has at least a level 3 (and preferably on some items a level 4) on the maturity levels, this risk is reduced because there is a described vision, including a strategy and commitment to achieve that described vision.

The way an Intent-Based Network operates also requires a high level of standardization for both configuration and procedures to be successful. (Each Intent is essentially a small piece of configuration that can repetitively be deployed on the network.) Inherently, IBN requires that same level of maturity of the enterprise for a successful transformation.

Therefore, one of the most critical and important tasks in this phase is to make sure that the enterprise at least has a maturity level of three and preferably four on certain aspects.

Phase One determines the current level of maturity. Table 8-1 describes which maturity level must minimally be reached within this task.

Table 8-1   *Overview of Maturity Levels to Achieve Within the Enterprise*

Aspect	Maturity Level	Remarks
Incident management	3	Written procedures for incident management provide the benefit of consistent workflow through incidents.
Change procedures	3	Change procedures within the network must be written down to increase the chance of a successful implementation of IBN.
Disaster recovery and risk management	3	Disaster recovery and risk management are often overseen as the network is usually very reliable. However, having a level 3 on this aspect provides the benefit that the business understands the risks and impact of a major failure in the network. (It also helps the business understand that networking is not a cost center but a business enabler.)
Lifecycle management	3	Lifecycle management describes at which point in time the hardware and/or software needs to be replaced within an organization. If this aspect is at level 3, processes are in place to initiate hardware and software replacements before a failure occurs or the support on the equipment has ended. A written and documented lifecycle management process proactively supports running modern and supported network equipment that is ready for adopting new technologies.
Design and configuration	3	Regardless of whether designs, configurations, and software images are standardized, documentation must exist for the IT environment to be able to standardize them.
Vendor and product selection	4	The transition to an Intent-Based Network takes a long time. It is important to have a written vendor strategy including a consistent product selection that focuses on the future usage as well as hardware replacement.
Generic IT vision and strategy	4	IBN might require new hardware to be procured. Having a generic IT vision and strategy for the upcoming five years will benefit both in procuring new hardware as well as keeping commitment from management during the transformation.

Implementing (and supporting) change inside an organization commonly takes a much longer period of time than the technical implementation that enables that change. For example and from personal experience, technically connecting an enterprise to a trusted supplier to automatically send purchase orders and receive invoices electronically might only take two months. (The actual link takes even less time.) But it will probably take the staff of the individual departments of each organization at least a year to get accustomed to that automated behavior and that faxing/mailing or phoning an order is no longer required.

This example is common for any change, and a parallel can be made in achieving higher maturity levels within an organization. Changes take time both in writing down visions, strategies, and procedures and in allowing staff to get accustomed to them. The end result will be that the quality of the organization as a whole will improve as well.

It is, of course, not required to overspecify all aspects in tightly written procedures where the procedures have become leading over the processes. Keep the written procedures pragmatic and manageable; procedures must always be supportive of the processes and not vice versa. A pragmatic approach to the procedures will not only keep the organization lean and flexible, but make it much easier for the employees to follow those procedures and therefore adopt the change more rapidly.

Resource Availability

Traditionally, projects are set up to implement changes for an organization, whether this is the upgrade to a new mail system or replacing network equipment at a specific branch location. In most cases, project managers are given a limited budget (often too little), a critical deadline, and a number of external resources. Sometimes the project manager has an incentive to deliver the project on time (via a bonus or an even bigger project).

What happens is that after the project is finished, the project is signed off with possible shortcuts and open items, and the operations team is faced with these open items. The operations team is given yet another new tool to manage a small piece of the network, and they have to deal with it on a day-to-day basis, while the project team is disbanded and the project manager has moved onto the next project.

A Cisco DNA is designed not only for the digital business to succeed, it also defines a design for a network infrastructure that is easy to understand and resilient for changes and specializations, while remaining as standardized as possible. Intent-Based Networking (IBN) is a perspective to that architecture; it describes how you can operate and manage a Cisco DNA. IBN is essentially written and targeted for the network operations team so that they can cope with the challenges and changes they are facing or will face in the near future.

IBN is also about changing the operation itself, leveraging the power of tools to do repetitive work consistently and predictively and to be easily scalable. The operations team needs to manage and operate those tools on a day-to-day basis, as well as they need to undergo changes. Their jobs will not be lost, but their tasks and responsibilities will change over time.

Conclusively, it is a requirement that all tasks related to the preparation and implementation of an Intent-Based Network need to be executed in a close relationship with the network operations team, or preferably by the network operations team itself.

Unfortunately, the operations team is often already overloaded with delayed work and responding to incidents. If a person has too much on his or her plate, that person only has focus for the work that needs to be done. The person often literally does not have time to consider changing certain aspects of the work at all.

Ideally, all phases are to be performed by the operations team so that the team can take ownership of the transformation. The operations team needs to see that the required changes are beneficial to the team.

Therefore, it is an important requirement to get commitment from management to make resources within the network operations team available for the different tasks related to the transformation to an Intent-Based Network. One of the possibilities to achieve this within the network operations team is to add extra (external) staff to the operations team so that the workload is shared among more staff, which results in increased availability within the network operations team. That allows the network operations team to perform the tasks necessary for transformation themselves.

Alternatively, the operations team supports an external project team for the transformation, where the operations team has a (semi-) final say in specific choices as long as these decisions benefit the ultimate goal of implementing Intent-Based Networking.

In conclusion, two organizational requirements must be met within this task:

- The organization needs to operate at a certain maturity level that encompasses written and documented visions, strategies, and procedures. It is clear that the organization also adheres to and follows the vision and procedures in the day-to-day operation. Changing an operation to that level of maturity can take some time as it demands commitment from management and behavioral change from staff. While an increase in maturity will bring documentation in the form of designs and procedures, these documents must never become leading; rather, a pragmatic approach should be taken so that the steps toward the desired maturity level are small.

- Instead of having external project teams execute changes isolated from the network operations team, the network operations team is deeply involved, preferably fully enabled, to execute the different projects and tasks to transform to Intent-Based Networking.

Network Infrastructure Requirements

Another aspect of the task to match requirements is to meet the requirements on hardware and software for an Intent-Based Network, because IBN is based on Cisco DNA. Cisco DNA sets forth a number of requirements in both hardware and software for the network infrastructure devices. For example, not all network devices can run virtual network functions or support virtual routing and forwarding (VRF) to isolate logical networks on the IP layer. The task continues on the inventory of hard- and software that was made in phase one and mandates that all network equipment used for IBN meets the requirements.

Phase one produced two tables related to the inventory task executed. Table 8-2 and Table 8-3 are a copy from the example provided in phase one.

Table 8-2   *Overview of Installed Hardware and Software*

Device Family	Device Type	Device Name	SW Version	Update SW Required?	Install Date	Replacement Required?	Replacement Moment
Routers	C2951	C1-RT01	15.2	No	Jan 2016	Yes	Jan 2021
Switches	WS-C3650-24PS-S	C1-AS01	3.7	Yes	Mar 2017	No	
Switches	WS-C6509-E	C1-DS01	12.2	N/A	Oct 2014	Yes	ASAP
Wireless	AIR-CT5508	C1-WS01	8.5	N/A	Jan 2017	Yes	ASAP

...

Table 8-3   *Aggregated Overview of Campus Network Hardware*

Device Family	Device Type	Total Switches	IBN Ready	Remarks
Switches	WS-C3650-24PS-S	40	Conditional	Max 3 VNs*
Routers	C2951	2	No	
Switches	WS-C6509-E	3	No	End of life
Wireless	AIR-CAP2602I	200	No	End of life
Wireless	AIR-CT5508	2	No	End of life

...

*IP Base of the Catalyst 3650/380 provides maximal 3 virtual networks (or VRFs); switches running IP Services (ending with E in the SKU) can have maximal 64 virtual switches.

The specific actions related to this task are dependent on the contents of these two tables. If all hardware is IBN ready, but not running the appropriate software, then a plan should be written and executed to upgrade the devices to a software version supported for IBN. For example, IOS-XE version 16.6 or higher is required for Model-Driven Telemetry. This plan should be written and executed in close cooperation with the operations team.

However, it is quite realistic to state that besides software upgrades, the hardware, for example, switches or wireless controllers (or even access points), needs to be replaced as well. In that case, the upgrade plan needs to be combined with an investment plan.

The investment plan needs to be written in a clear and concise manner where several priorities should be organized and matched against the available budget, available resources, state of equipment (install date, end of life), and impact. As an example, replacing a Cisco Wireless Lan Controller (WLC) 5508 would be of a higher priority than replacing a Cisco Catalyst 3650 switch with a Cisco Catalyst 9300 switch because the WLC 5508 is end of life and does not support assurance, whereas the Catalyst 3650 switch is supported for IBN and the first steps to IBN can be taken with that 3650 switch. The execution of this task to replace the necessary hardware and upgrade the software can span multiple years because the investment cost can exceed the maximum IT budget for a year. Also, fiscal administrative rules and regulations can dictate that the hardware can only be replaced when the hardware is fiscally written off. A complete investment plan should be defined that contains all hardware that needs to be replaced. Whether this investment plan spans multiple years is based on the depreciation value of the devices, the available IT budget, the number of devices to be replaced, the different branch locations, and the resources available. If the investment plan covers multiple years, it is important to obtain commitment and approval for those planned years by management beforehand to keep the transition at an optimal momentum.

In case this task spans multiple years and the maturity level of the organization is approaching the minimal level, it is possible to combine this task with the subsequent tasks and next phases.

Use Case: Importance of Lifecycle

SharedService Group manages a worldwide network of equipment. The network originated from mergers and acquisitions. As such, some locations were IBN ready, while many others were not. Although formal lifecycle management was lacking, SharedService Group leveraged ITIL processes for incident management and had standardized on incident management. After they ran an inventory of their equipment and matched these against the IBN requirements, it became clear that some isolated branch locations were able to migrate to IBN while others would require hardware replacement as some of those locations had end of life equipment installed.

Internally a program was created to execute lifecycle management on all locations that had older hardware. The program considered both the operational end of life/end of support status as well as the administrative status of the equipment.

With the appropriate budget, the program was set up, and management decided, in close collaboration with operations, that the program would not only physically perform hardware replacements but also document the processes for lifecycle management so that operations could continue the same approach after the program was finished.

It was also decided that those locations that were IBN ready would move toward the next tasks and phases in parallel to the program. Once a location was physically IBN ready, it would immediately receive the most current configuration and adopt IBN.

The execution of the program in parallel with a limited set of branch locations moving toward IBN was only possible because of the maturity level of SharedService Group in combination with commitment from management.

As you can see from the use case, it is possible to run a number of tasks or even phases in parallel; however, this is possible only if the enterprise is at a minimal maturity level with sufficient commitment and resources available. If this is not the case, it is recommended to perform tasks and phases sequentially as much as possible.

If an enterprise does not have a lifecycle management procedure, however, it is possible to combine the upgrade plan and the investment plan with a set of procedures to create and develop a lifecycle management process. This is beneficial as the effort within this task can assist in obtaining a higher maturity level for that aspect.

A lifecycle management process describes the full lifecycle of any product or service, from inception to the end of its lifetime. Lifecycle management is common for manufacturing companies but is also applicable for any IT-related product. Figure 8-1 displays a state diagram for an example lifecycle management process.

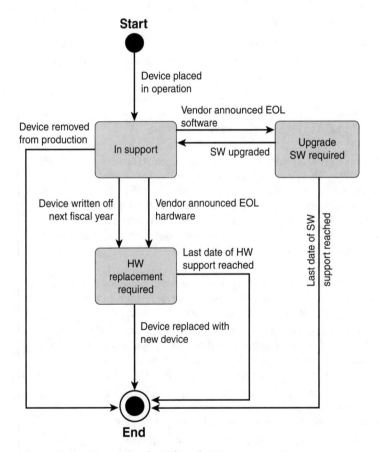

Figure 8-1   *Example of a Lifecycle Management Process*

This state diagram displays the "lifecycle" state of a device within lifecycle management based on a number of principles that are common within IT.

In general, each IT product consists of both hardware and software, whether this is a phone, laptop, switch, or router. Vendors provide support on both the hardware and the software. At a certain moment in time, the software might reach end of life and support is no longer provided for that software version. In that case, the state transitions from "In support" to "Upgrade SW required." Once the software is upgraded, the state goes back to "In support."

Similarly, if the vendor announces an end of life for the hardware of the device, the state of the device transitions to "HW replacement required." If the support date is passed, the lifecycle of the device is ended as well, as there is no support for the device anymore.

In parallel, administrative regulations often dictate that investments above a certain monetary value need to be written off in a number of years. In other words, the costs related to the investment are often equally divided over five years instead of having the costs in a single year. If the device is written off and still in production, the support for the device will reach the "HW replacement required."

Although this task is solely about matching the necessary requirements for the network devices to run an Intent-enabled network, this sample state diagram combined with the output of this task can be beneficial for defining and implementing a lifecycle management process.

Standardization of Campus Configuration

If you go through all the layers and functions of an Intent-Based Network from a configuration perspective, the requested Intents are translated into small pieces of configuration that are pushed onto the required network devices using automation. In other words, within IBN, the campus network consists of a standardized configuration as foundation, and the specific Intents or purposes are dynamically added to or removed from that foundation. To have a successful transformation to IBN, the configuration of the network infrastructure devices in the campus needs to be standardized.

This step is designed to convert the traditional specific port-centric configuration of switches to a policy-driven configuration with a highly standardized templated configuration of the switches and controllers in the campus network.

Migrating from Port Centric to Policy Centric

Often the campus network has evolved into a network with static and specific port configurations for the endpoints connected to that port. A port is commonly configured for a specific role, for example, an IP camera or a printer. The VLAN is configured statically as well as possibly some security features. If the printer is relocated, the operations team would need to configure the new access port the same way as the old port, and once everything was tested, the old port would be cleared from the old configuration (which is not always the case). This change would require the cooperation of the persons executing the relocation of that printer as well. This method of operation takes a lot of effort and coordination, and generally is slow. The campus network is truly port-centric based.

An alternative evolution found in the campus network is the creation of completely separate functional networks within the campus as a whole. If a network would be required for IP cameras, a separate physical network would be deployed only for those IP cameras. The ports are all statically configured for the IP cameras, and other types of endpoints are not allowed. The printers might be shared with the office network, but other types of endpoints such as sensors or logistics would each have their own physical network. Although this approach can be valid, it does introduce a number of limitations and restrictions.

For one, each network would require its own distribution switch (and possibly access switches). This adds up not only in installation cost but also in management of the network. Instead of managing a single campus network that meets all functional requirements for that branch, each network needs to be managed separately.

Second, if a new network is to be introduced on a specific location, a complete new network is built for just that purpose and added to the WAN router. This adds up to a highly complex and more difficult-to-manage network.

Third, like the previous example, relocating a printer would now not require a change of configuration, but a change of patch cables from one switch to another.

In summary, both campus network designs are not scalable and are essentially port-centric driven configurations. Without any form of standardization these networks are doomed to fail and will not be able to run as an Intent-Based Network.

However, over the past decade more and more campus networks have also introduced network access control, leveraging the IEEE 802.1X network access control standard.

The IEEE 802.1x standard provides network access control in any wired or wireless network. It consists of a number of components and several protocols. Figure 8-2 provides a schematic overview of the required components.

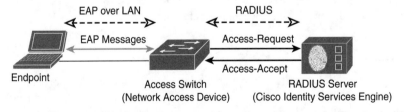

Figure 8-2 *Required Components for an IEEE 802.1x-Based Network Access Control Deployment*

The IEEE 802.1X protocol is explained in detail in Appendix A, "Campus Network Technologies." In general, the switch tries to set up an authentication session with the endpoint and acts as a proxy to the central policy server using the RADIUS protocol. The RADIUS server provides the authentication (which device or user is connecting to the network), authorization (what is allowed on the network), and accounting (what has the device done) roles.

It is possible to define several authorization rules in any RADIUS server. The results of these authorization rules are added as RADIUS attributes in the Radius-Accept response back to the switch. One of the most powerful features in this authorization is the capability to dynamically perform a VLAN assignment for that specific endpoint for the duration of the session. Cisco provides a detailed guide for these types of authorization rules with the Cisco Identity Based Network Services 2.0 model.[1]

In other words, if a Cisco switch receives that VLAN assignment (using a Vendor-Specific-Radius attribute), it overrides the VLAN configured on that access port with the VLAN received from the RADIUS server, essentially placing the endpoint in a different logical network. This feature enables the possibility of removing the specific port-centric VLAN assignment from the switch and placing it into the central policy server. If this transition is executed for every VLAN, the port-centric configuration of the campus network is essentially migrated to the policy server.

Cisco provides this functionality using the Identity Services Engine (ISE) solution. The Cisco Press book *Cisco ISE for BYOD and Secure Unified Access*, 2nd edition, by Aaron Woland and Jamey Heary, provides a great overview on how to introduce a RADIUS server into the campus network and leverage the VLAN assignment functionality to standardize the access port configuration.

If the organization does not use a network access control server, the first task within this step is to introduce that function into the campus network. The introduction of this functionality is not like a next-next-finish approach, but rather a phased step-by-step approach, which requires the cooperation of all teams inside the organization, as network access control touches all divisions (workstations, printers, servers, compute, networking).

Note   A next-next-finish approach is an analogy to how users install applications. They start the installer, click Next a number of times, and then click Finish to finish the installation, assuming that it can be installed and working correctly with little to no configuration.

Although IBN is also focused on security, in the situation where the enterprise lacks a network access control server, it is possible to only use the policy-assignment feature at first to enable the migration to a policy-centric deployment. The IEEE 802.1X access control standard can be deployed at a later stage.

---

1 https://www.cisco.com/c/dam/en/us/products/collateral/ios-nx-os-software/identity-based-networking-services/aag_c45-731544.pdf

> ### Use Case: Migrating from a Port-Centric to a Policy-Centric Design
>
> LogiServ Inc. provides network and IT services for roughly 250 employees at 30 locations in the campus network. Besides two larger campus locations, the other locations are serviced by a single access switch and an access router. The access router provides in general the Layer 3 access on each branch location using subinterfaces. Only in situations where multiple access switches are used (for example, in warehouses) is the Layer 3 terminated on the distribution switch. Traditionally when a new location needed to be added to the network, an IP network was selected from the IP plan and the router was configured with the appropriate IP space and a new access VLAN specific for that location/company. The configuration of the access switch was essentially copied from the latest location and manually adopted. Changes to locations were happening frequently but not on a daily or weekly basis. An automation tool to automate changes on the network was therefore not directly required. The network was port-centric configured.
>
> However, as the number of branch locations was growing at a rapid pace and employees started to move between shared locations, the need for a standardized configuration was increasing to facilitate the roaming employees without any changes on the network infrastructure by the operations team.
>
> Unfortunately, there was no budget available for a Cisco Identity Services Engine deployment; the use case was more on the automation side rather than security at first. Also, not all endpoints were able to use the IEEE 802.1X standard, and thus a different approach was taken.
>
> As the use case was to migrate to a policy-centric network configuration and not security, the MAC address of a device can be used to identify the device and push the appropriate VLAN as authorization to the network switch. The VLAN assignment would only be required for special endpoints, such as access points, IP cameras, and printers. Fortunately, the VLAN number for these devices was the same across all branch locations.
>
> PacketFence, an open source RADIUS server appliance, was deployed to the network. Several groups (roles) were defined, and each group would have its own VLAN assignment.
>
> After importing the MAC addresses into the PacketFence database and enabling 802.1X with MAC Authentication Bypass on the switch, the VLANs were automatically assigned for each special device.

LogiServ clearly made a decision to start standardizing the network with VLAN assignments based on the MAC address of the devices that would require a special VLAN. It was understood that extra work was required by registering all MAC addresses of the special devices, but this weighed up against the current manual work.

The implementation of PacketFence provided the necessary capabilities to create a default access port configuration on all switches and let PacketFence override the VLAN if required.

The standardization of an access port configuration greatly improves the standardization level of the switch configuration and is a great benefit to automation and the transformation to Intent-Based Networks.

This same principle can be used with Cisco Identity Services Engine as well to convert the campus network from port centric to policy centric. For Intent-Based Networks, the preference is to deploy a Cisco Identity Services Engine as Cisco DNA Center integrates with ISE. This integration requires ISE version 2.3 or later. (At the time of writing, the ISE version 2.4 latest patch is the long-term supported stable version.)

If a network access control server is already deployed in the campus network, then use this server and introduce dynamic VLAN assignment to standardize the access port configuration of the campus network.

VLAN Numbering

The previous task within this step enables the campus network to move from static port configurations for each device to a policy-centric campus network. Intrinsic to this change is also that the VLAN numbers across the campus network need to be consistent for the same roles.

It is important (and also scalable and convenient) to use the same VLAN ID for each function of the network, so that the authorization policies inside the RADIUS server are independent of the location and thus more scalable. The access points are always connected to VLAN 2001, while management is VLAN 981, workstations in VLAN 100, and so on.

This task is used to identify VLAN usage mismatches and standardize the VLAN numbers across the campus network.

The complexity of this task is dependent on the diversity and evolution of the campus network for the specific organization. In general, the following actions can be executed sequentially to perform this task:

Step 1.   Identify all VLANs used in the campus networks.

Create a table of all VLAN numbers used in the campus network across all locations. Also write down which VLAN is used for which type or group of devices. If it is known that certain endpoints are on fixed VLANs for a specific reason, make a note of that as well. Also note the VLANs that are used to connect the campus location to external WAN providers because they can also be standardized.

Step 2.   Set up a unified VLAN numbering plan.

Just like an IP plan, analyze the results from the previous step and create a unified VLAN numbering plan. The key requirement is that the VLAN number is the same for each group of devices, regardless of the location.

Step 3.   Define gaps/transition projects.

Use this action to create a list of old VLAN numbers and the new VLAN numbers per location. This list can be used for a project per branch location, including the appropriate change procedures.

One aspect that needs special attention is that with the introduction of standardized VLAN numbers, the VLANs will become available at all locations within the campus network. This means that all the VLANs need to have IP connectivity over the WAN as well. Use this action to introduce the necessary IP networks as well.

If a device is placed into a VLAN at a location without any IP connectivity, well, it will not have access to any resource and an incident will be raised.

Also consider when the changes are performed, if the configuration changes are deployed via an old VLAN that is to be removed, to prevent a lockout during the change. Also analyze the possibilities to change the VLAN numbering with minimal impact.

Step 4.   **Implement projects.**

In the last step, the change procedures defined from step 3 will be implemented. Unfortunately, as the Layer 2 of a network is changed, this change will have impact on services provided to the end users. Part of the implementation project is the validation that the new VLAN plan is completely and successfully implemented, resulting in a consistent VLAN plan across the campus network.

Once these steps are completed, the VLAN numbers used within the campus network are standardized and a specific endpoint will now always be placed in the same VLAN.

Standardization of Configuration

The previous steps within this task have been focused on migrating from a port-centric configuration to a policy-centric deployment. VLAN assignments are handled by a policy from the central RADIUS server, and the VLANs are standardized across all campus locations. The configuration of a Cisco switch essentially consists of a global configuration and interface-specific configurations, such as access ports or uplinks. This step is used to standardize the global configuration for the network infrastructure devices commonly found inside the campus network.

Access Switch

In most campus networks the access switch is configured as a Layer 2 switch with a single IP address for management. Endpoints connect to the access switch, and VLANs are used to logically separate the broadcast domains and forward traffic to the distribution switch. This concept makes the access switch perfect to be standardized across all campus locations. Technologies like Spanning Tree, Switch Integrated Security Features (SISF), RADIUS configuration for IEEE 802.1X, and VLAN numbering are the same for all access switches. Only the management IP address, the switch name, and the domain name are different between all access switches. This makes the access switch a perfect fit for the definition of a first template. Once this template is created, the template can be deployed across all campus switches to standardize the configuration.

Note   A template in this context is a piece of Cisco CLI commands where specifics are defined as variables that can be entered by the operator when the template is deployed. The code in Example 8-1 is a template that can be used within Cisco Prime Infrastructure, Cisco DNA Center, and Cisco APIC-EM. The template is used to configure NTP and syslog.

Example 8-1   *Template to Configure NTP and Syslog*

```
ntp source $mgmtVLAN
ntp server $ntp6Server
ntp server $ntp4Server
ntp update-calendar
clock timezone CET 1 0
clock summer-time CEST recurring last Sun Mar 2:00 last Sun Oct 3:00
logging trap warnings
logging origin-id hostname
logging source-interface $mgmtVLAN
logging host $syslogHost
```

Within this template, the $ sign before a name denotes a specific variable. At the deployment of the template, the system asks the operator to enter the appropriate value for all variables in the template. The variable $mgmtVLAN describes the VLAN ID for management. Cisco DNA Center remembers the variables once deployed to a specific device.

Distribution Switch

The distribution switch in a campus network typically provides the IP connectivity to the different VLANs in which endpoints are connected. Also, the configuration of a distribution switch is also dependent on the size of each branch location (how many access switches are connected). However, a large part of the global configuration, such as the IP addressing, Spanning Tree configuration, and security technologies such as management access, can be configured using templates as well. Ideally each distribution switch will have the same set of basic templates and a single template that defines the unique aspects of a distribution switch for a specific branch location.

Wireless Network

Wireless networking is much more complex than a wired network. The primary reason is that the Radio Frequency (RF) spectrum is dynamic and each client can behave differently. Because the VLANs are standardized across the campus network, each local controller can now be standardized for several wireless settings, such as the SSIDs being broadcasted, the VLANs used, and the security configuration. The only aspect that is dynamic per location is the RF configuration. Tools such as Cisco Prime Infrastructure and Cisco DNA Center are excellent in creating and deploying a set of templates for wireless controllers to standardize the configuration of the wireless network.

At the end of this step, all switches and wireless controllers within the campus network have been configured using a minimal set of templates to standardize and harmonize the global configuration. Preferably, all access switches have the same template with only the IP address and switch name being different.

The distribution switch is a bit more complex but also capable of being standardized on portchannel numbers and other global configuration aspects.

Also, all VLANs are now available at all campus locations, and the central policy server is assigning the appropriate VLAN based on the identity of the endpoint. The campus network configuration is now prepared for an Intent-Based Network.

Introducing Assurance/Visibility

Within most enterprises large changes in the IT environment, whether a new application, hardware replacement, or a software upgrade, are executed in projects. Often these projects are resourced with external resources as the operations team is overloaded and cannot provide resources to support the project and keep an active association with the project.

Consequently, if problems arise in the project (like a special management tool is required for new hardware or an application is not working the way it is supposed to), the project team makes a decision based on the project requirements and deadlines and often cannot oversee the consequences of that decision for the operations team after the project is finished.

So at handover, the operations team is faced with those decisions (and leftovers) and needs to deal with them without control. And as the operations team was busy to start with, the new tool will probably not be used and the operations team will over time get annoyed over new projects.

To change this mind-set and behavior, a good association should exist between project teams and the operations team that will become responsible for day-to-day management after the project is finished. This association requires time from the operations team, and thus time needs to be made available from the day-to-day operations.

The network analytics component of IBN is meant to proactively support the operations team in their day-to-day tasks. It should alleviate the time pressure on the operations team so that the team can cope with more connected devices and an increasingly complex environment. The analytics component itself does not have a direct impact on how the campus network is managed other than just some information from the network devices is sent to the analytics component.

The analytics component is thus a perfect solution to quickly reduce the workload of the operations team by intelligently supporting the team during troubleshooting. The assurance component of a Cisco DNA Center (DNAC) solution is a perfect opportunity to introduce analytics to the operations team.

Use Case: How DNA Center Assurance Assists in Troubleshooting

SharedService Group provides wireless connectivity to its end users. Larger office locations leverage the use of a local controller with local breakout. At one moment incidents were reported that there were issues with the wireless network at one of the locations. In the transition to Intent-Based Networking, Cisco DNAC Assurance was enabled for a number of wireless locations. Cisco DNAC Assurance confirmed, by the client health score, that a large number of wireless clients were not connected to the network or had lost connection. Figure 8-3 shows a screenshot of that event.

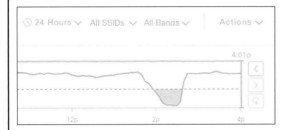

Figure 8-3   *Screenshot of Cisco DNAC Dashboard Related to Wireless Incident*

The operator is able to zoom in to a specific moment in time to analyze a problem. But besides manual analysis, Cisco DNAC Assurance leverages machine intelligence to correlate the data against a number of known issues to proactively support the operations team in defining open issues based on the network's configuration and behavior. For the problem at hand, an open issue was created as well. Figure 8-4 is a screenshot of an issue list that Cisco DNAC Assurance provides.

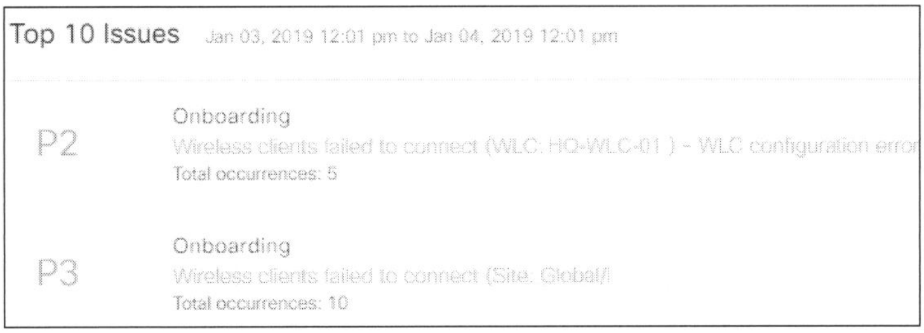

Top 10 Issues   Jan 03, 2019 12:01 pm to Jan 04, 2019 12:01 pm

P2   Onboarding
Wireless clients failed to connect (WLC: HQ-WLC-01) - WLC configuration error
Total occurrences: 5

P3   Onboarding
Wireless clients failed to connect (Site: Global/l
Total occurrences: 10

Figure 8-4   *Screenshot of Open Issue List*

Once the operator drills into the open issue, all information regarding that issue is displayed to the operator. The operator can quickly see how many users are affected and what the probable cause is. This is shown in Figure 8-5. As the data is smartly correlated, the operator is also shown when the issue occurred, which is shown in Figure 8-6. And to further provide support in fixing an issue more efficiently, a number of recommended actions are provided as well, which is shown in Figure 8-7.

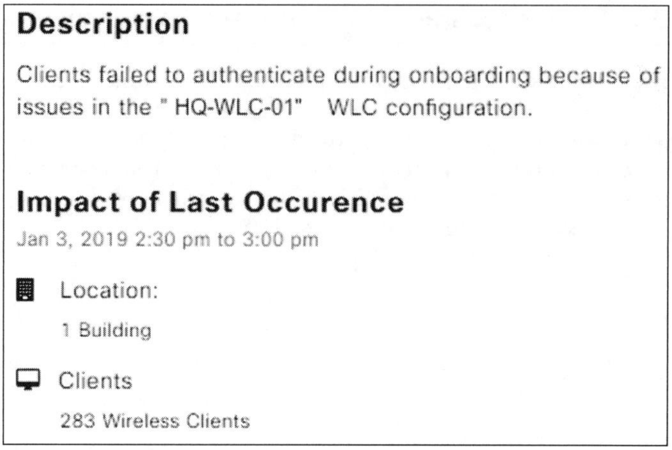

Description
Clients failed to authenticate during onboarding because of issues in the " HQ-WLC-01" WLC configuration.
Impact of Last Occurence
Jan 3, 2019 2:30 pm to 3:00 pm
Location:
1 Building
Clients
283 Wireless Clients

Figure 8-5 *Summary Description and Impact of an Open Issue*

Client Authentications (WLC: HQ-WLC-01)
Jan 3, 2019 3:00 am to Jan 4, 2019 3:00 am
Clients (#)
600
400
200
0
3:00a
5:00a
7:00a
9:00a
11:00a
1:00p
2:15p
3:3(

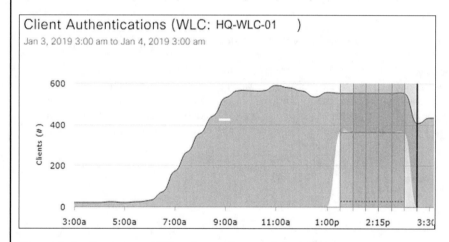

Figure 8-6 *Overview of When Issues Occurred Over Time*

Suggested Actions (3)
1 Verify if an AAA server is configured on the WLC "HQ-WLC-01".
2 Verify if the AAA server associated to the WLAN exists, and is operational and reachabl(

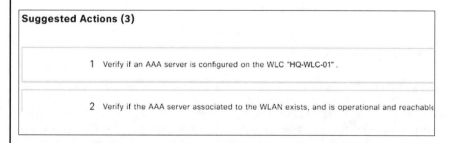

Figure 8-7 *Screenshot of Recommended Actions to Fix This Issue*

The open issue (from Figure 8-4) was created by Cisco DNAC Assurance as the wireless clients were not authenticating. The operator could now quickly dive into the open issue and check whether a configuration change was made and whether there were issues with the authentication server. As both were not the case, the operator moved to step 2, which was to validate the path between the controller and the RADIUS servers. At that moment it became clear that an uplink to the WAN (which was not yet included in the monitoring by Cisco DNAC Assurance) had failed, which resulted in the reported wireless problems by the user. Resetting that link resulted in the resolution of that incident.

As you can see from the use case, the initial reported problem about the wireless network being down was not the actual problem. It was the victim of a different failure where the controller could not reach the authentication servers. Although Cisco DNAC Assurance was assuming a misconfiguration on the Wireless LAN Controller, the correlation of the data did help the operations team to isolate the problem quickly. This increase in finding a probable cause will support the operations team in reducing the workload and thus increase the opportunity to enable cooperation with the project team that implements major changes. It could even be possible that some major changes are implemented by the operations team themselves.

Cisco DNAC Assurance is an integral part of the Cisco DNAC solution. As such, a Cisco DNAC solution needs to be installed into the network. Once the Cisco DNAC solution is installed in the network, it can be enabled. The advantage of Cisco DNAC Assurance is that you can enable it without using any of its other features.

Once Cisco DNAC discovers a device and device controllability is enabled (which is on by default), Cisco DNAC will configure that device for a form of assurance, which is covered in more detail in the following sections. In the case of a Wireless LAN Controller, the certificate of Cisco DNAC is installed on the controller, the proper URL is configured, and the controller is rebooted to enable assurance. Once assurance is enabled on the controller, the controller will connect to DNAC and use model-driven telemetry to send data to the controller.

It is important to note that Cisco DNAC is not polling or subscribing to a controller, but the controller is in fact a client connecting to Cisco DNAC Assurance. This can have an impact on the network policies deployed on the network to restrict access between network devices and management tools. A number of ports are used for Cisco DNAC Assurance communication as well. It is important to check beforehand whether those communication ports are open between Cisco DNAC and the controller.

Table 8-4 provides an overview of these ports in the case of Cisco DNAC version 1.2.

Table 8-4 *Overview of Ports Used Between DNAC Assurance and a Wireless Controller*

Source	SRC Port	Destination	DST Port	Description
WLC	any	Cisco DNAC	TCP 32222	Used by Cisco DNAC for device discovery
WLC	any	Cisco DNAC	UDP 162	Used to send SNMP traps to Cisco DNAC
WLC	any	Cisco DNAC	TCP 443	Sending model-driven telemetry
WLC/ Cisco DNAC	ICMP	WLC/ Cisco DNAC	ICMP	Used for checking reachability
Cisco DNAC	any	WLC	TCP 22 UDP 161	Used for configuration from Cisco DNAC

An additional caveat of leveraging Cisco DNAC Assurance as a solution is that it is based on big data and machine intelligence. The sizing of Cisco DNAC must be appropriate for the environment. Also, the device needs to be compatible with Cisco DNAC Assurance, so it is important to check the device compatibility list in detail before enabling assurance. For example, AireOS code 8.5 is minimally required for assurance, but the Cisco WLC2504 and WLC5508 do not support assurance, although they can run the 8.5 code.

Within this step, the introduction of Cisco DNA Center Assurance is used to reduce the workload of the operations team. Inherent to this use case is that the organization will choose the Cisco DNA Center solution for the transformation to an Intent-Based Network. If this is not the case for a specific organization, the same principle can be leveraged using another visibility tool as long as that tool is focused and capable of proactively supporting the operations team with troubleshooting. In that manner the workload of the network operations team is reduced with a quick win of introducing an analytics component to the campus network.

Introducing Automation

If automation is not yet used within the operations team, it is another factor to greatly reduce the workload of the team besides an opportunity to allow the network operations team to gain more confidence with using automation tools. As IBN relies heavily on automation tools, the operations team needs to start relying on (and thus trusting) automation tools. If automation tools are already used, then this step can be used to increase the use of the automation tool. As this step aims to introduce automation and gain trust within the operations team, it is important to let the operations team make as many decisions as possible and allow them time to learn to cope with automation while at the same time reducing the fears of losing their jobs over automation. More on the latter aspect is described in Part III of this book.

Before jumping headfirst into the automation tool that gets the most hits on a search engine, it is wise to perform a quick analysis of requirements, including the action plan and priorities from the previous phase, to decide which tool will best fit in the current phase of the transformation.

Depending on the situation of the organization, it could be considered to use two auto-mation tools in the transformation to IBN. If, for example, a large number of network devices need to be replaced, it is an option to start off with an automation tool already available (such as Cisco Prime Infrastructure, Cisco APIC-EM, or RedHat Ansible) and migrate to a Cisco DNA Center solution at a later stage. Similar checks and balances could result in similar decisions.

Once an automation tool is selected (or being reused), some operations can benefit from an automation tool.

Day-n Operations

One aspect of network operations that can easily leverage the power of automation to reduce the workload are day-n operations. The upgrade of switches is a task profoundly ignored by operations teams as the task to upgrade, for example, 200 switches to a new software version is often found to be cumbersome and laborious.

Automation tooling can provide a solution to this problem and provides a great way for the operations team to become familiar with automation tools. Both Cisco Prime Infrastructure and Cisco DNA Center have the capability to perform automated software upgrades, also known as SoftWare Image Management (SWIM). Although Cisco DNA Center uses a slightly different implementation of a software image management work-flow than Prime Infrastructure, the concepts are similar.

Figure 8-8 provides a screenshot of SoftWare Image Management within a Prime Infrastructure solution.

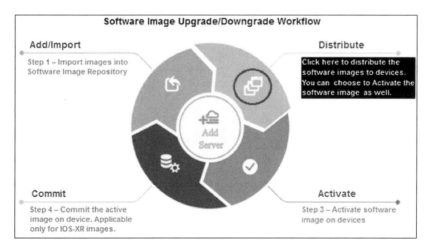

Figure 8-8 *Screenshot of SWIM Within Prime Infrastructure*

Both solutions leverage the concept of a repository and use a similar workflow. The repository is a location on the network where all the golden images for the different network devices are stored. Golden images (a Cisco DNAC-specific term) are those software releases selected to be deployed on the network. Other versions for the same switch type result in that switch being noncompliant. This repository can be the Cisco DNAC solution (or Prime Infrastructure) itself or an external FTP server. The following principal workflow is similar for both solutions.

1. **Import to repository**

   Import the image for the switches in the campus network to the repository. Both Cisco DNAC and Prime Infrastructure have the capability to download directly from Cisco Connection Online (CCO). However, in larger enterprises, a software release could have been tested in a lab environment before releasing it in production, so it is recommended to manually import the image to the repository.

2. **Distribute image**

   In this step the image from the repository is distributed onto the switches. It is possible to manually select specific switches or to allow the tool to push the image to all switches. The distribution step has the possibility to remove files from flash to create enough room for the new image to be copied. After copying the image from the repository to the switch, a verification step is executed to check whether the image was copied successfully.

3. **Commit**

   Once the distribution of the image has been successful, the image can be committed. In other words, the image is configured as a boot variable in the running configuration of the switch. The software is not activated. This step can be combined with the previous step, but it is also possible (for more control) to execute this step separately.

4. **Activate**

   The last step is to activate the new software image. By activating the image, Prime Infrastructure (and Cisco DNAC) saves the configuration, reloads the switch, and validates that the upgrade has been executed successfully. Besides possible caveats, a switch should return to a running state as the old version of the IOS image is still on the flash. So in case of a failure, the old image will be selected.

After the fourth step, the switches have been deployed with the new image. Although Cisco DNAC works in a similar method, the workflow is slightly different. As Cisco DNAC works with sites and network profiles, a golden image can be defined per site or globally. Once a golden image is defined for a specific switch type and role, some switches become noncompliant. Via an action in the interface, the operator can make all access switches compliant, and the above steps are executed automatically.

Use Case: Using Automation to Upgrade Switch Software

LogiServ Inc. provides IT services to a conglomerate of companies and manages approximately 40 switches. Although this is not a large number of switches, due to a history of acquisitions and mergers and specific industrial environments, approximately 5 different types of switches are deployed in the network.

In the past, LogiServ would update these switches by hand, logging in to each switch individually, copying and activating the image by copy-pasting commands in the evening or on weekends. The upgrade process would take close to two weeks of working in the evenings.

As Prime Infrastructure was used to primarily manage the wireless networks and monitor the routers, the SWIM process of Prime Infrastructure was used recently to standardize the images across all network devices.

During normal office hours the new images were distributed to the switches, where only one source image per switch was used. On a single Saturday, with announced downtime, the new images were committed and activated. Instead of working multiple evenings, a single Saturday morning was used to update all the switches in the network, including proactive comparison of the configuration after the upgrade.

As the use case demonstrates, the upgrade of switches is a typical task that benefits from automation. As this is a task that often does not have the priority of an operations team and in principle does not change the configuration, it allows the team to gain trust in automation tools and reduces the workload.

Day-0 Operations

Another aspect that can benefit from automation tooling are day-0 operations. In other words, automation can benefit the operations team greatly in the case of deploying new switches and configurations. However, this aspect is only beneficial if the number of new deployments is high—for example, because of lifecycle management to get all network devices intent ready.

If an automation tool is to be used for the provisioning of new network equipment, it also has the added benefit that the new devices will also receive a new standardized configuration.

This step leverages the capabilities of the Cisco APIC-EM and Prime Infrastructure, or Cisco DNA Center to provision configurations to new devices using Plug-and-Play (PnP). The step is explained using Cisco APIC-EM and Prime Infrastructure with an explanation of the differences based on a Cisco DNA Center workflow. A sample bootstrap configuration template follows.

In this workflow, APIC-EM's PnP application is used in combination with DHCP from a seed device to set up the device with an initial configuration that contains enough information so that the device can be discovered by Prime Infrastructure (or Ansible).

Prime Infrastructure's templating engine is then used to deploy a standardized configuration to the device.

As for requirements, Prime Infrastructure and APIC-EM need to be installed and deployed on the network, including the required integration between Prime Infrastructure and APIC-EM. Also, within APIC-EM, the PnP application needs to be installed and active. Once these requirements are met, the following workflow can be used to automate day-0 operations using Prime Infrastructure and APIC-EM. The workflow for day-0 automation contains the following steps:

1. **Define and import a bootstrap template.**

   A template that contains the bootstrap configuration is imported in a project within APIC-EM's PnP application. This bootstrap template configures the new device with enough information, such as hostname, SSH keys, and credentials, so that the device can be discovered via Prime Infrastructure.

2. **Enable PnP service with DHCP on seed device.**

   A seed device is required for PnP. This could be the distribution switch or the WAN router. On this device the DHCP service needs to be configured with the remember option and a specific DHCP option that PnP uses to discover the PnP server.

3. **Start up switches and provide them with the bootstrapped configuration.**

   Once DHCP and PnP are enabled, the new switches are racked and stacked. They can now be powered on. Once the switch is booted, a PnP process is started to attempt PnP. *This process will run as long as the boot process is not interrupted! So if you enter any key on the console, this process will be aborted!*

   The PnP process attempts to get an IP address via DHCP and will connect to the APIC-EM PnP server.

   Within PnP the device will be visible within the project created in step 1. The bootstrap template is applied and the required variables are entered by the operator. APIC-EM will in turn push the configuration, and if required the proper image, to the device and configure the device.

   At the end of this step the new switches have an IP address and are discoverable by Prime Infrastructure.

4. **Discover devices in Prime Infrastructure.**

   Once the switches are provisioned, a discovery rule within Prime Infrastructure is (automatically) started, and the devices are discovered and added to Prime Infrastructure. This step automatically places the devices in monitoring as well.

5. **Provision devices with appropriate template via Prime Infrastructure.**

   The last step deploys the appropriate configuration templates within Prime Infrastructure to the devices. These templates essentially finalize the configuration of the devices with the appropriate settings such as VLANs, logging configuration, and time servers.

After these five steps, the new devices are configured and provisioned. Although these steps might still seem to be a lot of work, the benefit of automation becomes true if multiple switches are to be configured at the same time, for example, in a new building. Field engineers can rack and stack the switches beforehand, and at a specific moment these steps can be executed for all switches by just powering them on; the operations team can perform the required changes remotely.

This process also provides the opportunity to have a more direct cooperation between projects (placing the new switches) and operations (managing the network).

Cisco DNA Center is the evolution of PnP from APIC-EM combined with templates of Prime Infrastructure. Within Cisco DNAC there is no need to define a project. New devices are placed in the inventory as new, unmanaged devices. Once the operator provisions that switch to a site, the network profile attached to that site will be applied to the switch. As the network profile contains a complete configuration for that site, including a golden image, the switch will automatically be updated to the correct image and obtain the correct information automatically.

DNA Center takes the automation of day-0 operations a step further.

The configuration template in Example 8-2 can be used for bootstrapping a new device.

Example 8-2   *Sample Configuration Template for Bootstrapping a New Device*

```
hostname $hostname
enable secret $secretPassword
service password-encryption
!
vtp mode transparent
!
vlan $MgmtVlanId
name Management
!
ip domain-name $DomainName
aaa new-model
aaa authentication login default local
aaa authorization exec default local
username admin privilege 15 secret 0 $password
!
int vlan1
 shutdown
!
interface Vlan$MgmtVlan
 description Management
 ip address $ipvAddress $ipv4Netmask
!
ip default-gateway $ipv4Gateway
!
```

```
ip tftp source-interface Vlan$MgmtVlanId
!
snmp-server group SNMP-MGMT v3 auth read SNMP-VIEW write SNMP-VIEW
snmp-server group SNMP-MGMT v3 priv read SNMP-VIEW write SNMP-VIEW
snmp-server view SNMP-VIEW iso included
snmp-server user prime SNMP-MGMT v3 auth sha $snmpAuth priv aes 128 $snmpPriv
snmp-server trap-source Vlan$MgmtVlan
snmp-server source-interface informs Vlan$MgmtVlan
!
snmp-server host $primeHost version 3 priv prime
snmp-server host $apicHost version 3 priv prime
!
ip ssh time-out 60
ip ssh version 2
line con 0
exec-timeout 20 0
logging synchronous
line vty 0 15
exec-timeout 20 0
logging synchronous
transport input ssh telnet
!
interface $Uplink1
!
switchport mode trunk
switchport trunk native vlan $MgmtVlan
channel-group 1 mode on
!
interface $Uplink2
!
switchport mode trunk
channel-group 1 mode on
switchport trunk native vlan $MgmtVlan
!
interface po1
!
switchport mode dynamic desirable
!
crypto key generate rsa mod 4096
!
```

Although the automation of day-0 operations might seem like quite some effort and not reduce the workload of the operations team, the opposite is true. Much effort is placed in the preparation of the day-0 operation. But once new switches are deployed, the configuration of those devices will occur semiautomatically and consistently because the same template is applied. In situations where multiple switches are to be installed, this automation step will save time.

An added benefit is that over time, the configuration of switches in the campus network will be standardized using the earlier defined templates.

Day-2 Operations

Some day-2 operations can leverage the power of automation as well. The common factor on automation is that the change itself can be defined as repeatable steps and needs to be executed on more than one switch. Changing a syslog server, adding or removing a user, and changing a RADIUS server configuration typically can benefit from an automation tool.

Use Case: Leveraging Automation for Configuration Changes

One of the companies I designed a network for was managed by three network engineers. For accounting purposes each employee was given a unique login and password. As the company grew, more network engineers were employed to monitor and manage the network. At one time, when an employee left the company, another engineer would log in to each individual switch and remove the user via the command line.

In today's networks, automation using Python can be used to automatically connect to all switches and issue the command **no user** *<name-of-employee>* automatically. By using an input file instead of hardcoding in the Python script, the automation tool can be used for other changes as well. This script would greatly reduce the time required to execute this change.

Although day-2 operations seem to be perfect for automation, it is important to consider carefully when to start using an automation tool for these kinds of changes. The phrase "one error is human; many errors is automation" rings true. Automation can bring down a complete cloud environment if executed incorrectly. And if such a change goes awry, the potential trust for an automation tool would be reduced dramatically within the operations team. Therefore, you can use day-2 operations to gain further trust in automation within this step, but only if the automation tool is readily in place and has proven successful with other operations in the past.

Day-1 Operations

One of the primary principles of an intent-based network is that Intents are provisioned to the network devices using an automation tool. These Intents are almost always day-1 operations on the network, such as adding a VLAN or performing a change on an access list. The automation of these types of tasks is actually the end result of the transformation. As such, these operations do not quickly reduce the workload of the operations team and do not fit in this phase of the transformation.

Summary of Automation

To summarize, the introduction of an automation tool to the operations team is both essential and important in the preparation for an intent-based network. This step aims for three goals:

- The introduction of an automation tool
- Gaining trust of the operations team
- Reducing the workload of the operations team

It is not directly required to automatically select the latest automation tool or immediately start using the automation tool that is the best fit for an Intent-Based Network (DNA Center). It is valid, based on a quick requirements and action plan check, to start the automation step in this phase using existing tools or technologies like Prime Infrastructure or RedHat Ansible.

It is important to perform this step in close cooperation with the operations team and allow for discussion and questions, as the past has demonstrated that the automation of anything will also introduce resistance and fear by the employees who execute those tasks. It is a valid strategy to take the least-liked "boring" tasks and showcase how the automation tool makes these tasks easier. Both day-0 and day-n operations are the best candidates.

Involvement of the operations team is important to reduce the fear and show the benefits. It is therefore recommended to not implement automation without members of the operations team, but rather allocate enough time and guide them to perform those changes via the automation tool. If there is a lot of resistance and fear, start with a change that is minor and does not have a great impact.

At the end of this step, there is a deployed automation tool that has proven its value, the workload of the operations team is reduced because of the tasks executed via the automation tool, and the operations team has a level of trust in the tool as well.

Risks of This Phase

Phase two encompasses all steps required to prepare the organization and the network for an Intent-Based Network. This preparation requires a number of small and big changes within both the organization and the network devices used within the campus network.

Some of the steps and tasks described in this phase can take some time, depending on the agility and maturity of the organization. Consequently, some risks can be associated with this phase.

The potential long time required for this phase is probably one of the most prominent risks that can be identified. If the maturity level of the organization needs to be increased, this means that the organization needs to change and start working with documents, procedures, and so on. Changing an organization takes much more time than the introduction of a new technology. Executing organizational changes can be compared with walking on a high wire. If the pace of change is too slow, management will either lose focus (and thus commitment) or get impatient. If the pace of change is too high, employees will stop cooperating, which will make change even more difficult.

In both situations, the commitment from management can fade, and as a result the transformation to an Intent-Based Network can be canceled. Another scenario is that, due to factors external to the IT department, the initial commitment for Intent-Based Networking is put on discussion, for example, because of strain on resources, lower budget, an acquisition, and so on. In summary, because of the long time it can take to change an organization, there is a chance that the transformation will be canceled.

A lack of budget or lower revenue can also result in being unable to replace network devices in the campus network for Cisco DNA-ready equipment.

To mitigate these risks, it is important to know and actively inform stakeholders so that management stays committed. A vision and strategy from management on IBN will reduce this risk as well, depending on the maturity and perseverance of management.

Another risk identified within this phase is to prematurely end this phase and declare that the campus network is prepared for an Intent-Based Network. All steps in this phase are meant to prepare the organization and the network for a successful Intent-Based Network implementation. Failing in, for example, the introduction of a standardized configuration with a central policy can lead to unexpected results when an Intent is working for one branch location but not another. Even worse is when an automation tool is not introduced properly with the operations team supporting that kind of automation. The team will not use the tool and will still work in an overloaded work situation with reduced faith in any attempt to reduce that workload. If the steps in this phase are not completed successfully, complex and unnecessary problems will eventually occur in phases three and four. These problems will reduce the success and potential of an Intent-Based Network.

Another pitfall and thus risk is to allow all steps and tasks in this phase to be executed by (external) project teams. Although this approach is common within organizations, not involving the network operations team is a big risk.

Part of this phase is to establish trust in a new method working within the operations team. If an external project team introduces a new tool, whether it is perfect or not, the operations teams will not have the time to investigate, learn, and really use the tool.

They are used to executing per-device changes or operating in a specific way, and they will continue to do so until something really bad happens or until they are led step by step into a different way of thinking. It is a human bias that facilitates this behavior. More information on this behavior is described in Part III of this book.

It is therefore important that management allocates resources to the network operations team, so that the network operations team can execute the tasks themselves with the support of a project team. The project team must be supportive to the operations team and not vice versa.

It is self-evident that the network operations team needs to focus on operating the campus network as well. Therefore, it is a valid option to introduce a dedicated project team, in which members of the network operations team participate and have the final decision on all choices related to operating the network.

This phase cannot be compared to a next-next-finish project. Each organization is unique in its own ways, culture, and methods. In some types of organizations, a directive approach can work better than a more subtle approach. Although in general, a subtle, gradual approach is most often beneficial to all, the proverb that each war strategy is thrown away when the first bullet is shot is applicable to this phase as well. It is important to keep a sharp focus on the expected end results of this phase while mitigating the risks and adapting to the specifics of each organization. In other words, manage for the expected outcome as described in the different steps of this phase.

Summary

The second phase in the transformation to Intent-Based Networking is about preparing the campus network and the organization for an Intent-enabled network. This phase might very well be the longest phase in the complete approach as both the organization and the network are prepared. There are four steps in this phase, and it is suggested to run these steps sequentially.

- **Matching requirements:** In this step the requirements for a successful transformation to IBN are met. These requirements are for both the organization (maturity level of organization and resource availability) as well as the network infrastructure (DNA-ready hardware and migrating from port centric to policy centric).

- **Standardization:** The configuration of network devices is standardized, and a standardized consistent VLAN numbering plan is introduced.

- **Introduction of automation:** Automation is introduced to gain confidence in tooling and reduce the workload on the network operations team.

- **Introduction of assurance:** To reduce the workload on the network operations team.

This phase is probably the longest in the transformation to IBN. The predominant reason is that both the hardware needs to be DNA ready (which takes time), and the organization needs to be at a certain maturity level (which also takes time). Therefore, this phase also has a number of risks:

- Lack of budget

- Premature ending of this phase

- Executing the required steps by an external project team

- Lack of resource availability

In conclusion, these four tasks (matching requirements, standardization, introducing assurance, and introducing automation) combined make up phase two and conclude the preparations for an Intent-Based Network. The time required for this phase can be considerably long for a number of reasons. A primary reason is that the organization needs to be at a specific level of maturity in regards to IT and IT management. Most aspects must be at level 3 (processes are documented and being followed) with preferably a number of aspects at level 4, where a vision and strategy are defined and adhered to by both management and IT staff. Improving an organization's level of maturity (and thus quality) will take a long time as it requires change within the organization.

Chapter 9

Phase Three: Design, Deploy, and Extend

All the hard work and effort will finally bring forth fruit with this phase. At this stage the network and enterprise are prepared for an Intent-Based Network and all aspects necessary for the transformation. Phase three will actually design, implement, and extend the campus network to an Intent-Based Network.

Because IBN is a philosophy, a number of design choices can be made upon which the transformation will actually occur. The transformation to an Intent-Based Network can be achieved via either a Software-Defined Access or a classic VLAN approach. Both journeys are valid, and each has advantages and disadvantages.

This chapter describes what steps to take in the transformation for each journey and covers the following topics:

- Lab environment
- Which technology to use
- Deploying a baseline
- Convert to Intents
- Extending the network
- Increase security

Lab Environment

It has been common in networking to deploy new networks and new services onto the production network without testing. New networks or functions would be deployed to the network, and if problems occurred, troubleshooting the network would solve those and fine-tune the deployment of that new feature.

But the network has become one of the most critical elements for any business. Also, deploying a new site using Intent-Based Networking requires a new method of designing, operating, and managing.

This makes running new features on the network virtually impossible.

If possible, it is strongly recommended to set up a lab environment that preferably represents the actual production environment and should at least have one of each model used in the production network. While it is possible to simulate the deployment using other models, there may be important hardware or software differences. The lab environment should also contain a WAN simulator, as well as a compute environment that contains ISE and a Cisco DNAC solution to test the changes and transitions the campus network will face during the change to Intent-Based Networking. It is possible to run Cisco DNA Center in a virtual environment, as long as the server meets the requirements. Figure 9-1 provides a sample lab topology that can be used for many campus networks.

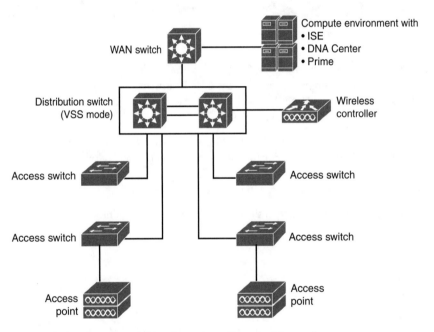

Figure 9-1   *Sample Lab Topology for a Campus Network*

In this lab environment, two switches in VSS mode act as a distribution switch. A number of access switches are wired to both distribution switches. A wireless controller with access points facilitates wireless networking. The compute environment, which simulates a datacenter, has a deployment (virtual) for Cisco DNA Center, ISE, and possibly Prime Infrastructure. This topology can be used for both classic VLAN networks as well as SDA. If SDA is to be deployed, the VSS pair needs to be torn down so that two individual distribution switches are realized, and each uplink to the distribution from the access layer would be a single Layer 3 link instead of a port channel.

Note   Most often the teardown of a VSS pair is a manual process, but as DNA Center receives new features with each new release, newer versions could include an automated process to do that.

Having a lab environment is not only beneficial for the transition to Intent-Based Networking. It also enables the operations team to get used to DNAC and test it out in a "safe situation," as well as the possibility to test out new features before implementing them in production.

Which Technology?

Cisco clearly states that implementing an Intent-Based Network is a journey. In other words, it is a process that takes longer and is much more than just technology; however, the choice of the network technology can either make or break that same transformation. In general, two concepts leveraging different technologies can be used to implement and enable an Intent-Based Network. The following paragraphs describe these two groups of technology and explain in which situations each technology can fit best for the transformation.

Software Defined Access

Software Defined Access (SDA) is the most commonly known technology that can be used for an Intent-Based Network. This is logical because the introduction of SDA coincided with the launch of Intent-Based Networking in 2017, and in due time SDA most probably will become the new default deployment for a campus network. SDA brings several advantages.

Furthermore, SDA is production ready, moving from early adopters to early majority in the technology adoption curve. Despite the advantages, however, some limitations might prove to be too restrictive for taking the first steps toward an Intent-Based Network.

Note The introduction and adoption of a new technology commonly follow a specific curve in which certain groups of users or organizations adopt a new technology. Figure 9-2 displays this technology adoption curve.

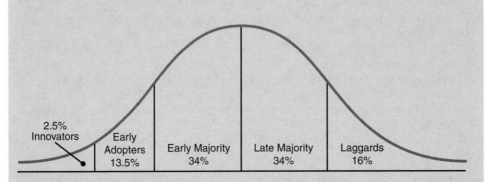

Figure 9-2 *Technology Adoption Curve, source: Courtesy of Everett M. "Ev" Rogers*

In general, new technologies are commonly adopted by innovators first; they know the technology is often still immature, and failure is an option. Once the technology evolves and matures, the technology is used by the early adopters. At the first stage of the adoption, the technology is still not production ready, but products start to be delivered with the new technology. As the product reaches production quality and maturity, the early majority group starts to adopt the technology. The technology has proven its value and is becoming mainstream. At 50% usage of the technology, the late majority group starts to use the technology as well. At the end, when the technology is already used by a majority, the laggards start to use the product as well.

Based on the culture and type of enterprise, each enterprise commonly falls under one of these categories in terms of the adoption of a technology. The culture of the enterprise must be taken into account as well to determine whether SDA is the right choice for the first Intent-Based Network in the organization.

As mentioned, SDA has a number of limitations that you need to be aware of when making the choice for the first intent-based network:

- **Cisco DNA Center:** The implementation of SDA requires a Cisco DNA Center (DNAC) solution installed. DNAC provides a number of advantages to the operations team, such as assurance and automation. But an SDA network will not be possible without DNAC. If the deployment of SDA requires high availability, a minimum of three DNAC appliances is required as well.

- **Size of DNA Center:** Early deployments of the DNA Center solution were limited to 25,000 endpoints and 128 virtual networks for a single DNA Center deployment. Over time, with new hardware and software features, these numbers are increased and different DNA Center solutions are available with different sizing limitations. The size of a DNA Center deployment itself is measured over 37 different aspects, such as number of endpoints, number of WLCs, number of switches, and so on. As these numbers change over time, because of optimizations, new hardware, and so on, recommended practice dictates that you validate that the expected total number of endpoints and devices fit within the DNA Center solution as a whole.

■ **Cisco Identity Services Engine:** The central policy server in the campus network must be a Cisco Identity Services Engine (ISE) solution running version 2.3 or higher. The policy defined in DNA Center is pushed to ISE via APIs. If the organization does not have an ISE deployment, deploying SDA with Scalable Group Tags (SGT) will be impossible.

■ **SDA-ready equipment:** Another limitation is that only the next generation of network infrastructure devices are able to run SDA to the maximum capacity. Although Catalyst 3650 and Catalyst 3850 switches are Cisco DNA ready and are able to run SDA, to run more than three virtual networks the IP Services license is a hard requirement for the Catalyst 3650/3850 series to meet. All Catalyst 9000 series switches are part of the next generation of network infrastructure devices and are capable of running SDA.

■ **Standard off-the-shelf campus network:** SDA is production ready for standard IPv4 (and IPv6) network connectivity. As SDA matures, more features like multicast and Layer 2 flooding are introduced. Check that SDA covers and supports all features that the organization is currently using on the campus network, specifically for the first Intent-Based Network location.

If these limitations are not applicable for the organization, then SDA can provide some advantages over using classic VLANs for the first Intent-Based Network. One of these advantages is that creating and deploying new virtual networks, or adjusting a policy, is much easier within the graphical user interface of DNAC compared to classic VLANs. DNAC has a specific appstack solely for deploying and operating SDA networks. Connecting multiple SDA fabrics using multisite SDA is also relatively easy.

SDA is continuously in development, and new features are introduced at a regular pace. It is important to match the enterprise's campus network against the current state of SDA at the moment of choice. Best practice is to use the different release notes (Cisco IOS-XE for Catalyst switches and Cisco DNA Center) to understand the features, limitations, and scalability guidance and match these to the enterprise campus network. If at this stage a number of limitations are applicable for the specific campus network, it does not mean that SDA is not possible. It might be possible to start with only a limited set of sites under SDA, or wait until most limitations have been solved and start with a classic VLAN Intent-Based Network and then migrate at a later stage.

Use Case: Analyzing and Coping with Limitations to SDA in an Existing Deployment

In the new branch locations SharedService Group leverages the Catalyst 3650 switches in the access layer. The switches are installed with an IP Base license, limiting the number of VRFs logically to three. The distribution switch manages the Layer 3 connectivity and the Layer 3 isolation using VRF-Lite. The switches have been standardized for new locations as well as a standardized IP plan, and SharedService Group has a large-scale Cisco ISE deployment. In summary, SharedService Group is in the perfect position to introduce Intent-Based Networks using SDA. The only limiting factor is that the 3650 switches are running IP Base instead of IP Services (IP Services allows for 64 VRFs and thus 64 virtual networks). SharedService Group was able to test SDA in a lab environment and was positive on the results. SDA wasn't completely production ready at the moment of testing, but it showed enough promise.

It was decided that the transformation to Intent-Based Networking would continue on two tracks.

One of the tracks would be to test the Catalyst 9300 switches for the access layer, and once they were accepted, the new branch locations would be rolled out with Catalyst 9300 switches and SDA. In parallel, the existing campus networks were being standardized and prepared for Intent-Based Networking using classic VLANs. Once lifecycle management dictated that the switches at a branch location had to be replaced, the site would be migrated to SDA as well.

Classic VLAN

An alternative for SDA is to use VLANs and VRF-Lite to configure an Intent-Based Network. As explained earlier, the intent is translated into small bits of network configuration and pushed onto the network using automation. Within SDA, one or more virtual networks are created, and devices are placed inside a virtual network. Scalable group tags provide the mechanism to define microsegmentation on a security level. With a classic VLAN deployment, a minimal foundation campus network is implemented with reachability to Cisco DNA Center (preferably in a separate management VRF). The automation tool, for example, Cisco DNA Center, pushes small templates to this minimal network to implement the intents, and as Scalable Group Tags are part of Cisco TrustSec, they can be applied to VLANs as well. VRF-Lite is used to logically separate the different networks and effectively be able to create the different virtual networks. The distribution switch would still be terminating on Layer 3, and VRF-aware routing protocols can be used to connect the logical networks (a single campus location) to the outside network.

An Intent-Based Network can be configured using classic VLANs and VRFs if the campus network can fulfill the following requirements:

- **VRF-Lite capable distribution switch:** The IP isolation of the different networks is handled with VRF-Lite, just as with SDA. Therefore, the distribution switch needs to be able to run VRF-Lite and be able to use VRF-aware routing protocols like OSPF, BGP, or EIGRP to route off the different networks over the WAN network to the datacenter.

- **No Spanning Tree in the campus network:** One of the advantages of SDA is that the links between switches are IP-based; no spanning tree is required. But in a collapsed-core campus design there are also no loops while retaining high availability. Besides that the Spanning Tree Protocol (STP) is not required in a collapsed-core design, there is a second, more important reason to disable Spanning Tree. With the exception of MST instances, when a VLAN is created or removed, STP will temporarily disrupt traffic on all links to set up a new topology. In an Intent-Based Network, you do not want to disrupt the network when adding or removing a VLAN from the network. For these two reasons, STP is not run on the network, and proper mitigation techniques such as BPDUGuard and Broadcast Storm Detection are implemented on the edge.

- **Single foundation network:** Analog to SDA, a foundation network, preferably in an isolated VRF, is used for management of the campus network location, so that Intents can safely be added to and removed from the network. The underlay network is Layer 2 based. This provides the benefit that most modern switches can be used in an Intent-Based Network using classic VLANs.

- **Normal network Intent:** A normal access VLAN terminated on the distribution switch is the normal regular network Intent. The VRF-Lite instance ensures that the network is logically isolated from other virtual networks. It is also possible to physically separate wired and wireless VLANs.

- **Layer 2 Intent:** A Layer 2 isolated Intent is absolutely possible within a classic VLAN. Actually a VLAN number without IP connectivity is a Layer 2 Intent, although it is not possible to (easily) stretch the Layer 2 Intent over multiple campus locations. That would require specific configuration of technologies such as L2VPN or manual VXLAN or GRE and need to be supported on the distribution switch.

- **Scalable Group Tags:** Just as within SDA, Scalable Group Tags can be leveraged to define microsegmentation policies, if Cisco ISE is deployed as a central policy server. It is possible to define the different SGT policies inside ISE as well, but it is absolutely possible to enable microsegmentation within a single VLAN.

- **Automation tool required:** Intent-Based Networks rely heavily on automation tools. This design is also based on leveraging automation tools. Cisco DNA Center might not be completely required, but it does provide extra added functionality, such as a simple-to-use interface, advanced templating for enabling intents, as well as Cisco DNA Center assurance for visibility. From that perspective it is recommended to leverage Cisco DNA Center in a classic VLAN-based approach as well. Alternative automation tools are possible but they will lack the ease of use that Cisco DNA Center brings.

These requirements combined make a valid design for an Intent-Based Network leveraging existing technologies such as classic VLAN and VRF-Lite. Functionally (and thus from a business perspective) this design can meet the business requirements and allow an organization to start the transition to Intent-Based Networking. Although this design is valid for our purposes, there are some limitations as well:

- **No overlay network:** One of the major advantages of SDA is that with SDA it is possible to create a single fabric network over multiple locations in the campus, as long as latency and other requirements are met. As classic VLANs do not leverage an overlay network, it will not be possible to stretch a single IP network across multiple sites. This also means that each campus location will need to have its own IP segments for each virtual network. This can bring extra tension on the available IP space within an organization.

- **More testing and templating are required:** SDA provides a single simple interface for defining and deploying new virtual networks to the campus network, including the relevant policies. An Intent-based design using VLANs would require more testing and knowledge of templates, as the templates that are to be deployed need to be defined by the organization. There is no ready-to-use templating mechanism to deploy or remove a template (and thus intent).

Use Case: Choosing the Right Technology for IBN

FinTech Ltd. uses Cisco Catalyst 2960G switches as access layer switches and Catalyst 3850 switches as distribution switches. The Cisco Catalyst 2960G switch itself cannot run any SDA network. But the switches are more or less standardized in their configuration, and a Cisco Identity Services Engine solution is deployed as well. The network team leverages Scrum/Agile methodology for managing the network. A transformation to Intent-Based Networking using classic VLANs is for FinTech the most logical choice.

By implementing an automation tool using templates, the company was able to implement its first Intent-Based Network.

In conclusion, designing and implementing an Intent-Based Network is absolutely viable using classic VLANs and VRFs for IP segmentation. The drawbacks are tightly related to the optimization that IBN will bring over time. At the first stages of IBN, the business requirements would be met with this design, and existing operations teams could run an Intent-Based Network leveraging existing knowledge. The impact of such a design is much lower compared to an SDA approach.

Both approaches to an Intent-Based Network have their benefits, and each approach (classic VLAN or SDA) has unique features and differences. It is also to be expected that over time SDA will become the common network technology used in campus networks. It is important to determine and decide which journey to start on for the first steps of configuring an Intent-Based Network. This decision should be made with the operations team and management of the organization, taking into account all the inventory and changes made in the previous phases.

As SDA leverages newer technologies, there is a higher risk of failure and disruptions. If the organization cannot overcome these first-time issues, it might be wiser to select a classic VLAN approach over SDA, even if the network itself, including Cisco DNA Center, is completely IBN ready.

The decision is also a no-regrets decision, as it is always possible to migrate a campus location from SDA back to classic VLANs and vice versa. This is also logical as the trend will be that campus locations will migrate to a form of SDA over time.

This decision is important as this will have an impact on the remaining steps within this phase to enable Intent on the campus network.

Deploy a Baseline

The next step in this phase is to design and deploy a baseline for Intent-Based Networking on a single campus location. If you are able to use a lab environment, the baseline and procedures will of course be tested and deployed on the lab environment first. Even if the baseline is tested in the lab environment, it is recommended to carefully choose the first campus location to migrate to an Intent-enabled network. The location is preferably nearby the network operations team and has friendly, constructive end users who are willing to provide honest and positive feedback and who are also prepared to experience disruptions if they might occur.

If a location is chosen, it is important to communicate and discuss the choice with the users, so they are aware of the upcoming changes beforehand, and they will not get into unexpected surprises. In general, unexpected surprises tend to escalate quickly into larger, unmanageable problems.

Use Case: Advantage of a Lab Environment

SharedService Group recently introduced a lab environment for testing out software and functions used within the campus network. The disadvantage of the lab is that it is not at a production scale, and it is isolated from the production network. So although it is possible to test functionally, truly testing performance or with a high number of endpoints connected to the network is impossible, even while using special test equipment.

To improve quality, the decision was made with management that after successful testing, the building in which SharedService Group was housed would always be the first building to roll out new software versions and features.

It was known by management that this decision could have the consequence that the building might have disruptions, but it would also be beneficial in communicating about the upcoming changes with other locations they managed.

The new feature or software was already running stably and successfully in their own building for a longer period of time, essentially providing a software guarantee to reduce resistance for updating configurations or software.

The example of SharedService Group is not unique. The "eating your own dog food" method has its benefits, and many technology companies leverage that same principle. For example, some business units within Cisco test their software or hardware inside a regular office building on the campus as well. One public example is the development of the Catalyst 9800 Wireless Controller. The engineers developed this new solution in their own building in India. The advantage was, of course, that high-severity caveats were potentially found and fixed sooner.

In conclusion, the choice of location for a first Intent-Based Network is important. The location needs to be large enough, with friendly users who are informed beforehand of the upcoming change. And disruptions on that network can be contained and are not too high of an impact.

SDA

The first step in deploying an Intent-Based Network is deploying a baseline for the network. Within SDA, the baseline is the underlay network upon which the different virtual networks are deployed. Figure 9-3 provides a sample SDA underlay network.

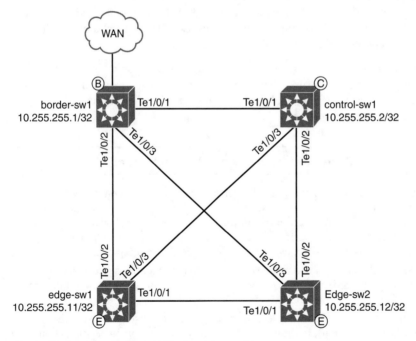

Figure 9-3   *Sample SDA Underlay Network*

An SDA fabric consists of edge nodes (where endpoints are connected), border nodes (connecting the fabric to the outside world), and control nodes (handling the lookups within the fabric). In this sample underlay network, a single control and a single border node are configured with two edge nodes. In this specific topology an extra link is created between the two edge nodes. The IS-IS routing protocol will solve this loop in the network as each link between the nodes is an IP link.

Two options are available to deploy the underlay network within SDA: LAN automation and manual configuration. The following sections briefly describe both options. The Software Defined Access Design Guide[1] and Software Defined Access Deployment Guide[2] by Cisco provide more detail about the required steps to configure an underlay network.

LAN Automation

LAN automation is introduced within SDA to automatically provision new switches in a fabric with the appropriate configuration for an underlay network. It leverages the PnP standard and process to discover new devices and configure them. To do that, a seed device needs to be configured manually with the appropriate options.

If you start LAN automation for a specific site, an IP pool is reserved for the underlay network. This IP pool is then divided into four equally sized segments:

- One segment is used for the loopback addresses of each node in the fabric.

- One segment is used for the configuration of the routed links between nodes (using /30 netmasks).

- One segment is used for defining the hand-off networks on the border nodes that link the fabric to external networks.

- The fourth segment is not used.

LAN automation works as designed, but some points require extra attention:

- **Size of IP address pool:** You have to carefully calculate the size of the IP pool used for LAN automation. Because it is divided by four, the IP space for the point-to-point links can quickly become depleted. And once a segment is depleted, the LAN automation will fail for the remaining underlay devices and they need to be configured by hand. The best method to calculate the size of the IP address pool is to identify the number of links in the fabric, multiply that by 16 (four to account for each /30 subnet and four because this segment is one-fourth of the address pool), and scale that number up to the first largest IP subnet. For example, if the fabric contains 7 links, the minimal IP space would be 7 times 16 equals 112. The first IP subnet would be 128. This would create space for one extra link.

- **LAN automation can run only once:** LAN automation leverages the PnP process and is assumed to run only once. Extra links added afterward—for example, adding a second border node for redundancy—would require manual configuration. The LAN

1   https://www.cisco.com/c/dam/en/us/td/docs/solutions/CVD/Campus/CVD-Software-Defined-Access-Design-Guide-2019SEP.pdf

2   https://www.cisco.com/c/en/us/td/docs/solutions/CVD/Campus/sda-fabric-deploy-2019jul.html

automation process cannot run that network. This point was specifically applicable to Cisco DNA Center 1.2. Later versions provide more functionality. Always read the release notes and guides for the specific DNAC version if this point is applicable.

- **Dynamic VLAN assignment for border nodes:** One of the earlier experiences with SDA is that LAN automation automatically selects a VLAN in the range 3000 and higher for the handoff between the border node router and the external networks. It is theoretically possible to have two border nodes use two different VLANs for handoff for the same virtual network. This was an experience found in the earlier stages of SDA, and it is expected that this will be changed over time. A test in the lab environment will determine if this is still the case.

- **Running out of DHCP addresses:** LAN automation leverages the PnP process. In other words, a DHCP server with a specific DHCP option is used to hand out IP addresses to the switches in the new fabric. If devices are already connected to that same fabric, they will be connected to the same VLAN1 that is used for PnP by default. This can have as a side effect that the endpoints claim all DHCP addresses, and the switch nodes are not getting an IP address. There are two workarounds for this potential issue. One is to disconnect all devices, which is difficult and requires extra work in an existing environment. The other is to use a different VLAN for PnP by leveraging the **pnp startup-vlan** *<vlanid>* command on the seed device. This option will enable PnP running on that specific vlanid instead of the default VLAN1.

In conclusion, LAN automation provides a clean method of deploying a new fabric; however, it can come with some drawbacks that require attention beforehand and during the rollout.

Manual Configuration

An alternative to LAN automation is to configure the SDA underlay network manually. You will recall that an SDA fabric consists of edge, border, and control nodes and uses LISP, VXLAN, and VRFs to create the different virtual networks. For the underlay network, SDA leverages numbered links between the switches, a VRF-aware routing protocol (best practice is IS-IS), and loopback addresses for management access and route exchanges.

Although manual configuration will take more manual work, you will not run into the attention points of LAN automation.

Besides regular global switch configuration, such as authentication, authorization, and accounting; management access; and enabling security features; the following configurations must be made for an SDA underlay network in addition to the generic global configuration of a switch in the campus network:

- Configuration of links
- Configuration of loopback0
- Underlay routing configuration

The following sections describe these configuration needs in more detail.

Configuration of Links

All links between the different nodes need to be configured as routed links with a /30 network link. The configuration in Example 9-1 can be used for each link.

Example 9-1   *Configuration of a Link Between Two SDA Switches*

```
interface $linkToNodeInFabric
 description link in fabric
 no switchport
 dampening
 ip address $localAddress 255.255.255.252
 ip pim sparse-mode
 ip router isis
 logging event link-status
 load-interval 30
 no bfd echo
 bf interval 500 min_rx 500 multiplier 3
 isis network point-to-point
 clns mtu 1400
!
```

The configuration in Example 9-1 combines a number of technologies or specific configurations for SDA:

- **No switchport:** Configures the interface as a routed port and disables all Layer 2 protocols

- **ip router is-is and isis network point-to-point:** Configures the interface to run IS-IS in a point-to-point network type

- **no bfd echo and bfd interval:** Bidirectional Forwarding Detection (BFD) configuration to allow for fast link-down detection in case of a failure

- **ip pim sparse mode:** Configures multicast on the interface to run in sparse mode to reduce multicast traffic

Configuration of Loopback0

Loopback0 must be used with an IPv4 address for management as the SDA fabric assumes that loopback0 is used for this purpose. By using a loopback address for management, the management tool (Cisco DNA Center) can connect to the switch regardless of the path (route) the traffic is taking. It is recommended to use loopback0 for all management and control protocols, such as SSH, HTTP, and RADIUS (for authentication). Example 9-2 demonstrates.

> **Note** Recommended practice dictates that you inject a summary route for the underlay network on the border nodes, so that each node is reachable from DNA Center and other network management tools regardless of which links are used within the fabric.

Example 9-2 *Loopback0 Configuration for Management Access*

```
Interface loopback0

  ip address $mgmtIPAddress 255.255.255.255

!

ip radius source-interface loopback0

ip ssh source-interface loopback0
```

Underlay Routing Configuration

IS-IS is the preferred routing protocol within an SDA fabric and must be configured on each node to learn about the underlay routes. Example 9-3 demonstrates the configuration.

Example 9-3 *SDA Underlay Routing Configuration Using IS-IS*

```
router isis

  net $isis-network_id_map

  domain-password $isisPassword

  metric-style wide

  nsf ietf

  bfd all-interfaces

!
```

Section Summary

In summary, there are two methods to deploy an underlay network for an SDA fabric. The manual configuration may have higher reliability and currently provide more robustness in the deployment, but it is also more error-prone and will require more manual work by the operations team, which is kind of counterproductive to one of the goals of Intent-Based Networking.

At the end of this task, the campus location is enabled with an underlay network for an SDA fabric.

Although the SDA underlay network is now configured, no endpoint can connect to that specific network location. At this stage, there are no services (virtual networks) designed and deployed to the fabric. The first step is to translate the existing network for that campus location (use the inventory from phase one and the lists for standardization from phase two) into virtual networks with basic connectivity policies using DNA Center. Once these virtual networks are provisioned, endpoints can connect to the newly created SDA fabric network.

Classic VLAN

An Intent-Based Network using classic VLANs and VRFs greatly resembles the standardized configuration established in phase two. That standardized configuration is essentially the Intent-Based Network with all Intents enabled. However, the standardized configuration from phase two might not be meeting all requirements set for an Intent-Based network using VLANs.

Therefore, this step is used to extract a baseline (for both access and distribution) from that standardized switch configuration and execute the necessary changes on the first campus location.

The baseline for an Intent-Based Network using VLANs is leveraging the loop-free and high availability capabilities of a collapsed-core campus design with some slight modifications to meet the requirements. Figure 9-4 shows the collapsed-core design used for a classic VLAN Intent-Based Network.

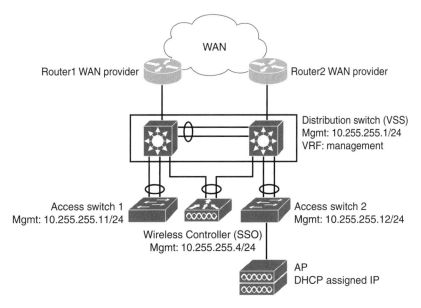

Figure 9-4   *Collapsed Core Campus Design for Intent-Based Networks*

The primary goal for the baseline configuration of this network is to have a minimal configuration for the switches. All configuration items in the baseline are as static as possible, because the baseline is the "underlay" network for an Intent-Based Network.

A single management VLAN is used for connectivity between the switches and DNA Center. This VLAN is logically separated in its own Management VRF. The WAN is preferably connected with two uplinks that support a VRF-aware routing protocol, such as Multi-Protocol BGP, to create virtual networks. This requirement is similar to the requirements for a border node on SDA. Spanning Tree is not used in this topology, but BPDUGuard and broadcast storm detection are enabled on the network.

Phase two established a standardized switch configuration for all services and functional networks on the campus. Although it is not an Intent-Based Network (just) yet, the result of this standardized configuration is effectively the same, having an operational campus network with a baseline and running all requested intents. The following sections describe how a baseline for this network can be extracted from the standardized switch configurations, which was one of the results of phase two.

Extracting a Baseline

For an Intent-Based perspective two roles exist within the wired campus network: the access switch providing the Layer 2 connectivity and the distribution switch to provide Layer 3 connectivity and virtual network isolation.

It is possible to use the same procedure to extract a baseline for both roles. At the end of this procedure, two templates (baseline and requested intents) have been created for both roles. The steps of this procedure are as follows:

Step 1.   Create two backups of the (running) configuration; these backups are the configurations that will be worked on.

Step 2.   Remove all VLANs and associated configuration to build a minimal (foundation) configuration.

Step 3.   Remove other configuration related to specific business requirements to further clean up the configuration.

Step 4.   Transform the remainder of the configuration to realize a minimal baseline configuration that can be deployed.

Step 5.   Save the baseline template.

Step 6.   Create an Intent template that contains all current implemented Intents on the network.

Step 7.   Validate is used to validate whether the extraction of a baseline template is missing functions or features.

Each step is explained in more detail in the following sections.

Step 1: Create Two Backups of the (Running) Configuration

The first step is to create two backups of the standardized configuration. One backup is used as the source for the rest of the steps below. If templates were created in phase two, these templates can be used as a source, but only the combined result of all individually created templates. In other words, the source for extraction needs to be a complete configuration for a single switch. The configuration can have variables (using templates as source) in it, but it must be a complete configuration.

Step 2: Remove All VLANs and Associated Configuration

Almost all VLANs in a campus network reflect a specific function or service provided to the business; a VLAN essentially represents a piece of Intent to be run on the campus network. In this step the source configuration is stripped of all VLANs and the related configuration so that the business-specific configuration can be separated from the minimal management configuration. The only VLAN that remains is a management VLAN and its associated IP address for management access. All configuration associated with a VLAN, such as routing configuration and VRF definitions, must be removed as well. The end result is that the source file now only can be used for management access to the device.

Step 3: Remove Other Configuration Related to Specific Business Requirements

It is possible that specific business requirements for the network are configured and are not directly related to the switch. An example of such configuration could be Quality of Service. Only user-defined or user-required features are to be removed. Global security features that need to be enabled by default, such as IPv6 RA Guard, IP DHCP Snooping, and IP Device Tracking, should be left inside the source template. The rule of thumb that can be applied in this step is that if a feature is applicable for all, it needs to remain in the template; if it is network- or user-specific, remove it.

Step 4: Transform Remainder of Configuration

The result of the previous steps is that the source configuration is stripped of all Intents created and deployed on the network. This source template can now be transformed into a baseline template for an Intent-Based Network. Use the following list to validate whether the source file covers the following features (if this is not the case, change the source file accordingly):

- **Connectivity to the network on management VLAN:** The management VLAN and its related settings (such as IP address, netmask, and routing information) need to be defined in the source file. Having a management VLAN is a requirement for a classic VLAN-based deployment for IBN. The management VLAN could be in-band with a dedicated management VRF or the dedicated out-of-band management port could be used with an out-of-band network. Both use cases are valid as long as the management of the devices is separated from other network traffic.

- **Restricted management access:** Management access to any device should be restricted. Configure the source file in such a way that management access to the device is restricted, and preferably clear-text management protocols such as HTTP and telnet are prohibited.

- **Disabled Spanning Tree:** Spanning Tree should be disabled on the campus network. The strong preference is to disable Spanning Tree completely and configure the source file to leverage BPDUGuard and storm control to prevent accidental loops. If, as an exception, a single campus location has physical loops in the access network by design, then MST should be configured with a single instance.

- **First hop security:** Security is an integral part of any Intent-Based Network. Configure the best practices for first hop security. This should include IPv6 first hop security as well, whether the enterprise consciously uses IPv6 or not (see below).

- **RADIUS configuration for IEEE 802.1x:** RADIUS is required for downloading policies and specific intents from the central policy server. Include the RADIUS configuration in the source file.

- **Standard access port-configuration:** Intent-Based Networking leverages the policy server to push policies based on the identity connected to a network. Consequently, a default access port configuration can be created and deployed. Use a macro to define the default access port configuration and leverage that macro in the deployment at an access switch.

- **Standard uplink port configuration:** Standardize the uplink port configuration for both the access switches as well as the distribution switch in the relevant source files. Standardize uplinks of access switches to PortChannel1, regardless of the number of uplink members. This approach will greatly benefit the standardization and validation of Intents. For larger deployments it is recommended to have a wireless controller on the location. Use a dedicated port channel number and configuration to connect the wireless controller. This again greatly benefits the standardization. An example could be that on the distribution switch, PortChannel1 and PortChannel2 are used for VSS, PortChannel5 for Wireless, PortChannel8 and PortChannel9 for uplinks to the WAN, and PortChannels to access switches are numbered sequentially from 11.

IPv6 First Hop Security

IPv6 is a separate protocol stack from IPv4 and is (eventually) the successor to IPv4. Some networks run IPv4 and IPv6 side by side (Dual Stack), but many enterprise networks primarily run IPv4. To smooth the transition to IPv6 networks, the RFC states that operating systems should prefer IPv6 networks and connectivity over IPv4, if that connectivity exists. To conform to this RFC, most recent device (or host) operating systems, connecting to the network, have IPv6 enabled by default. Even if the enterprise is not using IPv4 itself, IPV6 is run on the network because of these clients and the fact that IPv6 can be run without DHCP servers. As IPv6 is run, unaware of the security team, the behavior of IPv6 before IPv4 can be misused by a malicious user. Therefore, it is recommended to deploy IPv6 first hop security mechanisms in the campus network, regardless of whether the enterprise is operating an IPv6 network.

The distribution switch is used to provide IP connectivity for the different intents and potentially isolate the different intents leveraging VRFs. The source file for the distribution switch must also include the following aspects:

■ **Management VRF definition:** Management traffic should be isolated from running intents. It can be compared with the underlay network in an SDA deployment. Configure the distribution switch with the appropriate management VRF.

■ **VRF-aware route configuration:** As intents are deployed on the network, some of them will leverage VRF to isolate networks from each other. Create a standardized configuration for the routing protocol and include the management. Configurations deployed on the distribution switch for VRFs should easily be integrated with the routing protocol configuration. The most commonly deployed routing protocol for such situations would be BGP.

■ **Uplink to WAN:** The distribution switch is also responsible for the connectivity and uplink to the WAN. Create an uplink port channel configuration that allows for easy addition and removal of peer-to-peer VLANs for the connection of the different virtual networks to the WAN networks.

At the end of this step, the resultant source file can be seen as the baseline template for an Intent-based network. It contains all required configuration for management, globally enabled security, and network features. This source file creates the ability to add and remove intents onto the network.

Step 5: Save as Baseline Template

Review the result of the previous step and attempt to create variables for values that are specific for the organization. These variables commonly include hostname, domain name, log settings, management server IP addresses, and so on. Once these values have been defined as variables, save the result as a baseline template for the specific role (wired or wireless). It is recommended to explain and document the different created variables as well.

Step 6: Create an Intent Template

Now that a baseline template is created, the next step is to create an intent template that matches all current networks and services on the campus network. To create this template, compare the just-created baseline template with the second backup file. The differences contain all intents and potentially configurations that were intentionally removed in the baseline. Review the differences and remove those configurations. Save the result in an intent template that can be deployed. Appendix B, "Sample Configurations," contains a sample configuration for an Intent template for a new virtual network.

Step 7: Validate

The last step of the procedure is to validate whether the two newly created templates are valid for the existing network. This validation either can be executed in the lab environment or merge the two templates and compare that with the backup that was taken as the first step. Fix potential differences, specifically in user- or function-specific features such as VLANs, QoS, and so on.

The result of this procedure is that two templates have been created for each role (access and distribution). The baseline has been extracted from the standardized configuration from phase two.

Migration Strategies

There are two distinct options to deploy the just-created baseline to the first Intent-Based Network location.

Option 1: Using Automation

The easiest method of deploying this new topology is by leveraging Cisco DNA Center's templating capabilities in combination with PnP. Based on the previous steps, at least four templates have been created with the extraction of the baseline:

- Baseline template for access switch

- Baseline template for distribution switch

- Template with all running networks for an access switch

- Template with all running networks for the distribution switch

Cisco DNA Center PnP functionality allows you to define a bootstrap template for new devices (day0 operation) and assign templates to a site as network profile. Switches that belong to that site will get that profile (and thus associated templates) provisioned. This capability is leveraged in the process of deploying the templates to the first Intent-Based Network location in the following steps:

Step 1.   Define a network profile and associate the intent templates to the site.

Step 2.   Attach the baseline template for an access switch to that same site as the bootstrap template.

Step 3.   Configure the distribution switch cleanly using the baseline template for the distribution switch. This is a manual step as VSS requires manual configuration and reboots that cannot be automated using PnP.

Step 4.   Discover the new distribution switch and attach it to the site. This allows Cisco DNA Center to provision the intent template to the distribution switch.

Step 5.   Erase the configuration of the access switches and reload them to initiate the PnP process.

Note   To restart the PnP agent on access switches, the following files are to be deleted: running-configuration, vlan database, private-keys, certificates, and all files starting with pnp.

Step 6.   Leverage the PnP process to attach the baseline template to the access switches to provide the baseline.

At the end of step 6, all network devices are assigned and provisioned to the specific site. Because the templates are assigned to that same site, the transformation to an Intent-Based Network for that location is completed.

Although a lot of the transformation is automated, it does require a restart and therefore downtime on the campus location. That should be accounted for in the appropriate service windows. The procedure, just as the templates, should be validated in the lab environment first.

Option 2: Manual Configuration

Alternatively, if downtime of the campus location is not permitted, it is possible to configure the baseline using manual configuration. To do that, specific migration plans should be written that attempt to keep the disruptions to a minimum. The migration plan should have "before," "during," and "after" (migration) stages, and special consideration should be put in the migration guide to keep the period of "during" as short as possible, as that phase results in a mixed situation. Also, if changes are executed remotely and the management IP is changed, there is a risk of disconnecting the device and failing the change. In general, the manual configuration could take the following procedural approach:

Step 1.   Migrate management to the baseline.

Step 2.   Remove unnecessary services.

Step 3.   Prepare the distribution switch for new configuration (merge baseline into running).

Step 4.   Migrate access switches individually to the new configuration.

Step 5.   Remove the old configuration from the distribution switch.

Step 6.   Validate configuration and compare with the baseline.

In general, a manual configuration change takes more time in both preparation and execution. A balance should be made between the required effort for manual configuration and the disruption with a tested automated transition.

Regardless of the method, at the end of the migration, there is a baseline configuration deployed to the location, and two generic intent templates are deployed for that location. The first location is now converted to an Intent-Based Network.

Convert to Intents

At this stage, the first campus location is now running off an Intent-Based Network. The campus location is using a baseline configuration and quite possibly a single large intent running on top of it that covers all existing available services on the campus network for that location. And although the baseline is there, it does not completely make it an Intent-Based Network because that requires a number of intents that are applied to the network.

And as written in Part I, "Overview of Intent-Based Networking," Intent-Based Networking is about translating a business intent (or functional intent) into a number of building blocks of configurations that are pushed onto the network, while another process continuously validates whether those building blocks function and operate as intended. The goal of this step is to extract the different existing intents that currently run on the campus network of the organization. A similar approach is leveraged as to how wastewater is filtered at a treatment facility: the first filtering is for coarse material, and with each step finer material is filtered out of the water. To extract the different existing intents, the following four actions are used:

1. **Define intents for global services:** First define (based on the services currently running on the campus network) the globally available network services that can be defined as intents. DHCP and DNS are essentially network services that are commonly tightly integrated into specific functional networks and should not be seen as global services. Internet access could be seen as a global service.

2. **Define intents on the functional network level:** Define the different functional networks running on the campus network. Usually enterprises have functional networks for employees, guest services, IP cameras, physical security, printers, BYOD devices, wireless access points, and so on. If there are specific requirements for each functional network identified, these requirements should be identified as well.

3. **Define intents for groups of devices:** Intents at this level describe the required network functions and services for specific groups of endpoints within a functional network. An example would be a special IoT sensor network that is only allowed to communicate with its collector, or a specific controller that is only allowed to communicate with the light switches. Another example of specific intents could be to subdivide employees into manufacturing, sales, HR, and so on.

4. **Define intents for applications:** The finest level of intents are the requirements to the network from applications. The most common example for this is the requirement for Quality of Service for voice and video communication networks.

This model-driven approach to intents allows an enterprise to grow the concept of Intent-based networking as well as the ability to provide intents from generic to specific. All found intents are registered in a table, which not only describes the intent, but also documents special requirements. Preferably information such as whether the Intent is wired only, wireless only, or on protocol level is recorded as well. Table 9-1 provides an example.

Table 9-1 *Sample Table for the Definition of Intents*

Intent Name	Description	Wired	Wireless	Special Requirements
Internet access	To provide Internet access to all endpoints connected to the network	Yes	Yes	Traffic needs to be inspected by a next-generation firewall.
Guest access	Wireless guest access	No	Yes	Only access after a sponsor created account and acceptance of AUP.
BYOD access	Bring Your Own Device is allowed	Yes	Yes	Only allow access after successful onboarding to Cisco ISE.
Security cameras	CCTV for physical security	Yes	No	Special access for video wall; emergency response can connect after support requests.
Key-fobs	Key-fobs on all doors	No	Yes	Only allowed connection to door management system.

After the table of Intents is determined, the most difficult part of this step is to be executed: to use these intents and the running configuration of the campus location to extract templates for those intents. In other words, the intents described have been implemented by specific configuration items in the campus network. *The art is now to generalize the different intents into templates that can be reused over and over again.*

Although this step can be difficult, it will eventually make or break the power of automation and the success of deploying new intents onto the network. For example, for the campus network itself it is irrelevant if the requested intent is a wireless guest network or a wireless network for employees. They are both essentially virtual networks that should be separated logically. Similarly, depending on the security policy, a wireless BYOD network might be the same network as the wireless guest network, but they only require a different SSID. In conclusion, these three different intents can leverage the same template for virtual wireless networks.

Use Case: Extracting Intents from Existing Wireless Networks

At the introduction of wireless networks at FinTech Ltd., they deployed three wireless networks: one for visitors and external contractors, one for employees, and one special network for management. The reasons behind these three wireless networks were politics and security. They wanted to rotate the preshared key for the guest network every month without requiring employees to change the password as well. The political reason was to provide a bit more quality service (using a higher QoS level) to management devices. As security dictated that the wireless network was not allowed to be shared with the production network, all networks were terminated at the same Internet access outbreak, leveraging three VLANs, one for each wireless network.

At the time of transformation to Intent-Based Networking, it was possible to translate these three distinct wireless networks into a single wireless network template using variables as input parameters. The following parameters were defined:

Name: Name of the wireless intent

SSID: Name of the wireless SSID

BroadcastSSID: Boolean to determine whether the SSID is broadcasted

externalVLAN: VLAN to which traffic was terminated

preSharedKey: Preshared key to use for this wireless network

The other configurable items on the wireless network were the same. If the guest password had to be rotated, the template would be deployed again with a new value for the preSharedKey.

This use case demonstrates that generalization of specific implementations using templates and parameterization is essentially the power of Intent-Based Networking. If the operations team is experiencing difficulty with creating the templates based on the running configuration of the campus location, it is an option to temporarily acquire external skills to support the team.

For example, software designers are experts on translating specific use cases (intents) into logical programmable bits (templates). This process does require a special mindset and way of thinking, and getting extra support can be beneficial. The network operations team also benefits in their first steps to learn programmability.

Once the templates of the running intents have been completed, these templates can be imported into Cisco DNA Center (or another tool used to translate intent to automation). As these templates are imported, they will also be deployed onto the single campus location to bring the campus location to a fully Intent-Based Network.

Extend Intent Based

At this stage a single location of the campus network is deployed and configured as an Intent-Based Network. Some incidents or problems will occur during the transformation and identification of individual intents. Document the lessons you learned, and apply them as you plan to extend the transition further. The next step is to extend the Intent-Based Network in two directions: location and isolation of intents, as described in the following sections.

Location

The easiest direction to extend is the location. Use the same procedures and operations from the first location to transform other campus locations to Intent-Based Networking as well. Although this is a logical step, it is important to note that it is recommended to bring more locations into Intent-Based Networking in a controlled manner, one site at a time with enough time to fix specific site issues. The restriction of one site per migration reduces the impact of solving incidents (due to migration) at two locations at the same time, and experiences learned from one migration can benefit the next.

The WAN between the different Intent-Based Network locations uses VPNs to logically isolate the virtual networks over the WAN. If SDA is used for the Intent-Based Network, the concept of an SDA Distributed Campus (also known as SDA multisite) becomes an option. The SDA Distributed Campus concept defines a special transit network (SDA transit network) between the individual SDA fabric networks deployed at each campus location.

The SD-Access Transit network interconnects the border nodes of each fabric. The SD-Access fabric has a separate control node inside the fabric that is used to store and aggregate endpoint lookups from the individual control nodes in the individual fabrics. This exchange is achieved via communication to the border nodes of each individual fabric and the transit control node. Figure 9-5 displays a transit network between two campus locations.

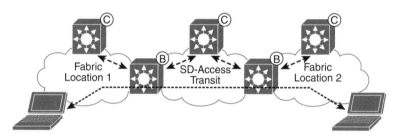

Figure 9-5 *Conceptual Overview of SD-Access Distributed Campus Deployment*

Because route information is exchanged, a border node in an individual fabric can look up a destination and send the packet directly to a border node of another fabric. This allows for a more direct communication path between the two nodes. Although there is a more direct path, the concept of encapsulation and decapsulation at the border of each domain remains, resulting in the three distinct encapsulation points (edge-to-border in location 1, border 1 to border 2 in the Transit, and border to edge in Location 2). Because the same mechanism as in an SDA fabric is used, an end-to-end security policy for point-to-point communication can be created. DNA Center manages the SD-Access transit network automatically. The SD-Access transit network itself can be an IP-based transit network (which will map virtual networks to VRF-Lite or MPLS networks) or be a separate SDA-based fabric. Deploying an SD-Access transit network provides an extra level of automation and security to the Intent-Based Network. Leverage this action to deploy an SD-Access transit network, if applicable.

Intents

Another direction to extend to is the isolation of intents. Although the individual intents have been defined with the appropriate templates with the previous action, there is a chance that each individual intent is run on the same IP network. In other words, there might be limited to no isolation of intents deployed on the campus network.

For example, different IoT network devices, point-of-sale devices in the cafeteria, and other third-party managed devices could be residing in a single Intent. The logical isolation of these functional devices will increase the security of the Intent-Based Network too.

This isolation of intents is that, regardless of whether classic VLANs or SDA are used for the new campus network, both have the possibility to logically separate and isolate intents that benefit from isolation, whether it is the risk of cross-infection or from a security perspective. Use this step to identify which intents can logically be isolated and perform that isolation by adopting or adjusting the earlier created templates.

Section Summary

In summary, both directions of extension should be executed in this task. At the end of this task, the Intent-Based Network is extended to all campus locations. Also if existing intents can be logically separated, for security or other reasons, this task is used to achieve that goal as well. The complete campus network is now operated as an Intent-Based Network.

Increase Security

At this stage within phase three, an Intent-Based Network is operational across all campus locations. However, an integral part of Intent-Based Networking is network security; it is enabled by default in the network.

In phase two it was acceptable to leverage the MAC address for assigning a specific policy to a specific device. This was acceptable to make the transition from port-centric to policy-centric easier and smoother.

However, a MAC address can easily be spoofed using simple property changes within Windows or using a CLI command on Apple macOS or Linux-based systems. MAC addresses cannot be used for authenticating a network device.

This final step in the transformation to Intent-Based Networking is used to refine and improve security in the campus network. The primary reason that this step is executed as the last step for this phase is that (possibly) introducing IEEE 802.1x has an impact on all connecting endpoints.

802.1x Security

As stated, the MAC address cannot be used for authenticating an endpoint (or user) to the network as it can easily be spoofed (faked). The mechanism to use the MAC address is also known as MAC Authentication Bypass (MAB), and it literally says quite clearly that authentication is bypassed. It is meant for situations where an endpoint does not support the IEEE 802.1x standard. However, IEEE 802.1x has been supported since Windows XP SP3. In other words, any modern operating system supports the IEEE 802.1x standard for authentication.

This task is only applicable if no IEEE 802.1x solution was deployed to the campus network and in phase two the MAC addresses were used to migrate from port-centric to policy-centric.

The implementation of IEEE 802.1x can have an impact on the user experience, as an endpoint needs to be authenticated before it is allowed onto the network. In other words, if the authentication fails, the endpoint is denied access to the network and the user will raise an incident. To keep the impact at a minimum, a phased approach introducing IEEE 802.1x is recommended. It is strongly recommended to use the lab environment in each phase before changes are executed in production. Besides keeping outages to a minimum, it assists in learning the process to test before running into production by the operations team.

Requirements

But before the first phase is to be executed, it is good to understand what the requirements are for the introduction of IEEE 802.1x onto the network. The following requirements are a minimum.

- **Support for IEEE 802.1x by endpoints:** This is, of course, an obvious requirement, but most devices must be able to support IEEE 802.1x with one of the authentication mechanisms. Most modern endpoints, such as workstations, IP cameras, printers, and IP phones, support IEEE 802.1x. Not all these devices support certificates for authentication, but they often do support username/password as a mechanism. All statements that an endpoint does not support IEEE 802.1x must be validated with the vendor, as firmware upgrades or unfamiliarity might trigger such a statement.

- **RADIUS server:** Another critical requirement for IEEE 802.1x is the central policy server running the RADIUS protocol. Phase two has made sure that a RADIUS server is already installed with policies for establishing a policy-centric model in the campus network.

- **Switch and wireless configuration:** The same is applicable for the access switches and the wireless controllers. The switches already have an active RADIUS configuration for receiving the policies for Intent. The wireless network might not be leveraging RADIUS yet, but it is by default capable of configuring IEEE 802.1x (see sidebar).

Note   IEEE 802.1x has been embedded in wireless networking since the introduction of WPA. IEEE 802.1x is an integral part of the WPA2 enterprise solution. And as such, all wireless devices support IEEE 802.1x username/password or certificates for authentication. It is important to note that it is best practice to not use Microsoft Active Directory credentials to access the corporate wireless network. The reason behind this is that the username and password will be stored by the wireless endpoint to prevent asking the user to enter the password every time the device attempts to connect to the wireless network. A smartphone often disconnects from the wireless network to save battery power and quickly connects in the background when the user activates the phone.

The wireless network name including the credentials are stored in a preferred network list.

A malicious actor can easily use the corporate wireless network name and broadcast that network in, for example, a restaurant. The smartphone is unaware that it is not at an actual corporate location but thinks it is because of the wireless network name. The smartphone uses its preferred network list and tries to connect. After a few retries the wireless network automatically grants access and the smartphone thinks it is connected.

Although the password itself is not sent wirelessly in clear-text to the malicious wireless network, there are easy ways to decode the password based on the information received by the malicious actor's access point.

If the Active Directory credentials were used for wireless access, this method would be easy to obtain those credentials and use them for other access as well.

This is the primary reason that a username/password is not recommended for wireless networks. Certificates are much more secure, as they leverage the asymmetric encryption characteristics for mutual authentication, and no credentials are shared.

Deploying certificates for wireless access is not difficult at all with modern solutions like mobile device management, AD group policies, and the BYOD PKI infrastructure within Cisco ISE.

Phase One: Introducing and Configuring IEEE 802.1x

Once the requirements are met, the network can be configured for the first steps in network access control. In phase two the network was configured to only use MAB for the authentication protocol. In this phase, the 802.1x authentication method, including tuned timers (for faster failover), is added to the default access port template. You can use the configuration in Example 9-4 to add 802.1x to the access port configuration. It is important that you disable port security as well because it conflicts with IEEE 802.1x and will cause problems.

Example 9-4 *Adding 802.1x to Access Port Configuration*

```
interface $AccessPort
 no switchport port-security
 authentication host-mode multi-domain
 authentication order dot1x mab
 authentication open
 authentication priority dot1x mab
 dot1x timeout tx-period 2
 dot1x max-reauth-req 3
!
```

The configuration in Example 9-4 tells the switch to first try IEEE 802.1x (dot1x) and then MAB. An alternative method for configuring IEEE 802.1X (and other switchport features) is by using Autoconf, which was introduced in Cisco IOS 15.2(2)E. Information about AutoConf is found in *Cisco Identity Based Networking Services Configuration Guide.*[3]

Besides the switchport configuration, the RADIUS server needs to be configured with the appropriate authentication and access policies. These policies must match the existing policies that leverage MAB.

The cooperation of the appropriate departments is required to configure the endpoints for IEEE 802.1x as well. Once they are configured, those endpoints will start to use IEEE 802.1x instead of MAB.

As the network was already configured properly with MAB, the risk of an endpoint not connecting to the network would be lower, as the fallback was already working.

Phase Two: Monitor and Improve

Once the network and endpoints are configured for IEEE 802.1x, the phase of "monitor and improve" is initiated. In this phase, the teams responsible for campus and endpoints closely work together. They continually monitor which endpoints should be able to authenticate using IEEE 802.1x but are using MAB. Each endpoint needs to be treated as an incident to be resolved. It could be that certain settings need to be tuned or other reasons.

Over time, the number of endpoints not authenticating using IEEE 802.1x will decrease to either zero or a limited number of devices that do not support IEEE 802.1x.

Phase Three: Optimize Policies

Once the number of endpoints using MAB is reduced to a minimum, the authentication and authorization policies in the RADIUS server are to be optimized. At this stage there

---

3 https://www.cisco.com/c/en/us/td/docs/ios-xml/ios/ibns/configuration/15-e/ibns-15-e-book.html

is essentially still a double set of policies: one for IEEE 802.1x and one for MAB. In this phase, the MAB policies that became obsolete will be removed and thus the policies of the RADIUS server will be optimized. Monitoring that this optimization of policies does not raise incidents is obviously an integral part of this phase.

After finishing phase three, the campus network has successfully introduced IEEE 802.1x to the campus network.

Scalable Group Tags

At this stage the campus is Intent-Based and groups of devices are divided into virtual networks based on their identity and authorization. Each virtual network has its own security policy based on the requested intents, IP addresses, and access lists.

Virtual networks alone might not provide enough security, however. It is possible, based on the intents, that within a virtual network, specific groups of devices are not allowed to access specific resources for a reason. For example, employees from sales are not allowed to access resources dedicated for human resources (GDPR being one of the reasons).

In other words, microsegmentation is required and is an integral part of an Intent-Based Network.

Scalable Group Tags (SGT, introduced as Source or Security Group tags with the introduction of Cisco TrustSec), are used to implement the required microsegmentation within a virtual network. Appendix A, "Campus Network Technologies," contains a detailed explanation of the concept and technology behind SGTs.

The key advantage of SGT is that a security policy can be defined based on a policy label (tag) and not on the IP address. This allows for a generic, simplified access policy and for microsegmentation.

Use Case: Example of Microsegmentation Leveraging SGT

SharedService Group is responsible for a large number of campus networks. SharedService leverages VDI to provide desktop services to its end users from consolidated datacenters. Because a large number of users are mobile and travel, most managed workstations accessing the network (via a docking station or wireless) are based on laptops with local profiles.

Fortunately, the campus network of SharedService Group was not hit with the nPetya outbreak in June 2017 or any other ransomware outbreak that distributes itself laterally through the network. But the risk of such an outbreak and the consequences were identified and mitigations had to be placed on the campus network.

As SharedService was migrating to Intent-Based Networks, they leveraged SGTs to provide a solution. An SGT-labeled managedWorkstation was created. Inside the policy matrix, a deny was defined for the communication from label managedWorkstation to managed-Workstation.

As devices are authenticated against Cisco ISE, they received this label. The access switches already downloaded the SGACL from Cisco ISE and are applied to ingress traffic from an access port, thus preventing horizontal communication within the virtual network for managed workstations.

Within this phase the intents for the campus network were identified in one of the previous steps. If microsegmentation is required for any of these intents, this step can be used to introduce and implement SGTs and the appropriate security policy into the network.

If the transition to Intent-Based Networking is based on classic VLANs, it is important to determine the support of SGTs on the different catalyst switches run in the access layer of the campus network. As a rule of thumb, any switch that is Cisco DNA-ready is capable of handling SGTs and SGACLs. Catalyst 2960 series switches are not Cisco DNA-ready, and special caution needs to be taken and support needs to be validated. The support for SGT can differ on the IOS version that is run on the switch.

With an SDA-based network, Cisco DNA Center can be used to define the microsegmentation policies if Cisco DNA Center is integrated with Cisco ISE. For classic VLAN deployments, both the policy matrix and the specific authorization policies need to be defined manually within ISE. As with any change to the network, it is recommended to test the new security policy on the lab environment first.

Risks

Phase three brings the tangible result of realizing an Intent-Based Network on all campus locations of the enterprise. All preparatory work comes to fruition in a smooth transition to an Intent-Based Network. Although this sounds positive, a number of risks are involved in this phase. The following sections describe these risks and how they can be mitigated.

Transition to SDA

From an organizational perspective, there are a number of reasons why starting Intent-Based Networking using VLANs is valid. Besides several hard reasons like cost of hardware replacement, there is also the cost of migration and operation. The step toward Intent-Based Networks using VLANs is lower and easier to implement, once the configurations are standardized.

However, Software Defined Access introduces a number of benefits in the long term that will make it the next evolution for campus networks. There is a risk that once the organization has implemented Intent-Based Networks using VLANs, it considers that the transformation is finished, which is not true at all.

The migration to Software Defined Access will, in due time, occur, also within the enterprise. It is important to periodically keep validating the features of SDA against the application and network requirements of the organization. Once the SDA features meet the specific application and network requirements of the organization, the approach described in this phase can be leveraged to introduce SDA within the campus network as well. The benefit of already running an Intent-Based Network is that the operations team is already accustomed to this new concept of operating the network and should have more time available to prepare the transformation tool.

It is important, until the migration to SDA has also been executed, to maintain communication with the stakeholders and management to reduce the risk of ending the transformation too soon.

Scalability

Phase three contains a step to decide which technology is going to be used for the transformation to Intent-Based Networking—Software Defined Access or a classic VLAN approach. Cisco DNA Center provides the most optimal solution for both types of transformation; however, in the early releases of SDA and Cisco DNA Center, the number of endpoints supported in an SDA fabric and DNA Center as a solution can be a restriction for larger organizations. As Cisco DNA Center and SDA evolve, the supported number of endpoints will increase over time as well.

Although the capacity is weighed in with the choice for which journey and for Cisco DNA Center, there is a risk that the expected number of endpoints used for the decision is underestimated. In other words, the number of endpoints will be higher than anticipated. This risk is heightened with the exponential growth of endpoint devices as well as the introduction of IoT devices. There are two mitigations for this risk, and both should be taken into consideration.

The most important mitigation would be to communicate the restriction and expected growth to management and keep informing them that Cisco DNA Center might need to be replaced at a faster pace than economically expected. This mitigation will bring cost with it, and communicating it in advance will pave the path a bit.

The second mitigation is to either double the estimated number of endpoints connecting to the campus and size DNA Center for that or leverage multiple DNA Center solutions to facilitate for the growth.

Training

An important task in this phase is training. An Intent-Based Network relies heavily on configuration abstractions, templates, automation, and leveraging analytics for faster troubleshooting. It cannot be said often enough, but for successful implementation of IBN it is critical that the operations team execute most of the changes in both the network as well as operation. This means that the network operations team needs to be trained in the different methods of operating the network, leveraging templates, possibly using scripts to program the automation tools, and so on. The operations team needs to execute the changes on the network differently.

Training is an essential part of learning new methods. It requires both background training (theory) and execution (practice). It is assumed (and strongly recommended) that most changes be executed by the network operations team, or they must be strongly involved. Essentially, they practice new methods while converting the campus network.

And although this is a great benefit, it also poses a risk. In many IT-related organizations (there are some exceptions), employers seem to expect that new technologies are to be learned in personal time and not immediately with formal training. For a successful transformation, (in)formal training on the used technologies, the flows, is critical for success. It is recommended to reduce this risk by planning training moments for the network operations team on Intent-Based and SDA, and use the training to get them more involved in the process as well.

Summary

Phase three starts when both the organization as well as the network are prepared to run as an Intent-Based Network. All the hard work on standardization and matching requirements is done, and now the network can actually start to run as an Intent-Based Network. Phase three is about introducing and expanding the Intent-Based Network onto the campus. To successfully execute phase three, six steps are to be executed sequentially:

Step 1. **Lab environment:** A strong recommendation is to set up a lab environment that reflects the campus network as a first step. This allows the team to test new technology, test out migration paths, and learn new technology.

Step 2. **Decide on technology:** Decide which technology is to be used for the transformation to IBN. Although SDA will over time be the next default configuration on a campus network, specific feature requirements or limitations could dictate that a classic VLAN approach is better suited.

Step 3. **Deploy a baseline:** Choose a first location in the campus network and deploy a baseline configuration on that location. Choose the location wisely because it is critical to success. After deployment, the campus network has a baseline configuration and a single Intent that covers all intents for that location.

Step 4. **Convert existing services to intents:** The single intent from step 3 that covers all network services is extracted to individual intents on the campus network.

Step 5. **Extend Intent-Based:** After a single location has been transformed to an Intent-Based Network, use the lessons learned to extend this Intent-Based Network to other locations and Intents.

Step 6.   **Increase security:** A key requirement for IBN is to use IEEE 802.1X for network access control; if the organization does not have IEEE 802.1X yet, this step is used to implement IEEE 802.1X. After IEEE 802.1X has been successfully implemented, leverage Scalable Group Tags to implement microsegmentation and increase security of the network.

This phase brings the tangible result of actually transforming the campus network to Intent-Based Networking. And a lot of preparatory work has been executed in phase one and phase two to make the transformation itself as smooth as possible. However, at this stage some things might go wrong, as a number of risks can be identified and mitigated.

■ **Transition to SDA:** Step 2 in this phase is to decide on a technology for implementing IBN. If classic VLAN is chosen, there is a risk for a sense of "accomplishment" and "finished" after the transformation, and focus on SDA will be lost and thus never be implemented. Keep validating SDA and communicating with stakeholders that SDA is the way to move forward in the long term to mitigate this risk.

■ **Scalability:** Early releases of Cisco DNA Center were limited in scalability. When selecting the Cisco DNA Center solution there is a risk that the sizing is underestimated (an increase in IoT devices could be one of the reasons), and the solution will not perform as expected, resulting in a less accepted and less successful transformation. To mitigate this risk, size the Cisco DNA Center based on a factor two for the number of endpoints. Actively communicate with management that the sizing is based on estimates and that the future can bring other sizing requirements.

■ **Training:** An important aspect of this phase is training. The network operations team is configuring and deploying the transformation to IBN. Although learning on the job is a valid training method, the risk of not reserving time for formal education on the topics can result in decreased performance and the occurrence of problems during transformation that could have been prevented. To mitigate this risk, allow for and organize formal training on the theoretical operation of IBN so that the team learns the foundational technologies behind IBN.

Chapter 10

Phase Four: Enable Intent

The campus network is now transformed into an Intent-Based Network. The campus network, based on a Cisco Digital Network Architecture (DNA) and Intent-Based Networking (IBN), is applied by the network operations team to implement changes faster and have intelligent support from that same network while troubleshooting. The transformation is not complete, however. Only the operations team is familiar with what an Intent-Based Network is capable of.

This is the last phase in the transformation toward IBN and is used to enable Intent throughout the enterprise and maximize the possibilities, opportunities, and capabilities of IBN in the campus network. This phase is not completely based on sequential sets of actions like the previous phases. It is a combination of descriptions as to why Intent needs to be brought to the enterprise, two actions that should be executed sequentially, and some examples of IBN.

This chapter covers the following topics:

- Why extend Intent to the enterprise
- APIs for Intent
- Bringing IBN to the enterprise
- Intent-Based examples

Why Enable Intent Further?

To recap, Intent-Based Networking is a perspective on how to manage and operate a network that is implemented based on the Cisco Digital Network Architecture framework. Cisco DNA defines a number of architectural building blocks, design principles, and how they all relate and cooperate with each component. Figure 10-1 shows the Cisco Digital Network Architecture building blocks.

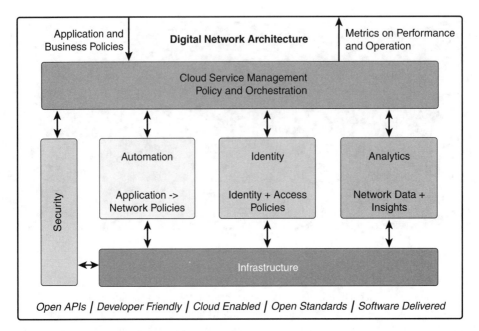

Figure 10-1 *Functions of Cisco Digital Network Architecture*

The previous phases of the transformation focused on how to deploy and manage the intents onto the network. In other words, the focus of the transformation was to leverage the tool within the Policy & Orchestration block to prepare and transform the campus network.

One of the tasks in phase three was to translate current functions and services on the network into Intents with corresponding templates. These Intents were then deployed on the network using Software-Defined Access (SDA) or classic VLANs.

With this step, the campus network effectively transformed into an Intent-Based Network, but it is only one part of the Cisco DNA story. The (technical) mechanisms of deploying an Intent onto the network are now completed, and the building blocks downward of the cloud service management block have been implemented.

An important key feature of Cisco DNA (and thus IBN) is the communication from the Policy and Orchestration block up to the business. In other words, the "northbound" part of Cisco DNA is what makes it the next evolution of networking in general.

With an Intent-enabled network, the business can request a business-based intent from the network. The Policy and Orchestration tool will take that business intent and translate it into the technical mechanisms and network Intents to satisfy the business intent.

Without enabling that key feature, the journey toward IBN is still not complete and is (still) focused on smartly managing and operating a network as an isolated silo.

Now, as the network and operations team is Intent-ready, it is time to communicate and share about the possibilities created during the previous phases. The start would be to incorporate the network (and its services) as an integral part of all business processes of the organization. This is an important final step to a complete Intent-Based Network. The two tasks in this phase describe an approach on how to accomplish this.

APIs for Intent

A key use case for Intent-Based Networking is a business process or business application that has a specific purpose, and to realize that purpose, specific network-related requirements and policies are required. Within a modern enterprise, the number and type of business processes and applications can become quite dynamic (digital business) and require a fast deployment (and removal) of those requirements on the network infrastructure. This is because the network is the connecting factor between endpoints that require access to specific applications or processes in the datacenter or the cloud. To achieve this use case, Application Programming Interfaces (APIs) are a key part of the solution.

APIs are the glue that bind the different building blocks within Cisco DNA together. APIs can be seen as external hooks to provide or perform a specific function or functionality. Traditionally, APIs were used by developers to integrate existing libraries with functions into their own application. In today's environments, APIs not only represent these internal integrations, but also the possibility to request or perform a function or service from a different application or service remotely. The latter mechanism is also known as REST-full APIs and is being used extensively in the application development world to provide or integrate cloud services.

For business intents to be serviced to the enterprise, business-driven intent APIs need to be defined and implemented on the northbound communication.

Use Case: Showcase Using Intent APIs for New Solutions

This use case is not based on one of the example organizations, but from a proof of concept the author wrote and presented at CiscoLive Europe in Barcelona 2019. Cisco introduced Intent APIs within Cisco DNA Center at Cisco Live Europe in 2018. These APIs allow software developers to request information about the network (and endpoints) available within Cisco DNA Center. This essentially allows a developer to request the same data that an operator sees in the Cisco DNA Center user interface. The intent APIs are primarily targeted to make the assurance-based information (analytics component within Cisco DNA) available.

In parallel, Apple made a framework (again using APIs) for Augmented Reality (AR) that included object recognition available in the same time period. Augmented Reality is in contrast to Virtual Reality, a virtual overlay in which software developers can provide a virtual world on top (mixed) of the physical world by leveraging the camera functions of iOS devices in combination with a virtual scene.

Object recognition allows developers to create object definitions of physical world entities, such as paintings in museums, and create content based on that recognition. For example, a painting in a museum can be recognized and a 3D virtual object or extra information could be shown to the user once the app recognizes the object. The best known AR application is Pokemon Go. This app allows users to find Pokemon in the physical world and play games with them.

I decided to combine both developments and demonstrate what can happen if these Intent-enabled APIs would be brought to app-developers familiar with user interfaces and leverage these new technologies to create user-centric applications.

In general, wireless networks are more complex than wired networking, which is also true for troubleshooting. Troubleshooting odd client behavior is rather difficult.

The combination of the Intent-Based APIs and the AR result in a proof of concept where wireless troubleshooting is made easier.

A network engineer can now launch the app and point the camera to an access point. The access point (AP) is recognized using AR, and other technologies are used to determine the name of that specific access point. Once the access point name is determined, the app connects to Cisco DNA Center and requests information on all clients connected to that access point. A summary of the information is shown to the user, and the user can tap to get all details such as signal-to-noise ratio (SNR), on-boarding errors, and other wireless specific issues. Figure 10-2 displays a screenshot of this app, recorded at the CiscoLive Barcelona venue.

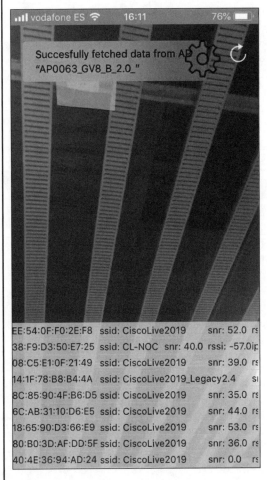

Figure 10-2   *Screenshot of iPhone App with AP Detection*

This use case demonstrates what power and possibilities APIs can bring to the business. A truly Intent-Based Network allows business intents to request the required network and security services to be deployed on the network infrastructure leveraging APIs. These APIs should be defined and provided by the tool(s) that implement the Cloud Service Management building block within Cisco DNA.

The following steps are used to determine which APIs are needed to allow business intents to be delivered via APIs.

Step 1: Identify Network Intents

One of the tasks of phase three was to identify which networks, applications, and services are deployed on the campus network. These networks, applications, and services have been translated into virtual networks or templates that were used to provision and deliver those same services.

Use that list of networks, applications, and services to create a full inventory of possible network Intents (including each individual requirement). Extend this inventory with required application policies, security policies, and other requirements as well. The primary focus should be the campus network, but if specific datacenter or WAN requirements come up, they should be registered in the inventory too. Although an inventory has already been made, it is not uncommon in enterprises that the specific requirements for application policies, such as Internet access and bandwidth requirements, are not known. Therefore, this task can take quite some time and could require support from the stakeholders to get this information available. The obtained information is paramount in order to move forward to the next step.

Step 2: Generalize Network Intents

Now that a full, extensive list of networks, services, applications, security policy, application policies, and requirements is created, this list should be validated against the business departments to verify it matches their needs (first step to business intent-driven services). Once the validation has occurred, use the list to define a set of generic services that can be used to implement all items on this list, including all restrictions, policies, and requirements.

This list of generic services should be set up in such a way that applicable restrictions, policies, and requirements can be defined using a structured description.

This generalization is similar to the creation of templates in phase three, except that this is one step further, and variables are replaced with generic constructs, structures, and abstractions. The ultimate goal would be to restrict the list of services to levels of network, network service, and application.

An example could be that for an organization, three logical, separate networks are required: one for security devices, one for employees, and one for guests and employee-owned devices. Although the services are different, they all share that they are based on a common virtual network and IP addressing. To generalize these three Intents, a single generic service called "virtual network" could be defined, with restrictions (for example, the maximum number of virtual networks to be deployed), policies (access rules), and requirements (IP address settings and DHCP server settings). Based on that generalization, it must be possible for each individual network to be defined and implemented.

Once this generic list of services is created, validate that all applications and possible new applications or networks can be defined with them as well.

Step 3: Define Concept API Definitions

In general API methodology, it is common to have a minimal set of API calls for the Creation, Reporting, Update, and Deletion (CRUD) of an information element or service. Combine this methodology and the list from step 2, "Generalize network Intents," to create a list of concept API definitions. These API definitions should have a description and structures for input and output that reflect the minimal list of services from the previous task. Table 10-1 provides an example of such concept API definitions for a network Intent. In this case the API definition is based on REST-full APIs.

Table 10-1   *List of Concept APIs to Enable Network Intents for the Enterprise*

HTTP Method	API Name	Description	Input Parameters	Output Parameters
POST	newNetwork	Creates a new virtual network	networkName: String site-specific: boolean sites: [String] nrClients: Int	networkId: UUID result: Int error: String?
POST	deleteNetwork	Removes virtual network	networkName: String deleteAt: Date?	result: Int error: String
GET	networkDetails	Retrieves details of network	byId: UUID? byName: String?	result: Int network: VirtualNetwork?

The table allows for creating, deleting, and searching for virtual networks. Some variables or structures are optional and end with a ? while others are required. The first example in the table defines an API call named **newNetwork**. This method creates a new virtual network and uses a number of input parameters, such as **nrClients**. This parameter reflects the number of clients that connect to the network, which is used as a number to request the IPAM service within the network for the appropriate IP network size. The API call **deleteNetwork** is used to delete a virtual network, either immediately or at a scheduled date or time.

These API definitions form the basis of APIs, which can be used by business intents to request network services from the campus network.

Step 4: Match API Calls Against Tool

A network that is designed around Cisco DNA can have one or more tools that allow for the provisioning of services onto the campus network. Cisco DNA Center is a great example of a tool that allows for the creation and deployment of a virtual network or a specific application policy. But Cisco DNA Center is intended for the enterprise part of the campus network. The security policies for the campus network can be defined within Cisco DNA Center (for SDA deployments) but are effectively configured on the central policy server (Cisco ISE). Similarly, an Internet access policy is configured via FirePower management or via vManage in the case of an integrated SD-WAN solution. Each of these tools has the possibility to be enabled to use APIs.

To recap, multiple tools can reside in the Cloud Service Management building block and can be used for different purposes.

In this task, the concept APIs from the previous step are compared with the available APIs of the network tools that are used within the organization. Append the earlier table with the name of the tool, the API call, and the API definition that will be used to define that generic service.

If a concept API definition is not implemented with one of the known tools, research whether multiple API calls or alternatives exist for that concept API definition. Document these API calls in the same list.

At the end of this step, the concept list from step 3 is extended with a list of existing APIs from the tools used by the campus network team.

Step 5: Create Network Intents Service Catalog

Based on the previous steps, a service catalog can be created for all network intents (network, service, and applications) that can be provided on the campus network. This service catalog essentially describes the technical services the campus network can deliver, including descriptions of how to request those services automatically using APIs. This service catalog not only contains a name and a description but also a list of API calls that are required to be executed by a software developer in case the intent needs to be requested via APIs.

If some services require manual configuration, this should be registered in the service catalog as well. (These are the gaps described in the previous step.) These services can still be provided by the network team, but take a longer time to deploy (traditional deployments).

This last step is used to create such a service catalog. See Table 10-2 for an example network intents service catalog. This service catalog represents confirmed definitions for the services that the organization is capable of running on the campus network. It effectively represents the northbound services and APIs available for the Intent-Based Network created with the previous phases.

Table 10-2   *Example Network Intents Service Catalog*

Service	Service Type	Description	API Name
network service	network	Creates a new virtual network service, wired and wireless. By default no access is allowed to any application. After creation of service, please add endpoints and application policies.	newNetwork
addApplication-ToNetworkSer-vice	application	Maps an application to a specific network service. Use this API call to allow specific application access.	addApplicationToVN(network Service: String, allowedProto-cols: [PortDefinition]
addEndpoint-ToNetwork	Security	Adds an endpoint to a specified network service. After assignment, this endpoint is always placed in this endpoint.	mapEndpointToVN(endpointId: String, networkService: String)
getEndpointsFor-NetworkService	endpoint	Gets all endpoints asso-ciated with a specific virtual network service.	getEndpoints(for: String)
...	...	...	...

Bringing IBN to the Enterprise

The previous task described how to create a service catalog of APIs that business application developers can use to automatically request the required services from the network. The service catalog describes which API calls are needed to request a specific service from the network.

But up until now, the primary focus of the phases has been to transform the campus network to an Intent-Based Network. The enterprise itself is unaware of the power and opportunities an Intent-Based Network can bring to the enterprise. So the next step is to bring that service catalog to the business in a manner that it will understand and can relate to.

It is important to announce that the service catalog is available and for both the opera-tions team as well as the enterprise to take small steps in adopting and using the service catalog.

Taking small steps will cut down on potential failures and expedite the incorporation of networking as an integral part of any business process.

Every new function or feature requires success stories to enable more success and accomplish innovative new methods. The following sections describe recommendations of how to implement the service catalog within the enterprise.

Communication Plan

Although the network has become an essential part of all business processes within the enterprise, it has also become so reliable and predictive that it is essentially invisible. Business departments view the network as a common facility like electricity or restrooms. For IBN to be successfully implemented within the business departments, they need to be aware that the network is actually performing some fairly complex tasks to bring resilient, reliable, and predictable connectivity services to that business department. The department also needs to become aware that it will experience a standstill if connectivity is not available.

Use Case: How Standardization and Design Benefit the Business

In the past, LogiServ managed a single IP network to which all endpoints and servers were connected. Every device was sitting in a single network, and all devices were able to communicate with each other. Over time the network grew, and more devices and types of devices were connected. But the network was still a single network. That old network worked but had its issues at times. Issues would be fixed in a reactive manner, fighting the symptoms, such as adding an extra switch if extra ports were needed for a new acquisition.

This approach is common in a lot of small businesses where IT is seen as a cost factor and not a business enabler.

When both the compute environment and the network were long overdue for a lifecycle management replacement, the choice was made to build up a new greenfield infrastructure next to the old network.

The network had grown over time, and the greenfield opportunity was also used to redesign and reconsider the businesses LogiServ was providing IT services to and to look at security risks, scalability issues, and risks of downtime.

Part of the design choice was to leverage Cisco IWAN technology to provide redundant connections from branch locations to the HQ for connectivity to the datacenter. Redundancy was another key design choice and aspect, where possible single points of failures would be removed by adding redundancy, whether this was an uplink, a power supply, or the Internet connection.

A few years after successfully migrating to the new network and the provided IT services, a conversation occurred between a business unit manager and a staff member of LogiServ. The manager told the staff member he did not know what they did with the new IT system and infrastructure, but they never had experienced any issues or downtime since they migrated.

The preceding use case was of course a big compliment for LogiServ and the transition. But intrinsic to that compliment was also the notion that the unit manager was not aware of what LogiServ actually did or was doing to operate that environment so successfully. This situation is often the case in networking. No employee or manager will give a compliment when the network operates without issues, but each will raise major incidents if there is a possible network issue.

A communication plan must be composed. This communication plan will be used internally to make the network more visible and to raise awareness to the importance of networks, connectivity, and the risks of no or limited security. The plan also covers opportunities and chances that an Intent-enabled network creates for the business.

The plan is similar to a marketing plan. Any knowledge and intelligence on marketing and communication should be leveraged, all related to the type of enterprise and its culture. Some enterprises might benefit from a large communication while others might benefit from smaller steps. Leverage the marketing knowledge internally or externally and emphasize the importance of the network.

Understand the Business

This is an often underestimated part of any IT-related project. Of course, employees from other business departments know what a computer is, but they do not know what a network is. Similarly, IT employees know the concept of a warehouse management system but might not know the importance to the business of a specific script once created.

It is recommended to talk with several employees in the different business departments and ask questions on what they do, how they do their job, and how IT can support them.

Understanding a business only brings benefits to IT, as IT starts to understand what drives the business, and only then can it truly support the business with the right technology.

The communication plan can also leverage knowledge gained from this step to share what kind of impact the network has on a specific process and how that was solved.

Set Up Pilots or Proof of Concepts

The communication plan and understanding the business help to identify pilot projects to create quick wins. Find out which business departments face certain issues or challenges that can easily leverage the capabilities of an Intent-Based Network. These business departments should be willing to test, use new technology, and accept failure in pilots as well. In other words, these business departments are usually at the front of the technology adoption curve.

The pilot is used not only to demonstrate that using APIs and the service catalog supports the business process but also for the network operations team to gain trust and experience in the fact that APIs can automatically request and remove applications on the network.

Build Apps/Portals to Support the Business

Once pilots are successful, use those pilots to build applications or portals that can be managed and operated in a production grade system. Also if small additions to a portal can bring great benefit to the enterprise, this should be a chance to show and demonstrate the power of IBN and the service catalog. An example could be the integration between Cisco ISE and the guest registration portal for the front desk security. An employee would then only register guests via the front desk security portal, while in the background the necessary guest credentials are created automatically for the registered guests.

Share Successes and Failures

An integral part of bringing the service catalog to the enterprise and using the communication plan is to share. Share the success stories of pilots and changes that were made because of IBN. But also share failures, mistakes, and lessons learned. Share the success after applying the lessons learned from a failure; it shows that the IT department is human.

These recommendations are intertwined with each other and run sequentially as well. That makes the execution of these steps perhaps rather difficult, and specialists in communication and marketing can be of great support in this task. The end goal for this task is twofold: raising awareness of the network and having a number of business departments or processes leveraging the Intent APIs for their network services. This is the only way to integrate IBN into the enterprise: by continuously sharing, communicating, and integrating with the enterprise.

Intent-Based Examples

Once enterprises, partners, and industries understand that the network is programmable and consistent APIs are available, several new types of functionality or use cases for Intent-Based Networking can be defined and created. The following sections describe a number of use cases or examples for applications that leverage the power of an Intent-enabled network.

Response to Security Incidents

Network security has become increasingly important to most enterprises. The impact of ransomware, malware, and other malicious intent can have drastic consequences for the functioning of the enterprise.

Security operations can benefit from an Intent-Based Network as well. When an indication of compromise (IoC) of an endpoint is seen on the network, a manual intervention needs to be executed to have that endpoint isolated (quarantined), investigated, or ignored. This requires close cooperation between security and network because these types of operations are commonly executed by two different teams.

With Intent-Based Networking, an IoC can trigger a push notification to an iPhone, just like a new text message is received. The security operator (for example, during night hours) can look at the IoC message and swipe to the left. The operator can then select quarantine, investigate, or ignore. Once the intent is known, the network is automatically configured for the intent for that specific endpoint, and the central policy server is used to trigger a change of authorization to effectuate that intent. There is of course reporting and communications between the two teams, but the incident itself can now be handled accordingly.

Organizing a Meeting

At larger enterprises the organization of a meeting with both internal employees and guests can take almost a day. Besides finding the date, an agenda needs to be set up, topics need to be prepared, and other non-content-driven activities must be executed, such as sending out invites, registering the guests and employees at security, organizing a meeting room, changing that room because more people join than expected, organizing the videoconference unit, organizing lunch, and managing Internet access for guests.

In summary, quite a lot of tasks are commonly manually executed using different systems. Most enterprises have a portal where you can register visitors in advance. Another portal would be used for creating guest access, and yet another portal to communicate with facilities for the meeting room and organize lunch.

With IBN and portals leveraging APIs, a lot of these tasks can be executed more easily, resulting in the following use case.

A user, organizing a conference, logs in to the facility's portal and checks for a room for a specific date, start time, and end time. The user selects the room and moves to the next screen. In that screen the user is able to register all employees and visitors for that meeting, upload an agenda, and select the checkboxes for lunch and Internet access. Once the room reservation is committed, the system creates a conference for the user and keeps it in pending. The system will send out invites with the agenda to the registered delegates, allowing them to register and confirm.

Three days before the event starts, the system will send out a notification to facilities to register for a lunch. The system also registers the visitors, on behalf of the host, with security. One day before the event starts, the system will connect to the Internet guest system and register guest accounts for the visitors who have confirmed the meeting. The Internet guest system will send out emails to the visitors with information on how to connect to the network.

One hour before the meeting starts, the system will ask the network to create a wireless network and associate the registered (and confirmed) employees as well as the visitors to that temporary network.

The network is now prepared for the conference, and within that conference that network can be used by the delegates to collaborate and share data and screens and be more productive.

Two hours after the meeting ends, the system will request the network to remove the temporary wireless network and its policies and to disable access for guest users.

This workflow or use case already exists in one form or the other. Several systems already provide parts of the solution, and these systems have APIs available. It is only a matter of defining a new portal and leveraging the APIs; all aspects are tied into a single workflow that makes the life of a host easier. It is even possible to build a mobile phone app that leverages the same APIs as the portal, so that the host can organize the event from his or her phone, using an enterprise-built app. Essentially, the business intent of the host is transformed into several actions, and some of them are deployed in the network and removed from operation when required.

Authorized Access

This use case is perhaps a bit more futuristic, but with the power of IBN (and enabling end-to-end Intent up to the datacenter) it is quite possible.

An employee would like to get access to a specific application—for example, a drawing application—because he or she needs to create a specific type of drawing for a project or a customer. The employee logs in to the self-service portal or app and selects the drawing application. Because the employee has enough App-Credits available, the request is automatically approved and added to the list of used applications for the license account report.

> **Note** App-Credits in this case is a fictitious credit system or point system inside the enterprise where a virtual number of credits is made available to the employee on an annual basis. Using an app "costs" the employee a number of credits per month, similar to how cloud services are consumed. App-Credits optimize the approval process by allowing employees self-service enterprise applications they need without manual approval of managers.

As the application request is approved, provisioning methods push the application toward all the employee's devices, including workstations, virtual desktop, and tablet. The network and infrastructure policies are updated so the employee now has access to the drawing application and the required shared data. The application itself is, via a policy, also allowed access to the user's directory to save data. Mobile endpoints are configured with the appropriate tunnels and policies to make the application accessible from anywhere.

The employee can now use the drawing application and creates a drawing or design.

When finished with the application, the employee will deregister the drawing application from her inventory. Once that is committed, the policies applied are removed, access to data is retracted, and the application is removed from the different devices.

The intent of the employee is to have access to a drawing application for a business-specific reason. The network and infrastructure are programmable, and the employee can be serviced automatically. APIs are used throughout the process to facilitate this intent.

Commonly, these types of workflows would require an approval and formal change requests on several aspects. But because the resulting components of the intent (pushing an application, setting up access policies) have been tested before, the APIs can be leveraged to execute this kind of workflow automatically without approval and deliver much faster.

With the programmability of the network, the number of use cases is almost unlimited, and many more use cases can be defined, described, or implemented. Some of these use cases have already been developed or will be developed over time. It is meant to provide insight into the power and possibilities that can be enabled now that the enterprise is Intent-enabled.

Summary

With the completion of phase three, the campus network is successfully transformed to an Intent-Based Network. The campus network is now based on the Cisco Digital Network Architecture (framework), and the network operations team managed the network by deploying intents onto the network while providing proactive feedback to the enterprise on the status of the network. Phase 4 is the last phase in the transformation and is used to introduce IBN to the enterprise to maximize the possibilities, opportunities, and capabilities introduced with the transformation.

This is achieved by performing two distinct tasks in this phase:

- Defining a **Network Intent Service Catalog** that describes which services are delivered and supported by the network operations team, including the APIs to be used

- Actively **bringing IBN to the enterprise** by leveraging a communication plan, pilot projects, and development of portals to support the business processes of the enterprise

As a final note, this chapter provides a number of examples on how IBN can be deployed within the enterprise. These examples are intended as concepts and a starting point for other IBN use cases. The possibilities are endless. The following use cases are described in detail:

- A mobile app that receives Indications of Compromise from endpoints and allows the security engineer to quickly determine the next course of action, which is in turn configured on the network

- An example aimed at making organizing a conference or meeting much easier

- An end-to-end use case for application access

Once the concept of IBN is successfully introduced and integrated in the network and business departments leverage the service catalog and APIs to automatically request network services to be enabled or removed, the transformation to an Intent-Based Network has completed.

Part III

Organizational Aspects

Part II provided a methodology on how to transform the campus network to IBN. Although the method primarily involves IBN and what is required for that transformation, it also provides handles and pointers to the changes required within the organization to have the organization benefit from IBN.

Many of the described tasks and steps involve a lot of effort and change within the network operations team. But the network operations team is not an entity unto itself; it is part of a larger organization, so the organization will need to change too. Also, IBN is not an isolated evolution; many other (internal and external) factors drive change within an organization as well.

Regardless of the driver (IBN or other factors), changing an organization or process is much more complex and challenging than introducing a new technology. It requires time, effort, persuasion, and enticement. As the lead in the transformation you will probably face resistance, intense discussions, and challenges too.

This part provides background information on different organizational aspects related to a transformation to IBN, regardless of whether IBN is a requirement, a cause, or an effect. The last chapter of this part also provides some recommendations that might be helpful in driving changes in an organization.

The chapters in this final part of the book are as follows:

Chapter 11   Architecture Frameworks

Chapter 12   Enabling the Digital Business

Chapter 13   IT Operations

Chapter 14   Tips to Make Your IBN Journey a Success

Chapter 11

Architecture Frameworks

Many organizations use architecture frameworks to model and organize their organization. This is also known as enterprise architecture, as described in Chapter 3, "Enterprise Architecture." The last phase of the transformation to Intent-Based Networking (IBN) introduced a service catalog and the possibility for business applications to request network Intents automatically under the supervision of the network operations team. Besides that this is an organizational and cultural change, what kind of impact does IBN have on the enterprise architecture? This chapter provides a summary of enterprise architecture and the impact of IBN on that model.

Enterprise Architecture

Many architectures, including the enterprise architectures, take a layered approach and are modeled around a specific domain. Each domain commonly has its own set of complexities and dynamics. In general, this approach is taken because the set of responsibilities can then be abstracted into functions that can be used by other domains. Enterprise architectures commonly take a four-layered approach, as depicted in Figure 11-1.

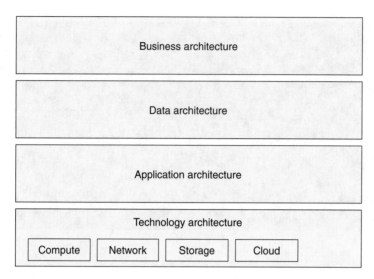

Figure 11-1 *Layered Approach of an Enterprise Architecture*

In this layered approach, four distinct (and isolated) domains are identified and modeled into an architecture:

- **Business architecture:** The business architecture describes how the business is organized around processes, departments, tasks, and responsibilities. For example, the HR department and its corresponding processes are described. The interrelationships with other processes and organizational elements are modeled and described—such as how HR provides services to other departments, or how logistics is responsible for the warehouse and the just-in-time shipping of goods sold by sales.

- **Data architecture:** The data architecture is probably the most difficult and abstract architecture within the enterprise. It describes all the data structures and elements necessary (and available) within the enterprise. It describes which process or department needs which data element and how the data elements are related. The data architecture is not a database model, but more an abstract description about what data is available within the enterprise. Database models can, of course, be used to model the data architecture. One of the common purposes of the data architecture is to remove as much redundancy in the data as possible.

- **Application architecture:** The application architecture describes which types of applications are required within the enterprise. The application architecture also describes how each application uses and modifies data within the enterprise. It also describes to which rules and guidelines applications should conform within the enterprise to provide a consistent approach to application usage.

- **Technology architecture:** The technology architecture describes how different software and hardware components are required to support the deployment of business, data, and application services. The technology architecture is traditionally the primary focus for IT departments, as they are responsible for the technology that the business needs to perform its tasks and responsibilities. Technology architectures commonly describe how the IT infrastructure should be organized, whether a single database server or multiple database servers are used, and so on.

In general, architectures (including these four) use a method of identifying a system and defining it as a collection of smaller components, where for each component its function, requirements, dependencies, input, and output are described. These components are commonly known as architecture building blocks. These components provide a number of benefits because they abstract complexity and are part of a larger system:

- **Flexibility:** Each component can be replaced by a different component, as long as the new component meets the requirements of the other component. It is not necessary to replace and rebuild a complete new system if only one component is to be changed. That component needs to be tested and then can replace the old component. The system as a whole remains operating as expected. It also provides customization options for customers while still maintaining quality standards. An example could be for a computer manufacturer to provide the new computer systems with more memory. They only need to replace the memory component instead of designing a complete new computer system.

- **Reusability:** By defining a system as a set of individual smaller components, it is possible to reuse a smaller component for a different application or system. This reusability results in lower costs of development for a new system because the wheel is literally not invented twice. A common example of reusability is found in the car industry where a chassis is developed once and reused for different car models.

- **Faster implementation:** If a system already has an existing set of tested modules, it is easier to define new systems or a new approach based on those modules. Only the new modules and new behavior require testing. Consequently, the new system is built and implemented faster.

- **Serviceability:** When every system is divided into logical components, it is easier to troubleshoot a specific problem once the component that is misbehaving is identified. Only that module needs to be analyzed and fixed instead of a complete system.

- **Possibility to change:** This is specifically true in larger complex environments. If a system needs to behave differently because of organizational change or business demands, it is now possible to reorder existing components, reuse other components, or possibly only introduce a new single component into the chain of existing components.

Combined, these four architectures (that exist of components with the benefits in the preceding list) form the formal description of how the enterprise is organized, managed, and operated. It is important to note that these architectures only describe each component functionally (and thus are rather abstract). The architecture framework might (and should) provide guidelines on how technology is procured and managed to provide a consistent solution for the enterprise, but no solutions are provided in these four architectures. They are only a description and model of the enterprise.

Many large organizations leverage some type of enterprise architecture, whether this is based on existing frameworks or defined internally. Although discussions exist on the benefits of an enterprise architectural approach, working via an architectural approach is common across several industries and has provided benefits to a certain level.

Impact of IBN

Architectures describe their functions abstractly; they do not provide a specific solution. One of the reasons for that is also the longevity of the architecture. Technology changes much faster compared to the architecture that describes the system. Cisco Digital Network Architecture (Cisco DNA), described in Chapter 4, "Cisco Digital Network Architecture," is no different. It describes how the next generation of network infrastructures should be designed. Cisco DNA, as an architecture, is commonly seen as part of the technology architecture of an enterprise; it specifically describes technology-related systems.

But is that really true? Because IBN, as a perspective to Cisco DNA, describes how that architecture can be used by the operations team. Could it be that Cisco DNA, because of IBN, is much more than just a part of the technology architecture at the bottom of the enterprise architecture? Cisco DNA does not only describe the network and how it should be organized, but describes four functions (described in the sections that follow) that should effectively be located in different architectures.

Analytics

The analytics function describes how data from the infrastructure devices are used in combination with other contexts (such as running configuration, identity of connected endpoints, applications found on the network, and other behavior analytics) to continuously validate whether the network is operating within normal parameters. Analytics uses several data models, such as Model-Driven Telemetry, NETCONF/YANG, NetFlow, Syslog, and others to perform this function. The analytics is truly a data-driven and data-based function, and key parts of the function are part of the data architecture.

Cloud Service Management and Automation

The Cloud Service Management is used by operations to define available network services. The cloud service management function then translates that into configuration changes that the automation function pushes to the infrastructure to perform the changes. These functions are effectively describing applications that use data and are effectively part of the application architecture.

Infrastructure

The infrastructure function within Cisco DNA describes the required network functions, requirements, and hardware. They truly are part of the technology architecture.

This means that Cisco DNA is not part of the technology architecture but is actually an architecture that transcends the different functional domains and is applied across all four domains. Figure 11-2 depicts the traditional enterprise architecture domains and how Cisco DNA should be seen in relationship to that model.

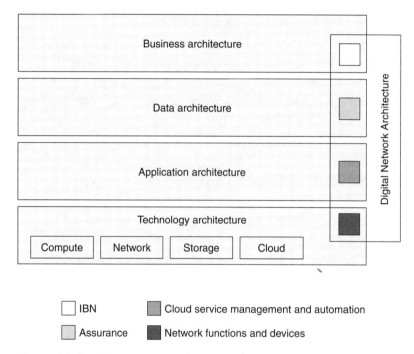

Figure 11-2 *Cisco DNA in Relation to Enterprise Architecture*

As you can see, Cisco DNA is really across the different architectures. *IBN itself is not a function of Cisco DNA, but it is a perspective on how the network is designed, managed, and operated.* It effectively describes the processes for managing a Cisco DNA-based architecture. Another reason why IBN effectively fits the business architecture is that Cisco DNA describes the possibility for other business processes to request network services automatically. Although APIs (technology) are used to describe that functionality, it is IBN that effectively enables that feature via the service catalog.

A good example of the fact that Cisco DNA and IBN are across all enterprise architectures is the salary-run every month by HR in an international organization. These salary-runs are run every month and need to have access to several systems to complete the run. Traditionally, the security policy within the network would always allow access between the systems. And if access would be required, it would be the HR department requesting access via the Operations (Ops) department, as shown in Figure 11-3.

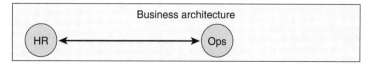

Figure 11-3 *Traditional Access Request*

After the access request is received, the operations team would use its internal systems to change the network and security policies. After the change, HR can perform that salary-run monthly. The responsibilities for access are clearly defined, and the communication between departments is represented in the business architecture.

But with IBN, the access to the different systems for the HR employee can be denied unless the HR employee wants to execute the salary-run (Intent), which improves the security of the network and organization. The sequence for this use case would be:

1. The HR employee wants to start the salary-run. The HR application makes its Intent available to the Cloud Service Management tool via APIs.

2. The service management tool approves the request and leverages automation to perform the change.

3. In the meantime the HR application validates, via APIs, whether the employee's intent is made available.

4. Once available, the HR application can execute the salary-run and then notify the cloud service management tool that the intent can be removed.

5. The service management tool will then remove the intent from the network and revert the access policies to normal.

Figure 11-4 provides a schematic approach to this IBN example.

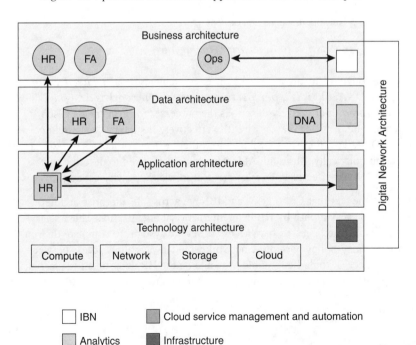

Figure 11-4 *Application and Data Flows for an IBN-Enabled Application*

There are, of course, many other examples possible, which proves that with IBN (and Cisco DNA), the clear borders between the classic four enterprise architecture layers will fade. IBN will effectively be one of the triggers to change the way enterprise architectures are modeled and designed.

Summary

Enterprise architectures are used within (large) organizations to functionally model and describe the organization. Just like any other architecture frameworks and architectures in general, complexity is reduced by introducing abstraction layers. It is common for enterprise architectures to define four layers of abstractions, which can individually be described without integrating them:

- Business architecture

- Data architecture

- Application architecture

- Technology architecture

IT-related architectures, such as Cisco Digital Network Architecture (Cisco DNA), and defined services that involve IT are commonly modeled in the technology architecture so that IT can provide the necessary technologies to the other architectures.

Cisco DNA is therefore also placed within the technology architecture because it primarily describes an architecture involving the network infrastructure. However, Cisco DNA is much more than just the network architecture; it provides information on how the network is operating, at a technical, application, and business level. It leverages the analytics component, which is strongly based on the data architecture. Also, the Cloud Service Management and automation functions are typically described as applications and are thus part of the application architecture. Refer back to Figure 11-2 to see how Cisco DNA effectively is layered across the different abstraction layers in the enterprise architecture.

IBN itself is a perspective to a Cisco DNA-based network infrastructure and describes how to design, manage, and operate such infrastructure. One of the true powers of IBN is that business applications or processes can request Intents to the network, automatically leveraging the power and functionality of APIs.

That means that with IBN, business processes (or applications) can now use those APIs to change the network (and part of its behavior described in architecture) dynamically without intervention of the network operations team, who is responsible for the network—for example, an HR application that dynamically requests access to financial data during a salary-run.

Because IBN provides this enablement, more and more applications will leverage these capabilities, and the distinct layers of abstraction within an enterprise architecture will eventually fade because of IBN.

Chapter 12

Enabling the Digital Business

One of the key trends over the past years for executives has been digitalization. Some industries already have seen disruption because a new player in that market introduced a new way of operation and created such a big change that it literally forced enterprises and markets into defensive modes, and they had to respond. In many commercially oriented markets, responding to a change often means the business is too late and needs to win back customers and business.

But how can an Intent-Based Network be a requirement for a successful digitalization of the enterprise? This chapter describes the concept of digitalization and a number of factors that support/enable digitalization, and it concludes with where Intent-Based Networking fits in a digital business.

This chapter covers the following topics:

- What is digitalization?
- Stages in digitalization
- Design thinking framework
- Intent-Based Networking
- Organizational impact

What Is Digitalization?

Digital transformation, also known as *digitalization*, is the concept of new technology being used to solve traditional problems. The concept itself is not new, but the process of *digitization* (converting analog information to digital information) has evolved exponentially over the past decade. The availability of digital information and the exponential increase in processing capacity have led to new solutions where new technologies and the digital data are used to redefine and solve traditional complex problems in an innovative way. This innovative approach is often also known as *disruption*.

Digitalization can be seen as the evolution of how businesses are organized and run. Digitalized businesses will bring changes to a lot of things in the world. But what, essentially, is a digitalized business? What makes it different from a traditional business? The following paragraphs provide a conceptual overview of the differences between a traditional business and a digitalized one.

Most traditional enterprises are organized around their business processes, in which the core business of the enterprise traverses those processes in a linear fashion, as illustrated in Figure 12-1. In this example, the sales process provides output for the production, which requires input from procurement, and after product generation, the products are delivered. Next to the primary business processes, several supporting business processes are defined with a primary purpose of supporting the primary processes. These business processes are commonly finance, product development, marketing, services, and IT.

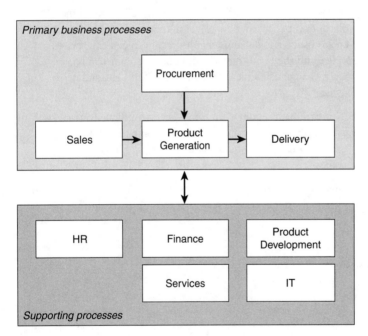

Figure 12-1 *Business Processes of Traditional Enterprise*

With digital transformation (digitalization), the business processes are modeled around data and technology. Technology is driving the business processes and vice versa in a continuous process, with a tight integration between the two at the end. Figure 12-2 provides a schematic overview of this concept.

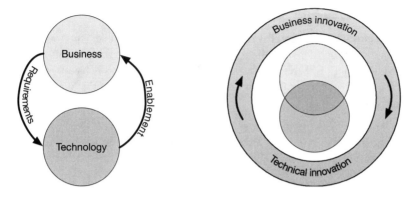

Figure 12-2 *A Model for Digitalized Enterprises*

The left model in the figure is a key principle for a digitalized business. Business processes define requirements, and technology will enable the business processes by meeting those requirements and providing the necessary tools. This mechanism occurs in a continuous loop, so if a requirement is changed, the technology will adapt and enable the business. Over time and innovations, these two distinct roles will merge, where not only business innovation will drive technology, but technological innovation will drive and change the business. The latter aspect is shown in the right model of Figure 12-2. Digitalization describes the process that an enterprise undergoes from traditional business processes to the tight integration between business and technology.

Stages in Digitalization

To have a digitized business (and thus successfully have digitalization), the enterprise will go through four distinct stages where IT (technology) integrates in the business. The sections that follow describe these stages in greater detail.

Stage 1: Business and IT Alignment

Perhaps the most difficult stage in digitalization is the first stage. It is common within organizations that IT has no direct feeling or understanding of the business processes and vice versa; the business processes lack an understanding of why specific technologies work in a specific way and what effort IT needs to make to successfully manage the ever-increasing complexity of IT systems.

But to leverage any technology at all, the business (processes) and IT need to be aligned with each other. So to move to the next stage in digitalization, the business side and IT side need to understand each other. Once they understand each other and that they require each other, they are aligned. Design thinking (described later in this chapter) can be beneficial in this process too.

Once this mutual understanding is achieved, the first stage of digitalization is completed.

Stage 2: IT as a Business Enabler

The next stage in digitization is when IT is recognized as a business enabler. Traditionally IT originates from the Finance department (as that was one of the first departments being computerized in the past). IT is therefore often seen as a cost center. This behavior is emphasized by the fact that a better IT service creates indirect benefits to the business instead of direct benefits.

Because of the alignment from the previous stage, business (and thus executive levels) will more easily understand that IT is not a cost factor, but it has become an essential and critical part of the business.

As soon as IT is seen as a business enabler, the organization acknowledges the importance of good running IT systems, which will result in appropriate funding for lifecycle management, innovations, and applying new technology to innovate.

Enterprises that see IT as a business enabler are also more prone to adopt newer technologies if these technologies are beneficial to the primary business processes.

Stage 3: IT Proactively Supporting the Business

The next logical stage is IT proactively supporting the business based on the tools and technologies available. An example of this is that data from IT tools is used to provide suggestions to optimize the order picking flow in a warehouse to reduce the time required between order picking and shipping to trucks. Or in a production facility, the data collected by sensors is used to raise an alarm that a critical process is overheating, which can in turn prevent a plant shutdown.

Use Case: How Information from IT Improves Services

SharedService Group manages a large wireless network. As with most wireless networks, the services are provided in both the 2.4GHz and the 5GHz bands. Because the 2.4GHz band is also used by Bluetooth, microwaves, and other devices, this frequency is often polluted.

As the wireless network in locations migrated to highdensity wireless networks (and endpoints having the opportunity of connecting to both bands), the 5GHz band was used more predominantly. However, data from DNA Center Assurance demonstrated that some (dual-band) endpoints were still proactively trying to associate to the less reliable 2.4GHz band while they had an excellent connection on the 5GHz.

To reduce this unnecessary roaming and improve the wireless service in general, it was decided to check whether the wireless network could be a 5GHz-only network. Other data from DNA Center Assurance was used to research whether endpoints could only connect to the 2.4GHz band.

It was determined that only a handful of devices were not (yet) able to connect to 5GHz networks. Therefore, it was decided to create a single 2.4GHz network for those devices and disable 2.4GHz for the regular wireless service.

Although an extra wireless network was created, the overall service and experience for users was improved by the change.

This use case demonstrates that the data collected by the network was used to optimize and improve the service provided to the business by disabling the 2.4GHz band on the general wireless network. The wireless network itself was not only providing the technical service; the data generated by the business using that service was used to improve this service to the business.

At this stage of digitalization, the role of IT is transforming. Instead of only providing technical services to the business process, IT is changing to become an integral part of the business processes within the enterprise.

Stage 4: IT Changes Business Processes

In the previous stage, IT systems and data within those systems are used to proactively support the business and provide suggestions to improve the business process. In the last stage of digitalization, the responsibilities between IT and business are reversed. Technologies, such as machine intelligence, combined with the available data are used to automatically optimize existing business processes or to define new business services and processes to create extra and new revenue streams for the enterprise. Machine intelligence systems are capable of finding patterns within big data that can be overlooked by humans.

At the end of this stage, the business is truly digitalized and run as a digital business.

Summary of Digitalization Stages

These four stages describe concepts and functions in a rather abstract manner. Not only have these stages already been proven successful for some industries, they also have a great parallel in how technology has changed the experience of driving a car.

The first stage can be compared with the introduction of digital components in the car. An internal network connects these digital components to execute simple things digitally instead of analog, such as electronic window openers, direction indicators, lighting control, or a distributed digital car entertainment system. For example, the Volvo V50 had a distributed entertainment system with a control end in the dashboard, while the radio tuner was in the back of the car and audio was transmitted digitally to the speakers.

Cruise control, electronic motor management, and electronic hand breaks are typical technologies that have a parallel with stage two. The technology is used to support the driving experience and makes driving easier and more comfortable.

Technologies like collision avoidance systems, power breaking systems, dynamic stability control, and traction control are typical systems for the third stage. Not only do these systems improve the driver experience, but in case of an impending accident these systems can proactively interfere with the actions of the driver to prevent the accident.

The concept of full autonomous driving is exactly the same as the final stage in digitalization. The technology is using data from digital sensors in the car to drive the car instead of the driver.

Although these four stages might not be formally defined, they provide enough guidance and handles for an organization to adopt and change into a digital business.

Design Thinking

Digitalization is about innovation and applying it to optimize or renew a business service or enterprise as a whole. A key part of that innovation is leveraging digital data, which becomes available due to digitization. But innovation is not just about data. The design of a new tool, solution, or process is important as well.

Design is a generic concept and is visible in all the things we as humans see, use, and apply. This ranges from driving a car or getting a cup of coffee from a coffee machine to complex IT systems that manage and operate complete power plants.

The beauty of a good design is that if it is thought through carefully and function meets purpose properly, nobody thinks about the design itself; using that object comes naturally because the design is perfect.

But if the design is flawed, it will confuse and even frustrate users when they need to use that tool or function with a flawed design.

Design Thinking is a human-centered approach toward innovation. It was first taught in the early 1980s at Stanford University as "a method of creative action" and later adapted for business purposes by design consultancy firm IDEO. Design Thinking provides a framework to help teams build products that solve real-world problems for users. As Design Thinking is becoming more common in IT environments, it can be used to support the innovation aspect of a digital business by enabling the organization to deliver high potential innovations at a high pace.

Any new tool or business process will require employees to use and operate them. By empathizing with the users and what they need up front, it is easier to understand what problems and frustrations they face and how to solve these for them by designing new products and tools. Because these products (or processes) are human-centric, the employees will love to use them, and this creates a faster success. Figure 12-3 shows where Design Thinking is focused: it is on the intersection of the domains Human, Technology, and Business.

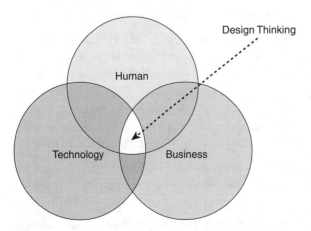

Figure 12-3 *Location of Design Thinking*

Design Thinking itself is a universal framework that can be applied in a broader area than just design, but also for understanding how a specific process works and where its flaws might lie. Leveraging Design Thinking will greatly support any enterprise in the different stages of digitalization, from alignment (emphathizing with the users and business processes) to supporting the business with better products and tools (stages three and four).

Cisco uses the Design Thinking framework throughout its organization to help understand users, emphasize their needs, and build tools and technological solutions to assist those users. Cisco has published a book called *Getting Started with Cisco Design Thinking* (https://cisco.mediuscorp.com/reference-guides/getting-started-with-cisco-design-thinking-c1334-prbklt-053) that provides a practical guide and pointers on how Design Thinking can be applied to solve complex problems. The following paragraphs provide a summary of the framework.

Cisco Design Thinking Framework

The Cisco Design Thinking framework has adopted the classic Design Thinking best practices with its own experiences and role as technological innovator. Figure 12-4 provides a schematic overview of the Cisco Design Thinking framework.

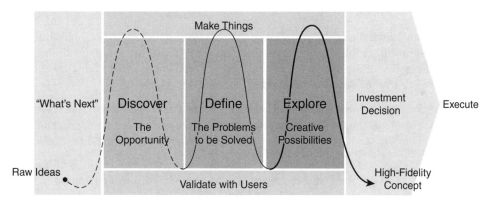

Figure 12-4   *Cisco Design Thinking Framework*

The Cisco Design Thinking framework can be used to create new innovative concepts (with a high chance of a successful implementation, defined within the framework as a High Fidelity Concept) that solve a problem for a user or process with a truly supportive design.

To achieve this, the framework defines three concrete Start, Finish, and Execute moments; three core processes to be executed; two guarding aspects to help focus within the core processes; and a Thread that walks through the different moments and processes.

Most design-based innovations begin with the "Start" moment. This is the moment where brainstorm sessions take place and attempt to create ideas for questions like "What's Next?" These brainstorm sessions result in a number of raw ideas to either solve a problem or define a new solution.

These raw ideas will then iterate through three core processes. These three core processes are at the heart of the framework and are executed sequentially.

- **Phase 1—Discover:** This phase is used to deeply understand the users or business processes and identify what the users need. The raw ideas can be used as input while communicating with the users. At the end of the process an opportunity statement is created by the team that clearly identifies the need of the user or business processes.

- **Phase 2—Define:** This phase identifies, documents, and prioritizes the "problems to be solved" based on the opportunity statement from the previous phase. Again, a statement is defined at the end of this phase called Problems to be Solved statement.

- **Phase 3—Explore:** This phase is used to explore what kind of solutions can be applied (or defined) to solve the problems from the statement. The objective of this phase is to identify which solutions will delight the users, solve their core problems, and claim the opportunity.

The "Finish" moment is at the end of phase three. Several solutions have been identified to solve a specific problem for the users. It is now time to make an investment decision and choose which solution will be executed, created, and implemented. This choice is of course made by the necessary stakeholders.

Once a decision is made in the "Finish" moment, a team can now "Execute" the solution and start developing and implementing the solution. The specifics for developing and implementing are outside the scope of the Design Thinking framework itself.

To prevent ideas, opportunities, problems, and solutions from diverging too much and to keep focus on solvable and user-centric designs, the Design Thinking framework mandates two guard rails. These two guard rails perform distinct functions that will not only keep focus but also assist in the goal of defining highly viable solutions.

- **Guard rail 1—Validate with users:** This is a fundamental tenet of Design Thinking. At each iteration or moment you must validate your ideas and conclusions with real users. Anything worthwhile to research further requires a validation with the users (the key stakeholders). It keeps the solution user-centric and thus design-centric.

- **Guard rail 2—Make things:** Another basic principle of Design Thinking is to make things. Sharing ideas with users is not enough for Design Thinking. Users will still interpret ideas differently. By making things to illustrate these ideas, users can respond to them, whether with confirmation or rejection. Software prototyping can be used as one of the methods to make things.

The Design Thinking framework defines the path that follows through all processes and bumps into the guard rails as The Thread. The Thread is shown in Figure 12-4 as the dotted line that flows through the phases. As you traverse The Thread, confidence is created within both the team and the users that the identified opportunities are indeed viable and solve a problem. This ensures that at the end of The Thread, there are one or more High-Fidelity Concepts that not only clarify a "what's next" but also drive the investment knowing it is really beneficial to users or business processes.

The previous paragraphs provide a brief overview of the Design Thinking framework. The framework itself of course provides more detail, principles, proven methods, and structures. The Cisco book on this topic is truly a getting started book that can open up a complete new world to you. As becomes clear from this overview, Design Thinking can be powerful and supportive for any enterprise in the digital transformation.

Intent-Based Networking

To recap Intent-Based Networking, it is a perspective on a network that is based on the Cisco Digital Network Architecture. It describes how the next generation of network infrastructures can be managed and operated while being able to facilitate an exponential increase in connected devices, an increase in requirements, and the requirement to be able to change the network at a faster pace, all while keeping the network secure as well.

To accomplish this set of requirements, an Intent-enabled network infrastructure uses a common generic underlying network infrastructure upon which Intents are deployed and removed on-demand. Network intents are descriptions of purpose or requirement that an application or business process has that can be translated into a small distinct piece of network configuration and policy. If the Intent is no longer needed, the Intent is removed from the network.

Several technologies and processes, such as automation, big data, analytics, and APIs, are used to make this type of behavior on the network possible.

While in traditional enterprises the business process is leading, and data, technology, and applications support the business, a digitalized business is about a tighter integration of data, technology, and business processes.

Data and technology are used to redefine the business processes, where innovation of each domain (technology and business) can drive each other forward.

In a digitalized business, applications and data are heavily used in the business processes as well. The network infrastructure plays a critical part in bringing these applications and data to end users.

As soon as a business process is changed, either manually or by technology, the intent for that business process is changed. The network should reflect that change to achieve that improvement.

An Intent-Based Network has the requirement to be capable of deploying and removing Intents via APIs, so it is possible an application can request a change of intent on the network without any human intervention or manual change. This is a typical example for a stage three or stage four change in a digital enterprise; an application or technology is forcing a change in the business process instead of a manual change.

In other words, an Intent-Based Network is a key enabler and requirement for any digitized enterprise as the network infrastructure connects data and applications and is therefore an integral part of the technology.

Organizational Impact

The process of digitalization will have a drastic impact on how an enterprise is organized as a whole. Traditionally, the enterprise is organized around processes that follow each other linearly. With the tighter integration of technology within the business processes, a more symbiotic environment is created where technology can change processes and vice versa.

Consequently, this will change the way an enterprise should and will organize itself around the processes.

The sections that follow highlight a number of organizational changes that will occur during the digitization of any enterprise.

Architecture

For example, an enterprise architecture is traditionally organized in a layered manner with four distinct architectures, as illustrated in Figure 12-5.

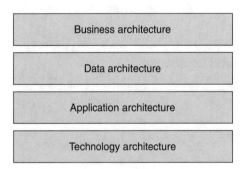

Figure 12-5   *Traditional Enterprise Architecture Modeling*

Building solutions leveraging architectures will of course still be beneficial as it provide flexibility by leveraging building blocks and offering abstraction to other building blocks. Leveraging building blocks remains beneficial to reduce complexity.

But with digitalization, the distinct layers between the different architectures will dissolve as the business will not be the only leading factor in an enterprise architecture anymore. In other words, an application can leverage data from other business processes to suggest (stage three) an optimization of a data model. Also, technology used in the enterprise will provide data that can be used by a business process for improvement or optimization. Figure 12-6 provides a schematic overview of how the domains (people, data, technology, and business processes) interrelate and integrate with each other.

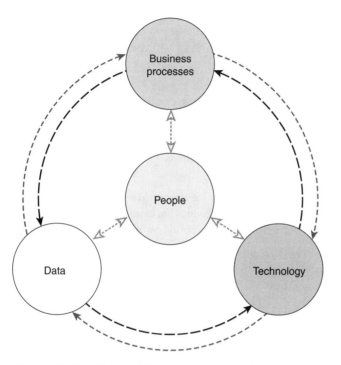

Figure 12-6   *Digitized Business Conceptual Overview*

With this model, data is generated by technology (for example, with Model-Driven Telemetry in a campus network) and can be used to drive changes in a business process, whether this is order picking or the wireless network service.

People can leverage machine intelligence (technology), which consumes both business process and data to optimize a business process or data model.

In other words, the classic hierarchical model of an enterprise architecture is about to change. It is important for architects or designers to recognize that different types of modeling and integrations are going to be possible, and they should embrace it.

Network Design

Traditionally, the design of a network usually takes a rather linear and sequential process, similar to how business processes are modeled. The first step is to obtain the functional and technical requirements, usually written down in a high-level design. Then a low-level design is created that translates those requirements into a design that contains specifics on network equipment and configuration elements. After the low-level design is defined, a new network is implemented and deployed. The network implementation document is created and contains the specific implementation and configuration details.

But within a digitalized business, the functional requirements can change rapidly over time. The cause of this change could be the result of data gathered on the business process, an organizational change, or any other external factor. The network itself could even suggest an optimization of the business process to optimize the flows of applications within the network.

In a traditional environment, these changes would lead to following the same sequence of a new design, obtain the new functional requirements, create a new high-level design, create a low-level design, implement, and document. This work is performed by designers and will take considerable time.

But in IBN, these functional requirements are just a small part of the intents that are deployed and run on the network.

The network design should not be focused on a single functional requirement, but on a generic network infrastructure that is capable of facilitating changing Intents on the network. This will require a different mindset from network designers.

Network designers will need to design a generic infrastructure once and after testing deploy it within the enterprise. Next to the generic infrastructure design, mini-designs will be created that can translate Intents into repeatable pieces of network infrastructure configuration, the network Intents available to business applications.

Network Operations

Intent-Based Networking is an enabler, or even a requirement, for a digitalized business. The foundation of IBN not only provides relevant data to the digital business, but is capable of dynamically adding and removing Intents on the network. In other words, if a process or application is changed within a business process (or enterprise), the network is prepared for implementing that new Intent.

As Intents are deployed and removed on the network dynamically, and preferably automatically by applications, this will implicitly have an impact on the network operations team.

Traditionally the network operations team would log in to the network devices and start troubleshooting an incident based on the configuration of network devices, the connected endpoints, the expected flow, and how the network views that specific flow (hardware caches, installed routes, and so on). In an Intent-Based Network, however, the configuration of a network device is no longer static. It is dynamic and can be changed overnight or even while troubleshooting.

The network operations team must change the way they troubleshoot incidents. They will have to migrate from on-box troubleshooting to troubleshooting via the network management tools deployed on the network. Preferably, these tools have a method to reflect the status of the network at the time of the incident, similarly to the capabilities of DNA Center. Over time, these tools will collect historical data (based on real-time modern Model-Driven Telemetry) such that the time-based approach for troubleshooting can even be used with complex models and Machine Learning to predict future occurrences.

The digital transformation of an enterprise has an organizational impact. Processes and models change from a linear approach where data and technology are subservient to business processes to a more circular model where data, technology, and business processes are tightly integrated and both serve and influence each other.

A key driver of digitalization is that data and technology can perform changes in business processes (automatically or semiautomatically).

Consequently to this driver, a network design might not follow the traditional High-Level Design -> Low-Level Design -> Implementation flow anymore. Because this is a manual execution of sequential tasks, this is not in line with a digitalized business. So network designers need to consider beforehand that the network infrastructure they design will have dynamic (tested) changes over time. This is also a requirement for an Intent-Based Network.

As the configuration of network infrastructure becomes more dynamic, network operations teams need to stop troubleshooting per device, but leverage the tools available within an Intent-enabled network to perform troubleshooting and continuously validate if the network is operating within normal parameters. IBN will proactively support that change.

Summary

One of the key trends over the past few years for executives has been digitalization. Some industries have already seen disruption because a new player in that market introduced a new way of operation and created such a big change that it forced enterprises and businesses into defensive modes. These new players not only had the advantage of starting with a blank sheet, but were based on a digitized enterprise.

Digital transformation, also known as digitalization, is a concept where new technology (digital) is used to solve traditional problems. These digital solutions are often the result of new types of innovation, creativity, or applying new technology to redefine a traditional process or problem. Quite often, data available within an enterprise or market is used by these digital systems to create the new digital solutions.

Chapter 13

IT Operations

Intent-Based Networking (IBN) describes how to manage and operate a network infrastructure. Traditionally, IT operations teams are organized around IT operations frameworks based on best practices. These kinds of changes would have to follow (strict) change procedures including approvals from the change advisory boards.

This often results in the fact that a relatively simple change (for example, in some organizations even a reload of a switch) will take much more time and require significant resources to write a change procedure, request the change to the advisory board, wait for approval, have a discussion about the denial, and then after a long period of time, be able to reload that switch in the evening.

Change procedures and change advisory boards are in general a good thing to reduce the risk of major disruptions and prevent two changes from different domains at the same time; however, organizations often overdo the implementation with a drastic reduction in flexibility and change agility as a consequence.

With a full implementation of IBN, applications leverage APIs to change behavior in the network automatically, without any human intervention at all. The organization of IT operations will need to change to keep the processes (and thus compliancy) in line with IBN and to achieve the maximum potential of digitalization and IBN.

This chapter provides background information on some common frameworks found within IT operations and their principles and how IBN has an impact on these frameworks. The second part of this chapter provides some recommended changes to IT operations to truly enable IBN:

- Common frameworks found within IT operations
  - ITIL
  - DevOps
  - Lean
- Recommended changes

Common Frameworks Within IT Operations

Many enterprises organize their IT processes around a set of common IT operations frameworks. This section describes (briefly) the most common operations frameworks that are used throughout enterprises. Within each framework, the challenge with IBN is described as well.

ITIL

Perhaps the best known and widely used IT operation framework is Information Technology Infrastructure Library (ITIL). ITIL is actually not a framework (containing a model, design principles, and so on) but a collection of concepts and best practices from the industry for delivering IT services to the enterprise.

The most recent version of ITIL is ITIL v4, which was published in early 2019. It is an update of the previous version, ITIL v3 from 2011. ITIL v4 uses new techniques to increase efficiency within IT while also being more aligned with other existing methods, such as Agile, DevOps, and Lean. ITIL v4 encourages, in contrast to ITIL v3, fewer silos, increased collaboration, and the integration of Agile and DevOps into IT Service Management (ITSM) strategies. ITIL v4 is more flexible and customizable compared to ITIL v3. Also, ITIL v4 and ITIL v3 are not mutually exclusive, and many parts of ITIL v3 can be used within ITIL v4 too, which is great because many organizations have based their IT operations on ITIL v3. This section is not intended to fully describe the ITIL v3 framework, but rather provide a conceptual overview to provide context where the ITIL v3 framework has a relationship with IBN.

Use Case: Overusing an IT Operation Framework

SharedService Group provides several IT services to its internal businesses. Some of these systems are Electronic Data Interchange (EDI) systems used by partners to submit data electronically to specific business processes within the enterprise.

EDI systems are used to automatically exchange information electronically (based on agreed and standard document formats) between systems at each communication partner without human intervention. A clear example would be the automatic generation and sending of an electronic invoice to a customer, which would automatically be received and processed in the financial system.

To gain more control of IT in general, SharedService Group decided to implement the ITIL framework. A project was defined, and after executing a number of changes, including significant restructuring of the organization to represent and divide several responsibilities, the project was a success. In general, IT services were described, and procedures could be followed to have applications or services changed within the enterprise.

However, part of the systems that SharedService Group was managing also included specific EDI applications that were critical to the business. These applications were used by partners of the enterprise to submit data electronically.

Part of that data were structured physical locations that were used within the logistics department for receiving and sending shipments. These physical locations were using a coding scheme that made each location unique; and the unique codes were shared throughout the different EDI applications, and were also used by the partners.

As ITIL was fully implemented, the addition of a new physical location would now require a full change procedure, including approval from the change advisory board, and several persons would need to validate whether the additional record was allowed as change to be executed in a change service window.

As long as the change was not approved, no shipment could be sent or received to that new location. This resulted in considerable business loss and business standstills.

Unfortunately, this use case example is not a story on its own. Often organizations perform a full implementation of ITIL, and because it is a collection of best practices in the IT, it is assumed best to incorporate it fully. Consequently, it essentially negates one of the key aspects of any best practice: only adopt them if the context and best practices are applicable for the situation.

Often ITIL is initialized as an attempt to improve service, but it also often ends in a paper tiger containing a lot of procedures and processes that do not directly improve the service experience for customers. It is always important to be very careful and balance between processes and actual operations when implementing a framework.

ITILv3 defines five stages that each define a number of subprocesses for that specific phase.

Figure 13-1 provides a conceptual representation of the different stages an IT service can follow throughout its lifecycle. The image represents a continuous process of (re-)defining and managing services.

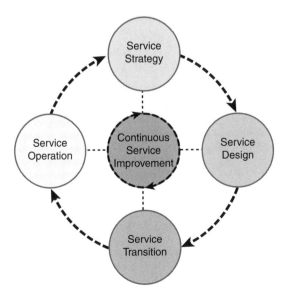

Figure 13-1   *ITILv3 Overview of Stages*

As you can see, the ITILv3 framework has a significant number of descriptive management processes and corresponding key performance indicators (KPIs). This section does not go into detail for each management process, but quite a few processes from the different stages, such as incident management, change management, problem management, and asset management, are familiar within IT operations teams.

Stage 1: Service Strategy

This stage determines which types of services should be offered to customers (or internally within an enterprise). Five rather generic processes are defined to describe this service strategy:

- Strategy management
- Service portfolio management
- Financial management
- Demand management
- Business relationship management

Stage 2: Service Design

The service design stage is used to identify requirements for the service to be provided and can also be used to define new service offerings as well as improving existing services. The following processes are part of stage two:

- Design coordination
- Service catalog management
- Service level management
- Risk management
- Capacity management
- Availability management
- IT service continuity management
- Information security management
- Compliancy management
- Architecture management
- Supplier management

Stage 3: Service Transition

The service transition stage is used to build and deploy IT services. Traditionally project management and improvements are part of this stage. The following processes are identified with this stage:

- Change management

- Change evaluation

- Project management (transition planning and support)

- Application development

- Release and deployment management

- Service validation and testing

- Service asset and configuration management

- Knowledge management

Stage 4: Service Operation

The objective of this stage is to make sure IT services are delivered effectively and efficiently. This would include fulfilling user requests, resolving incidents, and fixing problems, as well as executing routine maintenance tasks.

The following processes are defined within this stage:

- Event management

- Incident management

- Request fulfillment

- Access management

- Problem management

- IT operations control

- Facilities management

- Application management

- Technical management

Stage 5: Continual Service Improvement (CSI)

The last stage for an IT service is the concept of continual service improvement (CSI). The purpose of this stage is to identify repeating incidents or problems that can be solved by improving or changing the service (implementation). The following processes are part of this stage:

- Service review

- Process evaluation

- Definition of CSI initiatives

- Monitoring of CSI initiatives

Often the ITIL management processes used within operations are defined and document-based procedures. In other words, there are written steps to take when a specific action (within a process) needs to be executed. Usually these steps also include control points that require a human decision or validation by another team or group of persons.

Intent-Based Networking has some (interesting) cross-sections with different ITIL management processes. For example, the design of network Intent itself can have a strong relationship with the ITIL service definition stage as a whole; however, once a network Intent (service) has been defined, APIs and automation can be leveraged to deliver that service to the customer automatically. There is no written or documented process necessary; once the service is designed and defined, and applications are allowed to request that service and be deployed on the network.

A similar major difference (and strong relationship) can be seen with event and incident management.

Once a service is deployed, the IBN-enabled network uses analytics to detect and possibly autocorrect incidents based on triggered events.

ITIL and IBN are not mutually exclusive strategies; they can support and complement each other. Cisco DNA Center, for example, provides a number of APIs to tightly integrate Cisco DNA Center with IT Service Management (ITSM) tools that are based on ITIL process definitions. A good example of this is the software upgrade workflow within Cisco DNA Center. Once a (new) golden image is selected for a site within Cisco DNA Center, a change request can automatically be created in the ITSM tool. If the ITSM tool replies (via APIs) back to Cisco DNA Center with an approved service window, Cisco DNA Center can automatically deploy, update, and validate the software upgrade in that time window without human intervention, except when an incident is found while upgrading.

In conclusion, the ITIL framework itself is based on a set of best practices and is set around the definition and delivery of IT services. This is a common approach within any IT organization (or IT department within an enterprise). Intent-Based Networking will enforce that certain procedures will be optimized (or removed) and service delivery will improve.

However, with digitization and Intent-Based Networking as an enabler, the clear distinction between IT providing services and business applications/processes consuming an IT service will be removed. This process will in time result in a required revisitation of the ITIL processes as a whole. IBN can be an accelerator to this revisitation.

DevOps

DevOps, the concatenation of Development and Operations, is a methodology that has been driven by software development to be able to deliver new features and functions of an application or service faster to the customer. Within software development, the Agile software development methodology has proven to be very successful in delivering large IT software projects more efficiently and with increased customer satisfaction.

Being able to provide a new version of a software service every two weeks but needing to wait an extra week for operations to deploy that new version into production is counterproductive. As both worlds (development and operations) were increasingly using automation to release software and provision new services, the merger of the two into a single methodology was only logical. (Net)DevOps is in that regard the next logical step for Agile-based organizations, where network operations will be run based on the same Agile methodology.

But the Agile methodology itself (the basis for DevOps) can be applied to operations teams very successfully. The concept of having multidisciplinary teams that execute the work improves the efficiency as the accountability and responsibility are shared by the team. And although an operations team's primary responsibility is in operating and managing the network, the required work can be categorized into system management work (such as upgrades and changes), responding to incidents, and possibly project work.

One of the characteristics of project work and system management is that the required time can be estimated, in contrast to responding to incidents and problems. And because the work can be estimated and planned, it fits perfectly in the sprint capability within Scrum/Agile. (Sprints were explained in Chapter 2, "Why Change Current Networks? A Need for Change.")

Responding to incidents and problems is a completely different world with its own dynamics. Incidents and problems happen; they cannot be planned. So resources need to be allocated and made available beforehand to respond to the incidents. Kanban is a methodology (from Lean) that can follow Agile and is perfectly suited for incident response. Incidents are entered into the Kanban queue, and resources will work on the different items and effectively resolve incidents and problems.

To successfully implement Agile (and thus DevOps) into an operations team, it is required that the team be divided into two teams, where the teams alternate between sprints and Kanban work. Basically team one is working on system management tasks, such as regular updates and changes, using the sprints from Scrum/Agile, whereas team two is responding to incidents (if they occur) and assisting team one when required.

By allowing the teams to alternate between sprints and Kanban, there is always one team on incident response while the other team performs planned work. This method is very successful and helps employees keep focus. How often is a planned task delayed because a priority-1 incident occurred? In this method of operation, those types of delays are essentially removed.

This method of operation is very successful, and it is only a matter of time before more network operations teams will work on a similar basis, as DevOps is slowly but surely trickling to network operations as well.

However, DevOps is also based on the "fail fast" concept. In other words, deliver a new feature or function fast, and if it does not work, learn from it and fix it fast (in a next release). This concept provides some significant benefits as customers can see new features, test them, and provide feedback so that the solution can be improved. This is in contrast to more traditional software engineering methodologies such as waterfall.

But this concept is not very applicable to the network infrastructure, as a failure in a network configuration or service can have a dramatic impact on the business (even resulting in a business standstill). So fail fast is not really a success factor for network operations, but rather a risk.

Intent-Based Networking can be used to reduce that risk and still work within the Agile methodology.

In an Intent-enabled network, it is easy to quickly deploy network Intents on the infrastructure. To do so successfully, it is important to have those available Intents thoroughly designed and tested before release.

In that sense, the network Intents have a very large parallel to features within a software application; the Intents are features of the network available to be used.

And with that parallel, the tasks required for designing, developing, and testing network Intents are perfect for a Scrum/Agile methodology leveraging sprint items.

And once the network Intent (feature) is tested and approved, it can be released as a new available Intent and can then be used by applications and operations on the network. Because the Intent is tested, the risk of failure and a big impact to the enterprise is reduced.

In conclusion, the Intent-Based Networking concept fits very well within an Agile-based enterprise and operations team.

Lean

Lean IT is an extension of the Lean manufacturing and Lean service principles. It is focused on the development and management of IT products and services. Lean manufacturing, or simply Lean, was originally created by Toyota to eliminate waste and inefficiency in the manufacturing of cars. Because the principles were successful, many other manufacturers adopted the same principles, and Lean became the de facto standard for manufacturing. For many manufacturers, the adoption of Lean is critical in the competition against low-cost countries.

The ultimate goal of Lean is to eliminate waste, where waste is defined as the non-value-added components in any process, to maximize customer value. With every iteration of Lean in a process, the waste is reduced by bits and can be eliminated after a number of iterations. The iteration through Lean is defined with five key principles, which need to be executed sequentially.

Five Key Principles

The Lean Enterprise Institute (LEI), founded by James P Womack and Daniel T Jones in 1997, is considered the central location for Lean knowledge, training, and seminars. According to LEI, there are five key principles: value, value stream, flow, pull, and perfection. Figure 13-2 illustrates the flow of these five key principles.

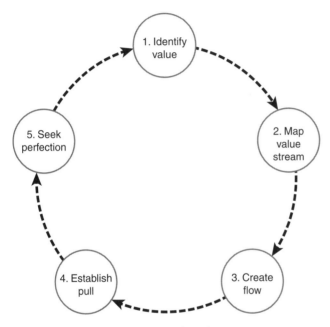

Figure 13-2   *Five Key Principles of Lean*

The sections that follow describe the five key principles of Lean in more detail.

1. Identify Value

Value is always defined as the customer's need for a specific product (or in the case of an IT service organization, an IT service). The value itself is not only monetary but also the timeliness of delivery and the quality of the product. What other requirements or expectations does the customer have for a specific product? These types of questions are used to define the value of a product or service. Once value is defined, it is effectively the end goal for the product or service.

2. Map Value Stream

Once the value (and the corresponding end goal) has been defined, the next step is to map the so-called value stream for all the steps and processes that are required and involved to actually define and make the product for the customer.

Value-stream mapping is a simple but often revealing experience that identifies which actions need to be taken to deliver the product. All processes required should be identified, including processes such as procurement, production, administration, HR, and delivery. The concept is to create a one-page map that contains the identified processes and maps out the flow of material/products throughout the process.

The goal is to identify all steps on that map that do not add value to the product and find ways to eliminate those wasteful steps.

3. Create Flow

Once the waste has been removed from the value stream, the next step is to validate whether the product flows through the remaining processes without any delay, interruption, or other bottlenecks. This step might require breaking down silos and making an effort to become cross-functional across all departments to optimize the value and keep the waste out of the process of creating value. This aspect of working across multiple domains and functional levels is one of the most difficult and challenging aspects in any organization, as it touches accountability and responsibility and requires change (of thinking).

However, studies show that overcoming a silo mentality can increase efficiency with double-digit improvement values.

4. Establish Pull

With the improved and optimized workflow to create the product, the time to market (or to consumer) for the mentioned product can also be optimized. This makes it easier to optimize the organization to deliver "just-in-time." It could literally mean that the customer can "pull" the product from the enterprise as needed, which results in shorter service delivery times (moving these delivery times from months to weeks). As a result of just-in-time delivery, the stock of materials required for the product can then be optimized to reduce the (often) expensive cost of inventory. This results in saving money for both the customer and the manufacturer.

5. Seek Perfection

Steps 1 through 4 already provide a good start and improvement to any production process, but the fifth step is perhaps the most important one: making Lean an integral part of the enterprise and corporate culture. Only when that strive to perfection (removing any waste in providing value) is an integral part of the culture and every employee thinks Lean can the waste be kept to an absolute minimum or ultimately no waste.

Lean can provide very big effects and increase customer satisfaction. Those effects will also fan out to suppliers and partners as they want to generate their own improvements, which will result in improvements for the enterprise too. But bureaucracy and unnecessary actions always lie around the corner, so these five key principles should be iterated frequently so that newly created waste can be removed, and the ultimate goal of providing maximal customer value with minimal waste can be achieved and maintained.

Lean for IT

Lean is originally focused on removing waste in the manufacturing of products and improving the value for customers. But in a sense the IT department within an enterprise, or an IT service company, also provides products, except these products are less tangible as they are focused on services.

Lean IT is an extension to Lean thinking and aims to adopt the framework to IT services. The five key principles are now applied to IT departments (or businesses) and how they provide the IT services to their customer, whether an internal or an external customer.

One of the differences is that the Lean IT extension predefines a set of identified wastes that affect customer satisfaction and service in general (and thus affect the value). Most of these waste types are recognizable within any IT operations team. The following waste types are part of that list and are (very) common within IT. These should be addressed with Lean IT thinking.

- **Defects:** Defects could be unauthorized system and application changes or substandard project execution. This would lead up to poor customer service (and satisfaction) and will increase cost of the service as more time and resources are required to provide the service.

- **Overproduction:** This occurs when IT services are deployed on oversized resources. For example, a branch office for ten Citrix users is provisioned with a 1 Gb WAN link as that is the predefined standard bandwidth for any location. This results in increased business and IT costs.

- **Waiting:** If an application or service provides slow response times, the customer is losing money (because of wait), and the customer satisfaction will be low as the product is not providing the value the customer requires.

- **Motion (excess):** IT operations respond to incidents as firefighters. They respond to an incident and repetitively fix the incident the same way and do not resolve the underlying problem that causes the incidents. This behavior results in reduced customer satisfaction and lost productivity.

- **Employee knowledge:** Perhaps one of the underestimated wastes in any organization is the waste of knowledge. It is quite common that employees on the work floor know where parts of the service or product are not optimized. But ideas and concepts to improve are lost when the information is sent up the hierarchy. And thus the waste remains. Another type of employee knowledge waste occurs when qualified staff executes non-service-related work or when they spend time on mundane and time-consuming repetitive tasks. This results in talent leakage (knowledge is lost) and low job satisfaction, as well as an increase in support and maintenance costs.

The same iteration of the five Lean key principles is executed to identify and remove waste in a service provided by the IT department. The previously mentioned waste types can be used as initiators to optimize request procedures and provide a better experience and service to the customer.

Transforming an IT organization to Lean can be difficult. Many IT organizations are cost focused, have service-level agreements (SLAs) with their customers, and have an internal "production quota" for billable hours. If a problem is found in a service, the primary focus is to restore service as quickly as possible. There is a slim to no chance that the service will be redesigned to prevent the incident from reoccurring.

When Toyota introduced this paradigm in the 1980s, when employees found a quality problem on the production line, they were required to stop the line and fix the problem but also take the time to prevent that quality problem from happening again. That principle is the road to increased quality and perfection.

Within IT service organizations, there is most probably a fear to report these types of quality issues and take a step back to improve the service and quality to the customer as that stop will affect SLAs, affect production quotas, and possibly result in lost revenue. That fear will have a negative impact on customer value and will greatly reduce the chance for maximizing Lean IT thinking potential.

Changing that mindset is difficult as it is also related to how well a business operates in the short term, and (upper) management needs to be aware that Lean IT thinking will have an impact on productivity in the short term to gain in the long term.

In conclusion, Lean itself is not an IT operations framework but more an organization-wide methodology that aims to create the best value for customers. For a network or IT operations department, the best value would be to provide the best IT service with a highly effective and efficient balance between customer needs and available IT resources with a minimum overhead on the service.

Intent-Based Networking is a methodology that fits very well inside the Lean IT thinking methodology. One of the drivers of IBN is that the number of connected devices and services (intents) on a network will increase exponentially, while the operations staff will not be able to follow that same growth pattern. In other words, IBN will result in an increase in efficiency and thus support Lean thinking in the enterprise.

Also, IBN allows business applications to request and consume network Intents automatically, removing waste from the services provided. IBN also allows the operations team to leverage the data gained from operating the network to fix incidents faster and more efficiently, as well as a continuous validation of Intents on the network. That is effectively also a reduction of waste.

For organizations that are fully Lean, IBN is a very good solution to remove waste from the IT services provided within the organization.

Summary of Common Frameworks Within IT Operations

In summary, ITIL and DevOps are probably the most commonly found and applied frameworks within IT operations. And although Lean IT might not be that common within IT operations, it is a method of thinking that has a lot of traction within enterprises.

There are, of course, many other frameworks available that can be used to describe how to manage and organize the IT operations team. Other common frameworks within IT are the ISO standards (ISO 20000 describes the standard for IT Service Management, and ISO 19770 describes asset management), whereas the Six Sigma for process improvement and PRINCE2 for project management with the goal to deliver projects with minimal risk, and too many other frameworks to mention as well.

All these frameworks have in common that they describe a model or abstract of the enterprise using processes and sequential steps; they are process-oriented. The identification of processes is used to abstract complexity as well as to introduce the demarcation of responsibility. Also, in these frameworks, the processes are defined and executed sequentially to keep focus and clarity.

However, the implementation of an Intent-Based Network will over time have an impact on those frameworks as the operation of the network is changed and will not adhere to those frameworks.

The biggest example is how changes occur on the network. Traditionally, changes require the submission of a change request that follows a (strict) change procedure. That change procedure attempts to assess the risk and impact and provides an approval or denial for that change. Often that decision is made by a change advisory board that meets once or twice a week.

But with an Intent-enabled network, an application can request a new network Intent via an API and get that Intent automatically deployed on the network. In essence, the application is performing a change on the network without following the paper-based change procedure.

There are other differences between IBN and these frameworks, such as the design of a network infrastructure. If IT operations are strictly organized around these frameworks, they will effectively block a successful implementation of IBN. Some parts of IT operations need to be changed to fully enable IBN.

Potential Conflicts and Recommendations

For those enterprises that have organized and implemented their IT operations around these common frameworks, the implementation of IBN will create potential conflicts within the IT department and the network operations team. As each enterprise is different, the impact of that conflict will vary as well. A complete list of conflicts between IBN and all frameworks is impossible to provide; however, a number of recommended changes in IT operations can be described and motivated. The section that follows describes the causes of potential conflicts and provides some recommendations to overcome these.

Common Design Patterns Change

One of the most common approaches to IT operations in general is a sequential approach. A problem is identified, the requirements are identified, a solution is designed, and then the solution is implemented and managed. This approach is so common that many frameworks and project steps take a similar approach.

Thus the organization (and operation) is defined in a similar approach, where designers and architects listen to the business. They identify the problem, determine the requirements, and design a solution. Network engineering will then implement the solution, and operations will in turn operate that solution. Often new networks are designed and implemented in this manner to solve new functional requirements as the existing network cannot be matched to these new requirements.

The approach in IBN is quite different. With an Intent-enabled network, there is a common existing underlying network infrastructure upon which Intents need to be designed and implemented. So instead of designing a new network, the designer needs to define the solution as part of the existing network, but it needs to be designed in such a way that it is easy to deploy *and* remove the Intent from the network. Designers need to change their design patterns and consider not only the deployment of the Intent, but also the removal. All network Intents must be designed as service blocks that can easily be reused.

There will, of course, be times when the organization wants to have an Intent-enabled network in a greenfield situation. In that case, the network architect or designer should focus on creating a minimalistic underlay network upon which a diverse variety of Intents are possible. The traditional limitations of designing a network for a single purpose or focusing on a single problem are not applicable; instead, the basic underlay network must be designed in such a way that it can facilitate for that single problem and for other Intents that are to be deployed on the network. In this situation (where a new Intent-Based Network needs to be designed), the network architect should not only look at the new required network infrastructure but also services and applications running on the network.

Management by Exception

The IT operations team (specifically the network operations team) is responsible for the proper operation and management of the network infrastructure. Traditionally, the network operations team is in control of the network and its configuration. Best practices and validated designs are used to guarantee that the configuration and operation of the network are as optimal as possible. Often the operations team will state that it can only be responsible (and accountable) for the network if it has full control and operation of the network. Every change on the network must be under the auspices and approval of the operations team.

In principle, the operations team is somewhat correct. To take responsibility, there needs to be control; however, with IBN, the control of the network configuration is split between the operations team and any application or business process that is allowed to request and remove Intents on the network. When this functionality is enabled (key component of IBN), the absolute control of the network is effectively given out of hand. That aspect will be a driver for fear and resistance from the operations team to share control with an external entity, as the operations team remains responsible and accountable.

This fear and risk of losing control is mitigated by leveraging two paradigms and changing the way responsibility is organized and documented.

To restrict the number of allowed changes on the network and prevent chaos on the Intents, only approved and tested Intents are allowed on the network (quite possibly with a limitation). In other words, the network operations team will define, in collaboration with network designers and architects, which Intents can be requested and deployed. These Intents must, of course, be well defined, well designed, and properly tested in a lab environment. Part of the requirements will be that a single Intent cannot interfere with other Intents.

This process will initially limit the number of available Intents, but it will also provide control back to the operations team because it controls which Intents can be provided as a service.

The other paradigm is called management by exception. Management by exception has both a general business application and a business intelligence application. Its principle is common in industries where the flow of information or the flow of goods is so complex that managing them individually is impossible. The basic principle of management by exception is the assumption that the generic process itself is well-defined and that 99% of the flow is going according to the process and plan. Specific tools, metrics, and procedures are defined that are activated in case something goes wrong. The performance of the actual operation would continuously be validated against the expected metrics, and if a deviation is found, the focus will be on that deviation.

Another example of management by exception is within logistics, where the amount of goods being transported is so high that it is impossible for public safety organizations to inspect every item being transported. Instead, they rely on profiling and smart usage of data to identify potentially interesting transports and will inspect them.

Sales organizations could rely on that same principle where the metrics are based on the number of units sold and the average selling price. If a single product underperforms in a quarter, management is informed and appropriate action can be determined and executed.

This approach is also common within IT for service monitoring in combination with SLAs. A probe periodically validates the performance of an application; if the performance is outside the allowed bandwidth, it will be reported and acted on.

This management by exception principle is actually an integral part of an Intent-Based Network. The tooling within an Intent-Based Network continually validates the successful operation of the requested Intents, and if an Intent is not performing as expected, the operations team is informed. In other words, an IBN has, by design, implemented the management by exception paradigm. It is important that the operations team is made aware of this concept and embraces that principle because the exponential growth of devices connecting to the network will make classical full control management impossible to maintain.

Work Cross-Domain

In a digitalized enterprise, business and IT are becoming aligned, and technology will support and drive business process changes. Part of that aspect is that business and IT need to understand each other. IBN is an enabler for the digitalization. IBN allows network Intents to be deployed onto the network, but IT is not only the network. It also comprises compute, storage, cloud, security, and application development.

It is common for organizations to organize their departments and processes around these different domains and fields of expertise. In other words, a dedicated team is responsible for server management, whereas a different team is responsible for workspace management. Although this is good for the organization of responsibility, it is bad for customer experience and innovation as they are essentially silos. One of the things that DevOps/Scrum Agile has shown is that with multidisciplinary teams, a much better valued software program is created, as the different experts work together to implement a specific feature.

Intent-Based Networking dictates a similar approach. The network enables connectivity for the applications and services of the enterprise, but the intents need to be defined and designed based upon the requirements of the business, and they need to be aligned with the other IT expertise fields.

It is therefore recommended to open up as a network infrastructure team, and when defining intents, work across domain with all expertise areas, including the customer (business process) to define a network intent that truly creates value for the business.

Organizational Change

In conclusion, the existing (control) frameworks used within businesses to organize IT services and operations will generate conflicts of interest with Intent-Based Networking and the digitization process in general. To solve these conflicts, deviations from well-known and familiar processes and responsibilities need to be defined. These deviations will in turn force a change in how IT operations manages their responsibility and provides services.

It also means that the organization is consciously deviating from the existing frameworks, which will have consequences for businesses that are being audited. Therefore, these deviations need to be validated and documented.

It is only logical that as IBN changes the way a network is designed and operated, IT operations needs to follow, and over time the frameworks will follow suit. But changing operational processes is challenging and complex. However, these changes are required for IBN; therefore, it is important to have commitment from management.

Summary

IBN is the next evolution of networking. It describes a way to operate and manage the network to be able to cope with the external changes, such as the exponential growth of connecting devices and the digitization of businesses.

Traditionally, IT operations teams are organized around a number of well-known common frameworks. These frameworks typically take a process-oriented and sequential approach on how to manage, operate, and improve IT services.

As IBN takes a new approach on how the network is operated, it is very well possible that IBN will conflict with some of these common frameworks.

A good example of such a conflict is the change request procedure. In traditional environments, a change request is registered in an IT Service Management (ITSM) tool and follows a (strict) change procedure where the impact and scope of change are determined, and a change advisory board decides whether the change is approved or denied.

These procedures usually take time from both the IT operations team as well as employees who have a seat on the change advisory board (which probably only meets once or twice a week). And although the principle behind it is to prevent major incidents, the change itself takes time.

With IBN, an application can use an API call to the network controller to remove an existing intent from the network, which results in changes in the network configuration. The application bypasses the change procedure to get its intent enabled or removed.

So although these frameworks aim to provide better service quality, improve customer experience, and provide a faster delivery time, parts of processes around the design and operation of the network will need to be changed and accepted. With the preceding example, if the API call were placed on hold until the change advisory board approved it, then where would the gain of faster deployment be? As with every change, small steps provide the best chance of success.

If the organization has a strong ITIL-based process organization and the business adheres strongly to those processes, there will be no room for change, and the chance of a successful IBN implementation would be reduced. But if the organization is open to improvement (for example, via the Lean thinking principles or the introduction of Agile), then the chance of successfully changing the processes that involve IBN is much higher.

In conclusion, IBN will also force and drive change in the organization's processes and responsibilities. This need for change will create conflicting interests within frameworks commonly used by organizations to define and manage their IT environment. Conflicts of interest could arise, and you need to be aware of these.

Common Design Pattern Change

Traditionally, enterprises follow a sequential pattern to solve a problem or define a new service. The problem is defined, its requirements and limitations are documented, and a designer creates a solution to that problem. Once the solution is designed, engineering implements the solution, and operations manages it.

In the case of a network, it is relatively common that a complete new network design is created because the old network design does not fit all the requirements, or possibly the engineering heart plays up, and new technology is required.

But with IBN, newly requested network intents are dynamically deployed on the network; in other words, there is a common network infrastructure that carries the required intents. The consequence is that the design of new network functions needs to take into account the existing Intent-Based Network, and the solution must be based on a small service that can easily be deployed and removed on that Intent-Enabled Network.

In other words, designers need to start designing in small microservices on the network instead of a (large) new network where the key design principles of DNA and concepts of IBN are leveraged.

Another design pattern change is when a complete new network, such as for a new plant or warehouse, needs to be designed. In that case, the network designer should design a minimal baseline network infrastructure with the microservices on top that will match with the requirements set for that new network. The designer needs to be aware that other services, possibly unknown to him, can be added and removed dynamically.

Management by Exception

A business is organized around the aspect of responsibility and accountability. As a business grows, departments are created to delegate and split responsibility and accountability among these departments. Most IT frameworks take the same approach. It is common that accountability and responsibility can only be provided if the team has full control of the process. In other words, many network operations teams claim that they can only be held responsible for the network if they have full control over it.

But with IBN, part of that control is delegated to (business) applications and processes that can add and remove intents on that network. Some control is being lifted, so how can the operations team still remain in control?

Besides the fact that any allowed intent should have been thoroughly tested in a lab before being enabled on the network, a mental shift in thinking about responsibility is required. There should be a mental shift from management by control to management by exception. Management by exception has both a general business application and a business intelligence application. Its concept is common in industries and markets where the high volume of data or goods makes a control-based management concept impossible. This concept assumes that in general the process is working and operating as expected, and if something is out of order, an exception is generated and handled.

A good example is the Rotterdam harbor. They handled 8,635,782 containers in 2018,[1] which averages to 23,660 containers per day. Because as it is common to have multiple types of goods and transports inside a single container, it is impossible for authorities to inspect every individual item. Instead, the assumption is that everybody follows the normal procedures and pays their import duties. Profiling is used to find exceptions to the process, and those containers will be inspected.

Although the concept is not known as management by exception within networking, network monitoring systems actually take the same approach. They assume that the network is operating correctly, and probes are used to validate this assumption. If an error is found, an alert is generated so the operations team can take appropriate actions.

Management by exception is actually an integral part of IBN. The tools used for IBN continuously validate whether the intents are operating correctly on the network and actively report the event to the operations team. Machine intelligence assists to determine whether the exception needs to be aggregated to a site-wide problem.

This concept should also be applied to the way the network operations teams view the network and can still take responsibility by leveraging the assumption that all flows are working correctly, unless monitoring states otherwise.

Cross Domain

It is common for businesses to organize their teams and processes around specific knowledge (technology) domains; for example, a dedicated team is responsible for server management, a different team is responsible for network security, another for application management, and so on. Although this is good from a responsibility (and control) perspective, it is bad for customer experience, as these domains are essentially silos. Silos are proven not to provide the best customer experience or best service. One of the success factors of Scrum/Agile (and DevOps) is the power of multidisciplinary teams that

---

1   Source: https://www.portofrotterdam.com/sites/default/files/overslag-havenbedrijf-rotterdam-2018.pdf
or
https://www.portofrotterdam.com/en/our-port/facts-and-figures/facts-figures-about-the-port/throughput

jointly work on problems and incidents. It has proven to provide a more customer-focused solution and increases efficiency as well.

IBN dictates a similar approach. The network is the connecting factor between endpoints and application services. And the necessary intents on that network are defined and built upon business requirements and needs at that moment. As the connecting factor, that intent needs to be aligned with other IT expertise fields as well to provide a consistent experience and service to the business.

It is therefore recommended to open up as a network infrastructure team, and when defining intents, work across domains with all expertise areas, including the customer (business process) to define a network intent that truly creates value for the business.

Organizational Change

The organization will change because of IBN. That change is required to fully maximize the capabilities of IBN and prepare for the next steps in the evolution of technology.

This organizational change means that the organization will deviate from existing frameworks and suggested methods of operation to define new ways, just as with digitization. Most frameworks approve of that type of deviation, as long as its arguments are documented.

But many organizations that follow these frameworks often follow it by the letter instead of using the best practices specific for their organization (due to lack of understanding or lack of faith in their own organization's capabilities). Consequently, auditors can have comments on those deviations. It is recommended to not only keep commitment from management for those changes but also document them and change the documented procedures, including arguments for why the change was made.

Without that type of documentation and commitment, there is a risk the change needs to be rolled back because of an auditor who is not aware of IBN.

Chapter 14

Tips to Make Your IBN Journey a Success

It is now clear that IBN is not only about managing the network but also about changing the enterprise, its processes, and its employees. Some of these changes will go fast; some will go slow. This last chapter provides a set of recommendations and background information that will support you in driving for change and making the transformation to IBN more successful. The topics in this chapter are self-contained, and some might not be applicable at all. Recommendations and background information on the following subjects are covered in this chapter:

- Human change
- Fear
- Quid pro quo and incentives
- Challenge
- Failure
- Forward thinking
- Ownership
- Training and demonstration
- Lifecycle management
- Stakeholders and governance

Human Change

Many books have already been written on changing employees or teams, changing your own behavior (self-help books), and the psychology of the human being. This background information is not in any way intended to be complete; rather, it provides a brief description of two concepts related to human change.

It is important to know that the human brain essentially works in two modes: a very fast mode and a very slow and considerate mode. The slow mode takes all the things that it perceives in more detail and balances out before making a decision, while the other mode of the brain works so fast it can feel like nearly instant action. The latter one is defined as the limbic system but is more commonly known as our lizard brain.[1]

An example of the lizard brain is when you are walking in the park. We do not need to think about which signal is sent to which muscle at which moment in order to walk. But just try to take that same walk while trying to continually add up nonsequential numbers. For example, start with one and add three at each step. Eventually your pace will slow down because your slow and considering brain is taking over from the lizard brain as the task at hand becomes more complex.

As you can imagine, that slow and considerate mode of the brain consumes much more energy to undertake an action than the fast mode. To make the most efficient use of our energy, our brain is "programmed" to use the lizard brain as much as possible and will attempt to take shortcuts, which are known as human biases.

Our slower considered mode of the brain is used for learning new skills and making difficult decisions. But once something is learned, neurological paths in our brain are created, or programmed, so that our lizard brain can take over after we have learned a new technique or trick.

This background information is important to know when a change in human behavior is required, for example, in troubleshooting a network incident. If a major network incident occurs, a typical network engineer will ask for some context and start logging in to switches and analyze the network. The lizard brain is taking over, and the skills the network engineer has learned are being applied to solve the problem at hand.

It is possible to change these automatic pathways and behaviors, but it will take time and effort. It is a complete separate field of expertise to change human behavior, but for this paragraph, it is sufficient to know that there are several fields within human psychology that cover this topic.

To facilitate change it is necessary to be aware that automatic pathways are used for skills that someone has learned. Figure 14-1 displays a model commonly used to represent the stages somebody follows when learning and applying a new skill.

---

1   The limbic system is often referred to as the lizard brain because the limbic system is all a lizard has for a brain function. It is in charge of fight, flight, feeding, fear, freezing up, and fornication.

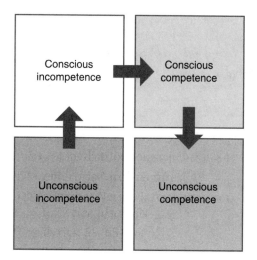

Figure 14-1 *Learning Stages of a New Skill*

The first stage is that you are unaware of a specific skill at all, so you are also unaware that you can possibly learn that unknown skill. The second stage is that you are consciously aware that you do not have that skill (yet), and you start to learn that new skill. Once you learn that skill, you will be consciously aware of that skill. You now know that you can apply that skill, and you set your mind to perform that specific skill. The skill is there, but you need to put your mind to it.

The last stage in learning a new skill is that you are not consciously aware of applying that new skill at all; you can now perform that specific skill without much thought. Your lizard brain now can jump into action and execute that skill automatically.

This information can be leveraged to support change in behavior. For example, somebody can be made aware that he or she automatically logs in to a switch when an incident is reported, while Cisco DNA Center assurance might already provide information without even touching the CLI.

Once somebody is made consciously aware that he or she followed an automatic pathway, it is possible to suggest alternative paths and allow the person to learn a new skill and thus adopt new (automatic) pathways.

It is important to support and guide the changes and learn new required skills.

And because learning new skills is performed by the slower brain, this change will take a lot of energy and concentration. That works great when there is no pressure, but as soon as pressure is applied almost everybody will revert to their old automatic patterns. This is perfectly normal human behavior; essentially the lizard brain kicks in and uses the automatic pathways and familiar behavioral patterns.

So even when training and coaching are being executed during the transformation to IBN, *once a major disruption occurs, or some other external pressure is applied, engineers (and designers) will fall back on their good old behavioral patterns. And it will appear as if all was done for nothing.* This situation will occur and should be allowed to happen. Ensure that there is room to make the "relapse" aware to the team and allow the team to learn and change again.

Fear

Another human aspect to change is fear. It is, again, part of our brain to react to a situation in either the "fight" or "flight" mode. Fear can be a difficult obstacle to overcome when not handled correctly. Fear can make somebody (or a whole team) go into a defensive mode, and they will do everything possible to keep things the same and might even sabotage changes to prove they are right.

Although many engineers are enthusiastic about any new technology or tool and their "engineer heart" wants to dive in immediately, the most common show of fear is with the introduction of automation into the network.

When automation is introduced into any environment, staff will almost instantly fear losing their jobs.

And although examples can be identified, in most situations where automation is deployed, old jobs will be lost, but new jobs will emerge as well. In other words, if you are able to change and adapt, you might find yourself in a new role with a different job description.

In summary, fear is a true risk to any change and is specific and real in the case of automation. To be able to cope with this risk, it is important to have both support and good understanding from upper management. IBN is not about how to do as much work as possible while reducing the operations team; it is to prepare the enterprise (and the network) for the upcoming changes with an already overloaded and understaffed operations team. It is important that upper management understands this and that IBN is an enabler for digitalization. Once that commitment is established, it is important to keep communicating and repeating that statement, specifically when introducing the automation component.

Quid Pro Quo and Incentives

A successful driver for change is the combination of quid pro quo and incentives. *Quid pro quo* is a Latin proverb that translates to "something for something." It is much easier to make a change successful if there is a beneficial element. That element could be something directly related to a person, or the removal of a boring part of the job that needs to be executed. Using benefits or incentives to drive a change is a common practice. The mechanism itself is very common, used throughout marketing and communications.

Use Case: How Quid Pro Quo Can Be Applied for Change

In my career I have participated in several projects, almost always IT-related but not always directly related to a network infrastructure. Quite a few of them were also about how IT can greatly reduce the complexity of a process or make work a lot easier. One of those projects was about the huge stack of travel documents that accompany a container vessel during the voyage (transport). At that moment in time, it was mandatory for each good being transported to have accompanying documents that detailed the sender, receiver, shipper, and type of goods. A typical container vessel would transport 200+ containers, which adds up to a lot of paper accompanying the containers.

Law enforcement, of course, had the right to inspect and validate those documents. It was common for law enforcement to board a container vessel during the transport and validate those documents. This usually took a lot of time and effort.

The captain of the vessel also received the cargo information digitally, because he had the obligation to report dangerous goods to other authorities as well (so that in case of a calamity, the appropriate emergency response could be provided, based on the dangerous goods information).

Within this project, the quid pro quo mechanism was used to introduce a new way of working. If the captain would voluntarily send the cargo information digitally to law enforcement, law enforcement would not inspect the containers during transport but during loading and offloading of the containers.

The advantage to law enforcement was that they received the information in advance, and the benefit for the captain was that his voyage (transport) was no longer interrupted.

Although this use case is not directly related to IBN, it displays how quid pro quo can be used to drive change when resistance or fear is a major factor. The transportation market is competitive, and cargo information is sensitive. But in this situation both parties benefited from a shared change.

Quid pro quo is a form of incentive where both parties benefit from a change. It can perfectly be combined with enticing a user or a team into change as well. The combination can be used to overcome tangible risks of fear and resistance in a team. It is used to reduce the level of fear and aims to provide a direct benefit to the team.

A good example where this can be applied is the introduction of automation. As automation is almost synonymous with the fear of losing a job, this mechanism can be used to encourage the team to use automation to get rid of boring tasks such as manually changing a Syslog server or updating 100+ switches manually.

Although this mechanism should not be overused (because of the risk of losing credibility), it provides a great method of gaining trust and introducing change.

Challenge

Another method or aspect to change is using challenges. Challenge a team or person on why a choice was made in the past. By challenging a design choice, or process, the person is triggered to think about that choice.

The challenge will trigger the brain to use the considerate mode and will likely use experiences related to that choice to determine whether that choice is still valid. Answers like "we have always done it this way" are not acceptable. Ask why that choice was made.

To keep the discussion open and alive, it is important to ask these questions and challenges in a noncondescending way. As soon as the challenge is perceived as condescending, people will go into a defensive mode and will not be able to approach the initial challenge differently.

Challenges can be executed by using the why question or by asking whether a different solution can be used to achieve the same situation. Different thinking can trigger changes as well.

Challenges (or disruptions) should also be just large enough to put somebody off-balance to trigger thinking differently. Change, though challenging, is a process that will take time, but it will provide the benefit that the support for doing things differently is greater than simply enforcing a change. Change should be intrinsic to the team, and challenging can help in adopting change. Also, do not create challenges too frequently, as people might completely go off-balance and then revert to old behavior.

Because this kind of change will take a longer period of time, it is possible that external factors will put pressure on the process of change. For example, a strong budgetary cut can easily put strain on the process, and a reversion to all methods will occur.

Use Case: Consistent Communication Important to Maintain Focus

FinTech Ltd. is operating in the financial market. As the financial crisis around 2010 reached its height, some business and revenue were lost for FinTech as well. This occurred in the middle of a transition with the implementation of network access control. As the revenue was reduced, budgets were cut across the board. The implementation of network access control was put on hold. Although management and the team found it important to implement network access control, there was initially no budget available for hardware and configuration.

In contrast, a consultancy firm was hired to analyze whether and how a restructure would benefit the organization and reduce the operational cost in general.

Although the project was put on hold, the internal communication with the team was kept active. This communication also included asking challenging questions to different stakeholders within the business as to why network access control was a good thing and what the risks were.

This strategy culminated in consistent communication during interviews with the consultancy firm. This resulted in the fact that the project was found important and beneficial enough to be continued, irrelevant of a possible restructure.

This situation typically describes an external factor that can put pressure and strain on any project and change. It is important in these types of situations to keep focus, consistent communication, and commitment to the changes already in progress. Some changes might take longer, but the commitment in combination with perseverance will eventually result in the desired change.

And as change is usually realized slowly, periodically try to step back and see the progress. Changes occur in small steps, and sometimes are even invisible.

Failure

It might be a platitude, but everybody learns the most from his or her own mistakes and experiences. The ability to recognize your own mistakes and learn from them is a separate skillset, and the most interesting stories are often from senior staff members who share war stories that also contain their own failures. Showing your own failures and mistakes is essentially a show of strength and not weakness.

A successful transformation to IBN is not complete without some type of failure and the experiences learned from them. This aspect is applicable to all facets of the transformation to IBN, from learning new technologies and new troubleshooting skills to changing teams and operations. If failures are not allowed during the journey, the chance of reverting to old behavior and patterns is very high. It is thus recommended to create an environment where failures in each aspect of the transformation are allowed. Inform stakeholders that mistakes and failures are an essential part of the process and need to be accepted without repercussions.

Forward Thinking

Forward thinking is a mechanism where a team is learning new skills or applying changes by guiding them through a number of smaller controlled steps rather than providing one big step. This principle is common in learning a new language. Instead of providing all grammar rules and vocabulary at once, smaller controllable steps are used to introduce new words and grammar rules to the student.

A similar approach can be taken for change. By continuously forward-thinking a number of steps toward an implementation, the team can take smaller, manageable steps toward that goal. By taking the team only on the first step (while keeping the second and third in the back of your mind), the team can take one small step at a time, making it easier while still being able to learn a bigger new skill.

The risk of not forward-thinking a number of steps is that after the first step a new path is taken to a completely different solution than originally intended and anticipated. By continuously predefining the next three to five steps, the path being taken becomes more controllable and manageable. Small diversions are allowed, as the second or third step will then be used to revert to the original strategy or implementation.

Although the steps are defined, it can be overwhelming to a team to know all the steps toward implementation. Sometimes it is better to not share all the steps, but allow the team to take one step at a time. This is specifically important if a large change in operation or design is to be implemented. Big changes tend to be more difficult than a sequence of small changes. And although the end result is the same, the risk of losing the team during the change is much lower with small steps than larger steps.

The process of defining the next three to five steps is rather difficult and requires some experience and knowledge. To prevent too small steps or taking a wrong path, it is recommended to periodically reflect the steps toward the intended change or implementation with peers using peer review and open discussion. These peer reviews could be with senior members of the team who are open to change or, in a more generic way, with persons who perform similar tasks.

It is important to periodically validate the end implementation with the stakeholders (and management) as they might have had a change of insight too.

Forward thinking can be seen as a key concept for the transformation to Intent-Based Networking. The end goal is an Intent-enabled network, which is a great change. By dividing it into smaller, manageable steps, it allows the team to take that journey and change more easily.

Ownership

Traditionally in larger enterprises, projects are used to drive change in an organization. Projects are used to deploy a new software solution, execute a large software upgrade, or select a new coffee vending machine. One of the reasons for this strategy is to keep operations running the business while a change is being executed in a controlled manner using project management frameworks. Although this strategy helps keeping a controlled scope and deliverables, this strategically will most likely fail for the projects related to the transformation to IBN.

Often these projects are defined with a specific demand. A project manager and project team are established to execute that task. It is common to hire external resources to execute the project to keep the operations running and not have the operations team worry about project-related tasks and project stress.

These project teams often have to make decisions during design or implementation that have consequences when the project is handed over to the operations team. These decisions are usually when the project faces problems, such as the application is not operating as designed or a special management tool is required for a new piece of hardware. Decisions are then commonly made within the project team without consulting the operations team and thus not overseeing the consequences of those decisions once the result of the project is handed over to operations.

Consequently, the operations team is faced with a project that is not delivering a solution that really helps operations, and operations needs to either use that tool or choose to ignore it as much as possible and move on to business as usual.

Also, project managers have a different task and responsibility than an operations team. Project managers have to finish a project within time and budget and often with limited resources and assumptions. Most often their priority is not completely in line with how the end result of the project is to be managed and operated after the project, but more on the project itself. Once the project is finished and delivered, they will move on to a new project.

From a management perspective that behavior can be a valid point to keep the project within budget and manageable. It often also leads to extra workload on the operations team to keep that new tool or system up and running.

Intent-Based Networking is primarily about how the next generation of networks should be managed and operated. It provides a way for the operations team to manage that network. Everything in the transformation is directly related to the operations team. To successfully perform that transition, the related projects must be executed by the operations team. Project managers and external resources can, of course, be used as extra support, but the changes and tasks should primarily be executed by the operations team. It is their environment that is to be changed. They should take and have ownership of the transformation.

Training and Demonstration

Perhaps one of the most underestimated aspects of any change is the power of training. We tend to forget that every existing operation (installing a new switch, configuring a new VLAN) is based on training and lessons learned (experience from that training).

Intent-Based Networking is leveraging new tools and methods to deploy and operate a network. Training and demonstration of new features or functions are great ways to make a team more comfortable with new methods of operation.

A variety of training methods can be used to demonstrate and learn new skills, including workshops, vendor-provided courses, role playing, simulations, and company trainings. Each type of training can have a different effect.

As a lab is recommended for the transformation to an Intent-Based Network, the same lab can also be used to as a training opportunity for the operations team. Simulate situations in the lab that reflect a small Intent-enabled network, and allow the team to analyze and troubleshoot it. Or use the lab to test new tools and procedures.

It is recommended to also use training methods to support change.

Stakeholders and Governance

Although the need for change should be intrinsic to the persons and units involved, there will be situations where the proverbial carrot proves insufficient and a stick is required. In that case it is important to have sufficient backup and commitment from stakeholders and upper management. They can provide a more directive approach to prevent situations in which people say yes to the change but act differently (for any number of reasons).

Leveraging management can in those situations be of assistance to keep focus and push a team into a change.

A good practice for stakeholder management is to not only have formal periodic meetings with stakeholders (usually per quarter) but have informal bilateral meetings with individual stakeholders at a higher frequency. As these meetings are informal and more frequent, lessons or experiences of what recently happened can be discussed, and actions can be taken to redirect or correct a flow or behavior. Make sure that these informal meetings are scheduled, and keep commitment to have these meetings, even if the only communication is that all is well.

These informal meetings will help in keeping management and stakeholders involved. Chances are that stakeholders will use those meetings as a form of peer review of their experiences.

Lifecycle Management

The concept of a lifecycle management process has been explained in Chapter 8, "Phase Two: Prepare for Intent." The lifecycle management process ensures that the network remains up-to-date on hardware and software via specified and committed procedures. As an Intent-Based Network is business critical in a digitalized business, it is a key requirement to keep the business going.

Use the experiences and lessons learned from the transition to IBN to set up a validated, proven, and supported life cycle management process. This benefits the enterprise on a number of levels, not only on a business outcome perspective (being able to execute change when required) but also the maturity level of the enterprise.

It also provides a warrant that when a specific new technology or solution can benefit the enterprise there is room and budget available to implement that new solution.

Summary

A key part of IBN is about change. Most of the changes in the transformation to IBN are not technically oriented but more organizational and behavioral. Making change happen is a complex process upon which many books have already been written. It requires a lot of adoption, flexibility, and focus from all parties involved. The information and recommendations described in this chapter are only a small part of a much larger toolkit with methods, methodologies, and concepts.

Determining when to use which aspect of the toolkit is a continuous balance based on past experiences, sensitivity, personal skillsets, and the available time and resources. You can use the recommendations and information in this chapter to facilitate that change.

Although a diverse set of recommendations and information was provided in this chapter, some aspects are slightly more important to focus on.

- **Ownership:** Perhaps one of the most important recommendations is that the journey to IBN is to be executed primarily by the network operations team. Try to avoid the use of separate project teams that do not involve the network operations team to prevent a solution from being presented that is not supported and beneficial to the network operations team. Project management is absolutely required for such a big transformation, but the executing staff of the identified projects must be the operations team. They are the ones who will operate and manage the IBN.

- **Positiveness:** The proverb "You can catch more flies with a drop of honey than with a barrel of vinegar" has a ring of truth to it in relation to change. Try to drive all changes with a positive attitude. Positive attitudes and providing (direct) benefits to changes allow for greater success and support within the operations team.

  Successful implementations (or parts) should also be celebrated with the team. This will provide a more positive vibe to the team.

  To celebrate successes, also allow for failures. In a sardonic way, failures can be celebrated as well to prevent a negative vibe around the failure that can create an implicit resistance.

- **Change is slow:** Successful changes take time. Regardless of the method, such as controlled disruption, quid pro quo, and challenging, each change is to be carried out by staff. Fallbacks to old processes will occur. Factor those in and be consistent, patient, and persistent to the changes. Make sure that the appropriate stakeholders are informed and that they stay committed to the transformation to IBN. Also, periodically take a step back and see what already has been accomplished.

- **Training:** Learning new skills equals training. Allow for enough training (including failures) on skills and changes required. The training should not only be on technology and tools, which is normal, but also on team building, learning new skills, and organizational aspects. If the role of employees changes, allow them to be trained on that new role as well.

- **Forward thinking:** A key recommendation to change is to foresee more steps that need to be taken. But keep those steps to a limited group of persons (to do peer review and reflect) while communicating the end strategy and the first step at hand. This is required to prevent losing the team by taking each step too fast.

In conclusion, organizational change itself is a complex task that requires effort, perseverance, patience, and commitment. It is also a different field of expertise with different knowledge domains. Leverage external knowledge and resources where possible, use personal experiences and soft persuasion, and apply pieces of the toolkit when and where necessary.

That will only help to accommodate the necessary organizational changes to successfully transform to IBN.

Appendix A

Campus Network Technologies

A campus network leverages several networking technologies to provide the required services of the network. Throughout this book a number of these technologies have been named and used within the campus network, varying from classic technologies like VLAN to new technological concepts like SDA. This appendix describes a conceptual overview of the technologies named and used throughout this book. The descriptions, although sometimes technical, are aimed to provide the reader with a conceptual understanding of the usage or workings of the technology. They are not a replacement for the technical documentation and technically oriented books available for studying and mastering new technologies.

The appendix is divided into groups of technologies and describes the following technologies:

- Common technologies for Intent-Based Networking

  - Network Plug and Play (PnP)

  - Zero Touch Provisioning (ZTP)

  - Virtual Routing and Forwarding (VRF-Lite)

  - IEEE 802.1x

  - RADIUS

  - Scalable Group Tagging (SGT)

  - Routing protocols

  - Software Defined Access

  - VXLAN

  - LISP

- Classic technologies

  - VLAN

- Spanning Tree Protocol

- Virtual Trunking Protocol

■ Analytics

- Syslog

- SNMP

- Model Driven Technology

- NetFlow

Common Technologies

Intent-Based Networking within the campus network can be deployed using either in a Software-Defined Access (SDA) manner or in a classic VLAN (non-fabric) manner. Both types of deployments are good for Intent-Based Networking, where over time more campus networks will evolve to SDA (as that is the next generation of technologies suitable for campus networks). Both types of deployments leverage common technologies in the operation and configuration of the Intent-enabled campus network. The following paragraphs describe the concepts of these common technologies.

Network Plug and Play

Cisco Network Plug and Play (PnP) is a technology that is used to (automatically) provision new switches or routers in the network. The technology is available within DNA Center as well as Cisco APIC-EM. The technology is used for LAN Automation within Software Defined Access; it is also used for non-SDA deployments. Figure A-1 provides an overview of how Network PnP within Cisco APIC-EM is used to provision a device.

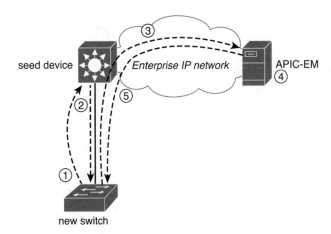

Figure A-1   *Flow of Network PnP with Cisco APIC-EM*

A field engineer racks and stacks the new network switch and attaches its uplinks to the distribution switch. In this case, the distribution switch is also the seed device.

Once the switch is started up, with an empty configuration, the Network PnP process is started in the background.

It is important not to touch anything on the console, as any character entered on the console results in aborting the PnP process.

The steps in this process are as follows:

1. Once booted, the new switch will perform a DHCP request using VLAN1 (untagged traffic as the switch doesn't have knowledge on VLANs yet) or a specific PnP-VLAN learned via CDP.

2. The seed device provides an IP address to the new switch from a pool. This can be a local pool or a central DHCP server. In the DHCP response, DHCP Option 43 is used to provide information to the PnP agent about how to contact the provisioning server, Cisco APIC-EM in this example.

3. The new switch parses the DHCP response, and if it contains DHCP option 43, it will parse the text inside to extract the required details to connect to Cisco APIC-EM. The new switch will use its serial number to register it with Cisco APIC-EM using the protocol and port specified in the DHCP option. If there is no DHCP option 43 specified, the PnP agent on the new switch will try to use DNS to connect to **pnpserver.customer.com** and use the DNS name of **pnpntpserver.customer.com** for the NTP server. Customer.com is the domain suffix as specified in the DHCP scope.

4. Cisco APIC-EM registers the new device in the PnP application. Specific SSH keys are generated in the communication between switch and Cisco APIC-EM to be able to securely configure the device. Once all device information is registered successfully, Cisco APIC-EM checks whether the serial number has an assigned fixed configuration. In that case, the switch is automatically being configured with the fixed configuration. If not, the device is set in the "unclaimed" state.

5. A network engineer selects the device and selects a template or configuration for that device. Once all required variables for the template are provided, Cisco APIC-EM will connect to the new switch and enter the configuration on the new switch.

This five-step process is used to provision a new switch into the network. The configuration (template) provided by the network engineer can be a full-feature configuration of the new switch or just a basic configuration, allowing other network configuration management tools such as Prime Infrastructure or Ansible to provide the detailed configuration.

DHCP Option 43

DHCP option 43 is used by PnP to tell the PnP agent how to connect to the PnP server, whether this is Cisco APIC-EM or Cisco DNA Center. DHCP option 43 is a string value that can be configured on a DHCP pool within the seed device, as demonstrated in Example A-1.

Example A-1   *Sample DHCP Configuration for PnP with Option 43*

```
ip dhcp pool site_management_pool
  network 10.255.2.0 255.255.255.0
  default-router 10.255.2.1
  option 43 ascii "5A1N;B2;K4;I172.19.45.222;J80"
```

The option 43 string contains a specific format, which is

- **5A1N:** Specific value for network PnP; this is a fixed value for PnP version 1 and in normal active mode. If you want to enable debugging, change this to 5A1D.

- **Bn:** Connection method; B1 is connect via hostname; B2 is connect via IP address.

- **Kn:** K4 means "connect via HTTP"; K5 "means connect via HTTPS."

- **I:** Contains the IP address of the PnP server (Cisco APIC-EM or Cisco DNA Center).

- **Z:** Optional field; the NTP server to synchronize time (for certification generation).

- **T:** Optional field to specify the trustpool URL to obtain a certificate.

- **J:** Field to specify the TCP port number, commonly J80 or J443.

A detailed explanation on Plug and Play is provided by Cisco in the Solution Guide for Network Plug and Play (https://www.cisco.com/c/en/us/td/docs/solutions/Enterprise/Plug-and-Play/solution/guidexml/b_pnp-solution-guide.html).

Differences Within DNA Center

DNA Center leverages the PnP technology for both LAN Automation within an SDA fabric-enabled network as well as provisioning new devices in non-fabric campus networks.

When PnP is used for LAN Automation, DNA Center facilitates the configuration of the underlay network of a fabric. A network device, usually one of the border routers or the control router, is used as a seed device. When switches are booted, the PnP process is used to connect to DNA Center. DNA Center uses the IP pool allocated for LAN Automation to configure loopback addresses on the switches as well as the numbered links between the switches in the fabric. It is important to know that only one IP pool (with a minimum netmask of 25 bits) is allocated for a fabric, and DNA Center divides this IP pool into four equal segments. One segment is used for the loopback addresses, one is used for the numbered links, and a third is used for the handoff networks on the border routers.

If PnP is used for non-fabric deployments, the functioning of PnP within Cisco DNA Center is almost similar to Cisco APIC-EM. In contrast to Cisco APIC-EM, it is not necessary to configure a new project. New devices are discovered and placed in the unclaimed state. They can then be provisioned to a network area (site), building, or floor. And the network profile for that specific location is then applied to the switch by DNA Center.

Zero Touch Provisioning

A lesser-known technology that can be used for day-0 operations is Zero Touch Provisioning (ZTP). ZTP is similar to PnP except that it does not require an operator to "claim" new devices and attach them to a bootstrap configuration. ZTP uses DHCP; a transfer protocol, such as HTTP (since IOS-XE version 16.5) or TFTP; and Python to configure the newly attached device. Figure A-2 provides an overview of how ZTP functions.

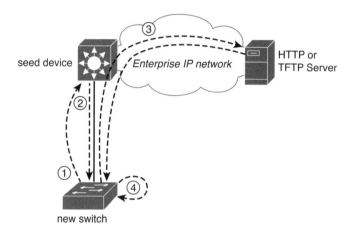

Figure A-2   *Operational Flow for ZTP*

Although ZTP is similar to PnP, there are a few differences. Once a field engineer has racked the new device and connects it to the network, ZTP kicks in with the following operation:

1. Once booted, the new switch will perform a DHCP request using VLAN1 (untagged traffic as the switch doesn't have knowledge on VLANs yet).

2. The seed device provides an IP address to the new switch from a pool. This can be a local pool or a central DHCP server. In the DHCP response, DHCP option 67 is used (with optional DHCP option 150 for TFTP) to inform the ZTP agent what the location of the Python script is to be executed.

3. The new switch parses the DHCP response, and based on the DHCP options, it will attempt to fetch the Python script from the management server.

4. Once the Python script has been downloaded, a guestshell is started on the IOS-XE switch, and the Python script will be executed. That python script contains several Python commands to set up the initial configuration of the device.

This four-step process is similar to Network PnP, but there are some differences. The most important one to note is that with Network PnP, APIC-EM or Cisco DNA Center is required, and the serial number is used as a unique identifier to replace variables with values set in the management server. With ZTP, no configuration is downloaded; a Python script is downloaded, which in turn performs the necessary commands to the switch.

Because it is a Python script, it would be possible to use other Python modules or code to tweak the bootstrap configuration (such as requesting a specific IP address from a different server).

DHCP Options

As described, ZTP leverages two DHCP options to define and locate the Python script. If the transfer protocol is TFTP, DHCP option 150 is used for the address of the TFTP server, and DHCP option 67 is used for the filename. If HTTP is used, then only DHCP option 67 is used with the full URL of the Python script.

Python Script

ZTP is based on copying and executing a Python script using the guestshell within IOS-XE. To execute configuration line commands to configure the device, Cisco provides a specific CLI module. The Python code in Example A-2 configures the switch with a loopback address and a specific username and password so that the new device is discoverable.

Example A-2   *Sample Python Script for ZTP Configuration*

```
import cli
print "\n\n *** Executing ZTP script *** \n\n"


/* Configure loopback100 IP address */
cli.configurep(["interface loopback 100", "ip address 10.10.10.5 255.255.255.255",
  "end"])
/* Configure aaa new-model, authentication and username */
cli.configurep(["aaa new-model", "aaa authentication login default local", "username
  pnpuser priv 15 secret mysecret", "end")
print "\n\n *** End execution ZTP script *** \n\n"
```

Summary of ZTP and Network PnP

Although both ZTP and Network PnP are protocols for automating day-0 operations, their use cases are quite different. Network PnP is available within Cisco APIC-EM and Cisco DNA Center and is an integral part of LAN automation. The inner workings of Network PnP are closed within these products, which is fine as it is part of the integral solution that allows for templating, variables, and tighter integration with the management tool.

ZTP, on the other hand, is much more open. It is possible to use any HTTP server for the automation of day-0 operations, but you have to program your bootstrap configuration and integration with the management server with a Python script. ZTP could suit Intent-Based Networks that leverage Ansible quite well.

VRF-Lite

Virtual Routing and Forwarding (VRF) is a technology that originated from the service provider world. It would allow several Virtual Private Networks with possible overlapping IP addresses to be routed and forwarded over the service provider backbone. Essentially, a VRF is used to create and isolate network routes in logical routing and forwarding instances in a router or switch.

Note   Although most service providers leverage MPLS to provide different Virtual Private Networks (and thus isolation) for their customers, this technology was not available in the datacenters. VRF was used for those areas where MPLS was not supported.

Traditionally, all routing and forwarding occur in a single global routing table. That global routing table is used to determine to which network an incoming IP packet would need to be forwarded. Two customers having the same internal IP address range (for example, 10.0.0.0/24) would cause routing issues to at least one customer, but probably to both. Because there is no distinction for the customer in the global routing table, a packet with destination IP address 10.0.0.5 for customer 1 could accidentally be sent to customer 2.

With VRF it is possible to create logically isolated routing tables where this problem would not occur. Each logical isolated table is referred to as a VRF instance. The number of VRF instances is dependent on the physical hardware (specifically the ASIC). For example, the Cisco Catalyst 3650/3850 switches have the capacity for 64 VRF instances, whereas the Cisco Catalyst 9300 series have a maximum of 256 VRF instances).

It is important to know that VRF only operates on Layer 3 (IP network) information. VRF does not provide logical isolation on Layer 2. In other words, although a switch might have VRF configured for separate IP networks, there is still a single global table for all Layer 2 information, such as MAC addresses and VLANs.

All DNA-ready Cisco switches support VRF, but it is dependent on the licenses installed on the switch. VRF is used within campus networks to logically separate IP networks from each other. Within Software-Defined Access, VRF is used to implement the different virtual networks that are to be deployed on the network. In a classic VLAN deployment of Intent-Based Networking, each logical network is also isolated using VRFs. Both concepts leverage the same principle that VRFs also isolate the logical networks (e.g., Intents for a separate network) from the underlay or management network.

To use VRFs in the network, the following steps need to be executed:

Step 1.   Define the VRF.

Step 2.   Define which IP protocols run within the VRF (IPv4, IPv6, or both).

Step 3.   Bind one or more Layer 3 interfaces to the VRF.

Step 4.   Configure routing within the VRF, which can be a dynamic routing protocol or static routing.

Example A-3 provides a sample configuration of two VRF definitions ("red" and "blue"), where VLAN100 is bound to VRF "red"; VLAN201 is bound to VRF "blue"; and static routing is used for both networks.

Example A-3 *Sample Definition for Two VRFs with Overlapping IP Addresses*

```
vrf definition red
  address-family ipv4
  exit-address-family
!
vrf definition blue
  address-family ipv4
  exit-address-family
!
interface vlan100
  vrf forwarding red
  ip address 10.1.1.10 255.255.255.0
!
interface vlan201
  vrf forwarding blue
  ip address 10.1.1.254 255.255.255.0
!
ip route vrf red 0.0.0.0 0.0.0.0 10.1.1.1
ip vrf route blue 0.0.0.0 0.0.0.0 10.1.1.1
!
```

Once VRFs are used in a network, it is important to know that when testing Layer 3 connectivity, or showing Layer 3 information such as the routing table, the VRF name has to be specified or else the global routing table (which still exists) is shown. It is crucial to train the network operations team on that, as many network engineers have made the mistake to forget the VRF name when troubleshooting a network.

IEEE 802.1X

One of the key principles behind the Cisco Digital Network Architecture (and thus Intent-Based Networking) is that security is an integrated component of the network infrastructure. Within a campus network, the identity (authentication) of the endpoint connecting to the network is used to apply a specific policy for that endpoint (authorization). Within the campus network this authentication and authorization use the IEEE 802.1X standard, which is commonly known as Network Access Control. Although the IEEE 802.1X standard is only defined for wired networks, the same concepts, principles, and flows are applied on wireless networks when the wireless network is configured to use WPA2 enterprise security.

The IEEE 802.1X standard, named Port-based Network Access Control (commonly known as Network Access Control, or NAC), defines a mechanism on how the identity of an endpoint can be determined before access to the network is granted. Its main use case is to prevent unauthorized endpoints from connecting to the network (e.g., a malicious user plugging a device into a wall outlet to gain access to the company network). Although authentication (who are you) and authorization (what is allowed) are usually combined in a single flow, IEEE 802.1X only defines the authentication component. Specific authorization (besides accept or deny) is outside the scope of IEEE 802.1X. NAC is based on a number of components that work together to establish the identity (authentication) of the endpoint. Figure A-3 displays the required components for IEEE 802.1X.

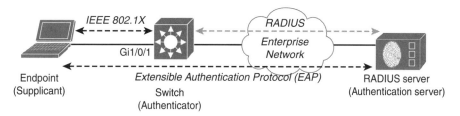

Figure A-3 *Overview Components of IEEE 802.1X*

The following components are part of IEEE 802.1X:

- **Supplicant:** This is a special software component on the endpoint that understands IEEE 802.1X. Although all modern operating systems support IEEE 802.1X, it is often required to manually enable and configure the supplicant software. The supplicant is used to provide the identity of the endpoint to the network.

- **Authenticator (switch):** The authenticator (the access switch) is an important component of IEEE 802.1X. The authenticator is the component that initiates the authentication process as soon as a link of an access port becomes active.

- **Authentication Server:** The authentication server is the central component of IEEE 802.1X. The authentication requests from all authenticators (switches) are handled within the Authentication Server. The authentication server determines, based on the identity of the supplicant, whether access is granted or denied.

To understand how these components interoperate with each other, the flow of operation for the authentication is explained below in a conceptual format. Figure A-4 displays schematically how the authentication process is performed using IEEE 802.1X.

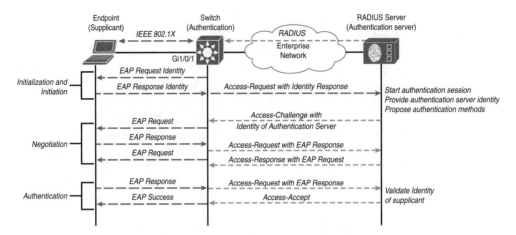

Figure A-4   *Flow of IEEE 802.1x Authentication Process*

A typical authentication procedure consists of four distinct phases:

1. **Initialization and initiation:** As soon as an interface (configured for IEEE 802.1X) becomes active, it will configure the port in an unauthorized state (dropping all packets except IEEE 802.1X) and will send identity requests to the endpoint.

2. **Negotiation:** The supplicant running on the endpoint receives the identity request and will start to establish a trusted (secure) connection to the authentication server and negotiate with the authentication server an authentication mechanism. The supplicant uses IEEE 802.1X frames (known as EAP packets) for that purpose. In this phase, the authenticator (switch) functions as a media-translator between the supplicant and the authentication server by transporting the different EAP packets via RADIUS to the authentication server.

   Once the secure tunnel is established (the supplicant can verify the authentication server's identity, via certificate), the supplicant and authentication server agree on an authentication method (which can be username and password or certificates).

3. **Authentication:** Once the negotiation on the authentication method is finished, the supplicant provides its identity (leveraging certificates or username and password) to the Authentication Server, and the Authentication Server will either permit or deny access to the network (using specific RADIUS responses). The authenticator will take the appropriate action based on the response.

The IEEE 802.1X standard relies heavily on the RADIUS protocol as an encapsulation (tunnel) for the communication between the supplicant and the Authentication Server. Only the resultant state of RADIUS (Accept or Reject) is used to inform the authenticator (switch) whether the authentication was successfully completed. The RADIUS protocol itself is not defined within the IEEE 802.1X standard; it is described using several Request For Comments (RFC). The following paragraph describes the concept of the RADIUS protocol.

Although IEEE 802.1X is originally a wired authentication protocol, a similar flow occurs on wireless networks configured for WPA enterprise. Once a wireless endpoint attempts to associate itself to a wireless network, the same flow of challenges and responses is used to determine the identity of that endpoint and whether it is allowed access to the network.

An Intent-Based Network relies on the IEEE 802.1X standard for two reasons. The first reason is to provide the identity of the endpoint connecting to the network and prevent unauthorized access (conforming to embedded security in a Cisco Digital Network Architecture). The second reason is to be able to assign the endpoint into its appropriate virtual network (authorization) and possibly apply microsegmentation or other security policies.

RADIUS

Remote Access DialUp Services (RADIUS) was originally designed by Livingston Enterprises and used intensively by Internet service providers to provide a central authentication and authorization service for their dial-up services. Over the years this concept of a central authentication service has been extended via Ethernet networks in ISPs to the enterprise networks where RADIUS has become a key component of Network Access Control. (See the previous paragraph about IEEE 802.1X.)

RADIUS is a concept that consists of three distinct features of access control:

- **Authentication:** Who is trying to connect to the network (the identity of the user or endpoint)?

- **Authorization:** What is that endpoint or user allowed to access?

- **Accounting:** When and for how long was the user or endpoint (identity) connected?

The RADIUS protocol implements these features into distinct flows. The first flow combines authentication and authorization in a single request-response loop. The Network Access Device (NAD, which can be a switch or wireless LAN controller) sends an access-request for a specific user to the RADIUS server, and the RADIUS server responds with an Access-Accept or Access-Reject message, which also includes specific authorizations. The second flow is also sent by the Network Access Device, which includes Accounting-Start and Accounting-Stop messages. These messages are received and processed by the RADIUS server. Figure A-5 provides a schematic overview of the RADIUS protocol.

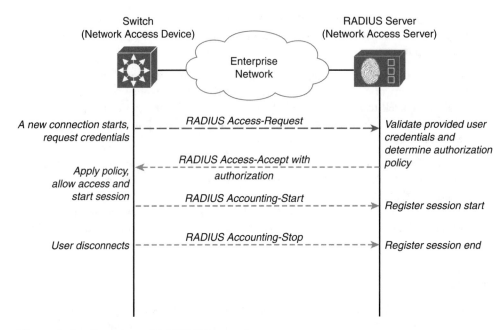

Figure A-5   *Overview of RADIUS Protocol*

The flow for RADIUS is relatively simple and consists of the following steps:

1. As soon as authentication is required, the Network Access Device (NAD, a client) sends an Access-Request RADIUS message to the Network Access Server (NAS). This message contains all required attributes for the authentication request, such as username, password, and other information.

2. The Network Access Server receives the Access-Request message and validates the NAD. Once the NAD is validated, it will look up the provided user and validate the password.

3. If the provided credentials are correct, the NAS determines the specific access policy and returns an Access-Accept message that includes the specific authorization policy by leveraging attribute-value keypairs. If the credentials are not correct, a simple Access-Reject message is sent back.

4. The NAD will parse and process the Access-Accept message and will apply the specific policy. The NAD will now send an Accounting-Start message to the NAS.

5. Once the session is closed, the NAD will send an Accounting-Stop message to the NAS to inform it of the closed session.

The RADIUS protocol was initially defined in RFC2058 in 1997. And although it is an old protocol, it is used in any campus network that uses IEEE 802.1X for Network Access

Control. The reason for that lies primarily in the fact that the RADIUS packet is defined using an attribute-value-pair model. Besides a control-part inside the RADIUS packet, the actual data to be exchanged between NAD and NAS (and vice versa) is modeled around an attribute type, the length of the value, and the value itself. Each RADIUS message consists of a number of attributes and its corresponding values. For example, attribute type 6 represents the User-Name field.

And although the protocol only allows 256 unique attribute types, one of them is called the Vendor Specific Attribute type (VSA, value 26). This VSA is used to realize the extensibility and flexibility of the protocol. This VSA allows a vendor to define its specific list of attribute-value keypairs that can be used inside the RADIUS communication.

Cisco, with vendor ID 9, follows the recommended format protocol : attribute sep value for its vendor-specific attributes. Table A-1 provides a number of examples for a vendor-specific attribute.

Table A-1 *Samples of Vendor-Specific Attributes*

Example	Description
cisco-avpair= "device-traffic-class=voice"	Assign the device into Voice class
cisco-avpair= "ip:inacl#100=permit ip any 10.1.1.0 0.0.0.255"	Apply an Access-list that only allows traffic to 10.1.1.0/24
cisco-avpair= "shell:priv-lvl=5"	Assign privilege level 5 to this session

This extensibility allowed for RADIUS to become the de facto standard for authentication and authorization services within network infrastructures, as each vendor is able to define extra attributes for its specific purpose. Over time, several extra attributes have been introduced by vendors. Within an Intent-enabled network, these VSAs allow the network operations team to define the policy at the RADIUS server (Cisco Identity Services Engine) and have the specific policy applied to the network port at the moment a device is connected and authorized.

Scalable Group Tags

Cisco introduced the concept of Source Group Tags (SGT; later known as Security Group Tags and now as Scalable Group Tags) with the introduction of Cisco TrustSec in 2007. In most network deployments, the enforcement of access policies is based on access lists that define which IP network is allowed to communicate with which destination and on which ports. Figure A-6 shows a typical enterprise network topology.

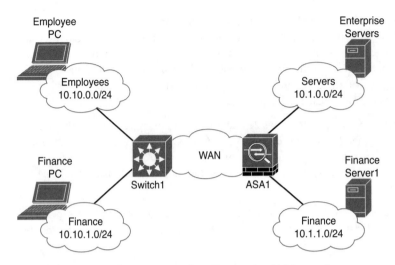

Figure A-6 *Sample Overview of an Enterprise IP Network*

In this example network, employees are connected to IP network 10.10.1.0/24 and are allowed access to the servers in 10.1.0.0/24. There is also a finance server network in IP network 10.1.1.0/24, and the finance employees are placed in IP network 10.10.2.0/24. If all employees are allowed access to the generic servers, but only the finance employees are allowed access to the finance server network, the access list on firewall ASA1 would be similar to that shown in Table A-2.

Table A-2 *Sample Access List for ASA1*

Source IP	Destination IP	Port	permit/deny
10.10.0.0/24	10.1.0.0/24	445,135,139	permit
10.10.1.0/24	10.1.0.0/24	445,135,139	permit
10.10.0.0/24	10.1.1.0/24	any	deny
10.10.1.0/24	10.1.1.0/24	445,135,139	permit

With more applications being enabled on the network infrastructure, these access lists grow explosively in both length and complexity. Because of this complexity, the risk of unauthorized access (due to errors in the access list) is quite realistic. The principle of SGTs is to remove that complexity of source and destination IP addresses and define an IP-agnostic access policy. In other words, the access list policy is based on labels instead of IP addresses. Table A-3 shows the same access list policy, but then based on SGTs.

Table A-3   *Sample SGT-Based Access List for ASA1*

Source Tag	Destination Tag	Port	permit/deny
Employees Emp-Finance	Serv-Generic	445,135,139	permit
Emp-Finance	Serv-Finance	445,135,139	permit
Any	Serv-Finance	any	deny

As you can see in Table A-3, the access list has become a policy matrix based on a set of tags or labels. Because the policy is now based on a tag, all employees can become part of the same IP network, which is also applicable to the servers. Figure A-7 shows the new network topology.

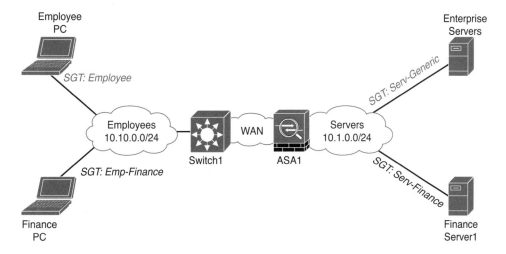

Figure A-7   *Sample Topology of Enterprise with SGTs*

The SGT concept is based on a central policy server (Cisco Identity Services Engine) in which the access policy is defined as a security matrix. The SGT assignment occurs when an endpoint is authenticated to the network; the SGT is added to the RADIUS authorization response. For servers, the SGTs are assigned manually within ISE, which could be based on a single IP address or a complete subnet.

Just as with VLANs, described in the section "VLAN" later in this appendix, the SGT is transported with the Ethernet frames received from the endpoint between Cisco switches.

Part of the Cisco SGT concept is that the same security matrix can be enforced on the access switch (to which the endpoints are connected). This means that the access switch has a downloaded Security Group Access List (SGACL) and enforces that on every packet that is received by the switch. This is, in fact, the enabler for microsegmentation (e.g., defining a micro security policy within a virtual network).

The Cisco TrustSec solution consists of more than SGTs, such as line-rate link encryption. Within an Intent-enabled Network, the concept of SGTs, in combination with a security matrix (defined in either Cisco DNA Center or Cisco ISE), is used to enable and implement microsegmentation.

Routing Protocols

Routing protocols are essentially the glue between different local networks. Routing protocols were developed and implemented so that different local networks could be interconnected to create a larger internetwork. Many books, such as *Optimal Routing Design* by Russ White, have already been written on routing protocols that provide in-depth coverage of the protocols, their mechanisms, and their technologies.

This section is not intended to provide a complete overview of the individual routing protocols currently available, but rather provide an overview of the concept of how routing protocols are used to glue local networks into a larger network and how that is related to IBN.

Concept of Routing Protocols

Common routing protocols, such as IS-IS, BGP, OSPF, and (E)IGRP, all have a single goal in common: they aim to provide a method to determine how a packet with a specific destination IP needs to be forwarded to which link. All these protocols aim to provide the most optimal route through this interchain of connected networks. Figure A-8 shows a sample network topology where several networks are interconnected with each other.

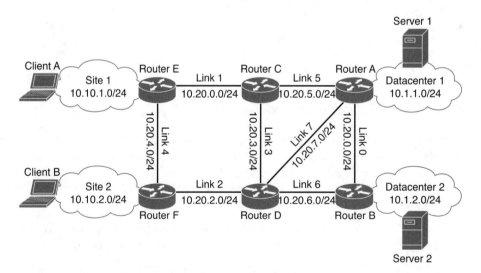

Figure A-8   *Sample Network Topology*

In this network, a sample enterprise, two campus sites (Site 1 and Site 2) are connected via a myriad of connected links to the two datacenters (Datacenter 1 and Datacenter 2).

To allow communication from Client A to Server 2, all routers in the network would need to know how to forward packets back and forth. In other words, they need to be aware of how a specific network is reachable (reachability) and which link to use to forward a packet (the topology of the network). And as there are loops in the network for high availability, the routers also need to keep that topology loop-free.

One option would be to configure all site networks statically on all routers so that the routers know the topology and the networks. But static routes do not scale well and can provide problems in case of link failures.

Routing protocols are designed to solve just that; they learn the topology and reachability information about the connected networks dynamically. There are two mechanisms for how routing protocols can learn the topology and reachability—link-state and distance-vector.

Distance-Vector

In a distance-vector routing protocol, each router in the network periodically shares all the networks it knows about with the associated distance (cost) to reach that network. The cost of a direct-connected network is, of course, the lowest. A distance or cost could be the hop count (for example, how many hops need to be taken before it can reach that network).

If a router receives a network update from a neighbor with a better cost, it will update its internal network database (topology) and will forward its updated network knowledge in the next update.

Over time, each router has learned all networks it can reach with the associated cost. As soon as a packet is received, its destination IP address is looked up in the topology database and is forwarded to the neighboring router with the least cost.

The distance-vector mechanism can be compared to road signs with the different cities (destinations) along the highway. If you were to drive to a specific city that required multiple highways, you would follow the road signs at each highway junction (router) to reach your destination.

The disadvantage of a distance-vector routing protocol is that it does not (always) take into account what the bandwidth and utilization of that link is. In the highway example, the distance-vector does not include a means to inform whether the highway is a two-lane road or a six-lane highway. It could result in packets arriving slowly because of congestion (traffic jams).

Link-State

The other mechanism that can be used to learn the topology and reachability is link-state. In contrast to distance-vector, the routers initially determine on which links they have neighboring routers (checking for reachability over a link). This reachability is checked periodically. Once reachability is established, the router floods its information about neighbors and networks (link-state) to all its connected neighbors. This leads to all routers having received information from all other routers and connected networks. Once this information is received from all routers in the network, each router will use an algorithm (Dijkstra's shortest path) to determine what the most optimum route is for each network. If a link fails, the link advertisements are sent again, and the topology is recalculated.

Effectively, link-state routing protocols maintain a database with all routers, the (connected) links to other routers, and the connected networks for each router, and use that to determine the topology and reachability.

Link-state routing protocols are common in smaller networks where the knowledge of all routers and connected networks does not lead to scalability and resource problems; if the number of routers in the network becomes too high, the cost of calculating the optimal route and maintaining that database takes too many resources.

A common example of the link-state mechanism is how a GPS navigation system determines the route from A to B within a city. Its map information allows creating a topology of all the roads (links) and their interconnections (routers) within the city. And the shortest path algorithm allows for determining the shortest path between two random points within the city limits. However, maintaining a full topology of all streets and their interconnections within a continent would be too large, and calculating the shortest route would take too long. Therefore, in these situations, most GPS navigation systems use hierarchies (network topologies on top of network topologies) to optimize the resources.

Every routing protocol used within a campus network is based on either one of these two mechanisms. For example, Open Shortest Path First (OSPF) and Integrated System-to-Integrated System (IS-IS) are based on the link-state mechanism, whereas Border Gateway Protocol (BGP) is based on the distance-vector mechanism. Cisco introduced Extended Interior Gateway Routing Protocol (EIGRP) as a combination of link-state and distance-vector mechanisms, which provides some unique improvements.

And although it does not matter which protocol is used for a traditional campus network, the choice of routing protocol does matter for an Intent-Based campus network.

In both a non-fabric as well as an SDA-based campus network, multiple virtual networks are deployed within the network. This means that the reachability and topology information needs to be exchanged within those virtual networks. The most commonly deployed routing protocol for that is BGP.

An SDA-based network adds the requirement for a routing protocol in the underlying switching infrastructure, as each link between the switches is IP-based. The most common routing protocol for the underlay network is IS-IS, where the IS-IS network itself is terminated at the border nodes of the fabric.

Software-Defined Access

Software-Defined Access is the next evolution of campus networks and combines several common technologies (IEEE 802.1x, VRF-Lite, RADIUS, and SGT) with relatively new technologies for the campus network environment. Chapter 5, "Intent-Based

Networking," described the design and concept of an SDA-based campus network. The following sections describe the two new technologies used within SDA.

VXLAN

Virtual eXtensible Local Area Network (VXLAN) is a technology that originates from the datacenter networks. The classic VLAN technology is restricted to 4096 different VLANs, thus limiting the datacenter network to 4096 logical Layer 2 networks. Another limitation of a Layer 2 network is that stretching it over multiple datacenters will introduce several complications, such as latencies, split-brain, and non optimal traffic flows. To overcome these problems, VXLAN was developed and introduced in the datacenter.

VXLAN itself is a network virtualization (overlay) technology that allows you to embed any Layer 2 packet into a logical network (virtual network id). VXLAN uses UDP to encapsulate those Layer 2 packets and forward them to the proper destination. The receiving switch decapsulates the original Layer 2 packet from the VXLAN packet (UDP) and forwards it locally as if it were a single logical network (like a VLAN). Figure A-9 provides an overview of how VXLAN is used to transport information across a different IP network.

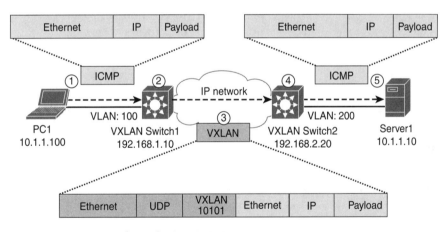

Figure A-9 *Output from the SIMPLE Program*

In Figure A-9, PC1 and Server1 are on the same logical IP subnet (10.1.1.0/24) but are physically separated by a different IP network. The VXLAN switches allow the devices to connect and communicate with each other. For example, PC1 sends a ping (ICMP) packet to Server1. The following flow happens:

1. PC1 sends an ICMP packet with destination IP address 10.1.1.10 onto the Ethernet connection to VXLAN Switch1.

2. VXLAN Switch1 receives the incoming ICMP packet from PC1 on VLAN 100. VLAN100 is configured to forward packets onto VXLAN 10101. This means that VXLAN Switch 1 will embed the complete ICMP packet into a new VXLAN network with VXLAN identifier 10101 (purple). VXLAN Switch1 uses a control-plane lookup to determine the destination of the VXLAN packet. For that lookup, it uses (in case of a Layer 2 VXLAN) the destination MAC address of the original (yellow) packet. Based on the control-protocol lookup, the destination IP will be 192.168.2.20, and VXLAN switch 1 will forward the packet based on the routing tables of the IP network.

3. IP Network will forward the new (purple) VXLAN packet through its network to its destination, 192.168.2.20.

4. Upon receiving the VXLAN packet, VXLAN Switch2 will decapsulate the VXLAN packet. Based on the VXLAN Identifier (10101) and its configuration, it knows it needs to forward the packet to VLAN200. Again, a control-protocol lookup (of the original yellow destination MAC address) will be used to determine to which interface the packet needs to be forwarded. Once the lookup is successful, VXLAN Switch2 will forward the original (yellow) packet onto the wire to Server1.

5. Server1 receives the original ICMP packet as a normal packet, and the response sent to VXLAN Switch2 will have to take the same path.

For PC1 and Server1, the complete VXLAN communication is transparent. They have no insight or knowledge that a separate IP network is in between them. An SDA network within the campus behaves in the same manner, where the switches where endpoints reside are named edge nodes, and the node where traffic is leaving the fabric is called a border node.

VXLAN itself allows for 16 million (24 bits) different logical virtual networks, identified as virtual network IDs. Within SDA, the VXLAN identifier is the same as the virtual network ID defined within Cisco DNA Center, which theoretically allows for up to 16 million virtual networks in a single campus fabric.

VXLAN itself is designed as a data-path protocol; in other words, its scalability and performance lie in the quick encapsulation and decapsulation of data-packets. A separate control-protocol is required to determine where each VXLAN packet needs to be forwarded.

LISP

SDA leverages VXLAN technology to define overlay virtual networks and transport them via an underlay network within a campus fabric. But VXLAN is a datapath technology; it relies on a control protocol for lookups and determining which destination IP address is used within the underlay network. Within SDA, Locator/Identifier Separation Protocol (LISP) is used as the control protocol.

LISP was originally an architecture (and protocol) designed in 2006 to allow a more scalable routing and addressing scheme for the Internet. Already at that moment, the number of IPv4 networks in the database of routers on the Internet was exponentially growing. The primary causes for that were the fact that there was an exponential increase in smaller IP subnets announced on the Internet, as well as that more organizations would be connected (and thus announced) via multiple providers.

Effectively in today's Internet, for each public IP network, the network and how to reach that network (location) is known. This is an integral part of the distance-vector routing protocol used on the Internet. And because every router on the Internet needs to know how to reach each network, each router effectively has a large database of networks and locations (how to reach those networks). And as the number of networks grows, the required resources to manage that increase too, which can also result in slower routing table loading times after a reboot or disconnect of a link.

LISP was designed to reduce that increase in complexity and increase in resource requirements. Conceptually, LISP achieves that reduction by both separating the IP networks (named endpoint identifiers [EID] in LISP) and how to reach those networks (via Routing Locator [RLOC] in LISP) information and moving that information into a smaller number of large database or mapping servers.

Routers in the network would inform that mapping server which endpoint identifiers (EID) were reachable via that router. And at the same time, if they need to know where to forward a specific packet to, they would perform a lookup in that LISP server to find which RLOC would be responsible for that network and then forward the packet to that specific RLOC. This results in a smaller, on-dynamic table on each router inside the network, while retaining full knowledge of where each EID (IP network) is located. Figure A-10 shows a (simplified) diagram of a larger Internet-network where two ISPs are used to connect several IP networks.

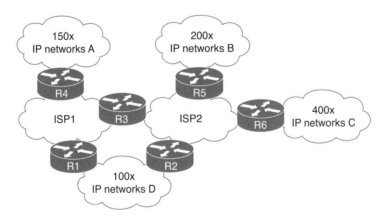

Figure A-10 *Traditional Sample Interconnected Network*

In the traditional (and today's Internet) network, each router would maintain a routing table containing all the networks and how they are reachable, such as Table A-4 for R6.

Table A-4   *Routing Table for Router R6*

IP Network (EID)	Reachable via (RLOC)
400x IP Networks C	Directly connected
150x IP Networks A	ISP2-R3
200x IP Networks B	ISP2-R5
100x IP Networks D	ISP2-R2
100x IP Networks D	ISP2-R3 ISP1-R1

Router 6 alone already has 950 routes in its database, with this relatively simple design. Every other router in the same IP network would have 950 routes, resulting in 5700 IP networks. Imagine what would happen with the numbers if this network would scale up to the size of the Internet with tens of thousands of service providers and enterprises.

Each router on the Internet would require the resources to maintain that kind of table.

With a LISP-based network, the network from Figure A-10 would look like Figure A-11.

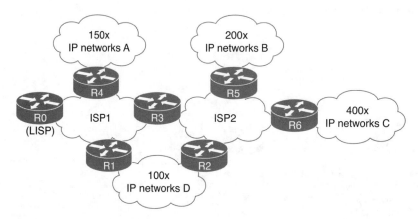

Figure A-11   *Sample Interconnected Network with LISP Enabled*

With LISP configured on the network, each router would provide its location identification (RLOC) and the connected networks (EID) to the LISP mapping server on R0. Table A-5 shows the mapping table on Router R0.

Table A-5 *LISP Mapping Table for Router R0*

IP Network (EID)	Reachable via (RLOC)
400x IP Networks C	ISP2-R6
150x IP Networks A	ISP2-R3
200x IP Networks B	ISP2-R5
100x IP Networks D	ISP1-R1 or ISP2-R2

The table itself looks similar to the table of Router R6. But instead of having each router maintaining that full table of IP networks, only R0 will maintain that table. Each router will only maintain a cache of table entries to reduce the number of routing tables. If from IP Network C most traffic flows to IP Networks A and B, the routing table on router R6 would only have 350 routers instead of 950 (full routing table). This results in a reduction of required resources on router R6.

LISP itself also contains other technologies and concepts to reduce the number of IP networks (prefixes) on such a network, such as tunneling traffic. But within SDA, the concept and principle of the LISP mapping server is primarily used within the campus fabric.

Within SDA, the LISP mapping server is named the control node. EIDs are the endpoint IP addresses (or MAC addresses for a Layer2 Virtual Network), and the RLOC information contains the lookback address of the edge node to which the device is connected. This mapping information is used to encapsulate the endpoint's traffic in VXLAN packets sent over the underlay of the fabric.

Classic Technologies

A non-fabric deployment leverages several classic technologies to enable an Intent-Based Network. The sections that follow describe the concepts of these classic technologies.

VLAN

One of the best known and most used technologies in a campus network is the virtual local area network (VLAN). VLANs are used to isolate several physical Ethernet connections into logical Layer 2 domains. The isolation could be because of a business requirement (isolation of printers from employee workstations or guest users), or to create smaller broadcast domains for manageability. The VLAN technology is defined in IEEE 802.1Q standard and is a Layer 2 network technology.

Traditionally, as shown in Figure A-12, every Ethernet device in the same physical network can communicate with each other. In other words, PC1 can freely communicate with PC2, the server, and other devices on the same switch.

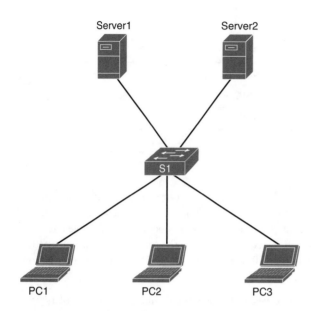

Figure A-12   *Single Ethernet Domain with No VLANs*

If, for any reason, PC1 and Server1 are part of the financial administration department, and PC2 and PC3 would not be allowed access, without VLANs these two devices would need to be connected to a different physical switch. Although this is a valid option, it is not scalable and is expensive. A VLAN is used to create logical switches within that single physical switch. To achieve that, each Virtual LAN is provided with a unique identifier, a VLAN ID. This VLAN ID ranges from 2 to 4095. VLAN ID 1 is the so-called default VLAN and is used for switches that do not support VLANs. Figure A-13 shows the same physical topology but now with a VLAN for Finance (red) and a VLAN for Employees (blue).

At this moment, the devices that are configured with VLAN 10 (Finance) can only communicate with each other, and those that are connected to VLAN 20 (Finance) can only communicate with each other. Because of this isolation, VLAN 10 and VLAN 20 will never communicate with each other. That also means that PC1 cannot communicate with Server2, because it is on a separate VLAN and thus a separate logical Layer 2 network. Only if the switch (or firewall or router) would have IP addresses in both VLANs, routing is possible on Layer 3 and communication can occur.

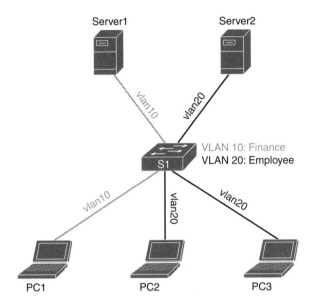

Figure A-13   *Switch Topology with Two VLANs*

The IEEE 802.1Q standard also describes how the Layer2 isolation principle works when multiple switches are connected and the Layer 2 isolation should be spanned across the switches. Figure A-14 shows the same topology, but now PC3 is connected to a separate switch.

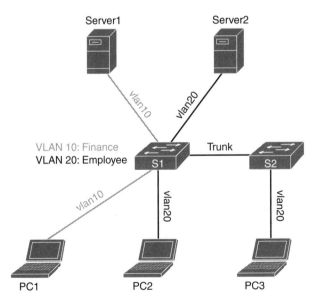

Figure A-14   *Topology with Two Switches and Two VLANs*

For PC3 to be able to communicate with Server2, the two switches are connected with a special IEEE 802.1Q interface. Within Cisco switches, it is called an Ethernet trunk. The Ethernet frames sent and received between the two switches also include the VLAN Identifier as a tag. It is also known as "tagged traffic." That way, if an Ethernet frame is received by S1 with Tag20, S1 knows which VLAN that Ethernet frame belongs to, so S1 can forward it to the appropriate logical network. The format of such an Ethernet frame is described in the IEEE 802.1Q standard.

In summary, VLANs are commonly and widely used technology for isolating Layer 2 networks. VLAN interfaces on switches (or firewalls or routers) are used to connect the different isolated Layer 2 networks for interconnectivity. Within an Intent-Based Network, VLANs are used in a nonFabric deployment to isolate the different virtual networks.

STP

Spanning Tree Protocol (STP) is a technology that is used to prevent loops in Ethernet networks. Although it was originally designed as a hack[1] to be able to create a single path from two nodes across multiple ethernets, STP has become one of the most common and widely deployed protocols in the campus network. The concept of STP is based on the premise that there can only be a single path between nodes in a redundant connected Ethernet network. To accomplish that premise, STP operates at Layer 2 (Ethernet) and builds a logical topology (based on a tree) on top of physically connected redundant switches. Figure A-15 displays a small switches topology.

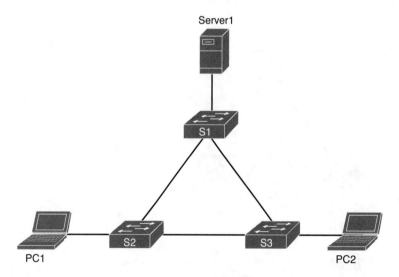

Figure A-15 *Small Switch Topology*

---

1 According to an interview with Radia Perlman, the designer of Spanning Tree, found at https://xconomy.com/national/2019/07/08/future-of-the-internet-what-scares-networking-pioneer-radia-perlman/

If STP would not be enabled in the above network topology, a broadcast storm would follow very soon. Suppose PC1 sends an Ethernet broadcast out to discover the IP address of Server1. That broadcast would be received by switch S2. S2 would, in turn, send that broadcast to S1 and S3. Both switches would, in turn, send that same broadcast to their uplinks. That would result in the broadcast S2 sent originally being received back twice (one via the path S3 -> S1 -> S2 and the other via the path S1 -> S3 -> S2). Because ethernet is a layer2 protocol, it has no concept of a time to live (or hop count), and within a matter of seconds the links between the switches become congested with a single broadcast.

Because STP is designed to only allow a single path for Ethernet packets, broadcast storms are prevented if STP is configured. STP achieves this design principle by periodically sending out special bridge packets to each interface, with an identifier of that switch and other information. As soon as such a packet is received by any other switch, that switch will stop processing all data and start a Spanning Tree calculation process. That process involves all switches in the network (which will, of course, also stop traffic). The received bridge packets are used to logically determine which switch will be the root of the Spanning Tree (the switch with the lowest MAC address and lowest priority). After the root has been determined, each switch builds up a topology of the network and uses the shortest path to determine what the most optimal path is to that root-switch. Once the shortest path has been calculated and determined, all other interfaces via which the root switch has been learned will be blocking inbound traffic to prevent loops in the network. The method used in STP is similar to the process of the link-state mechanism described in the routing protocols section.

Figure A-16 displays the same network topology but with Spanning Tree configured and active with S1 as the root.

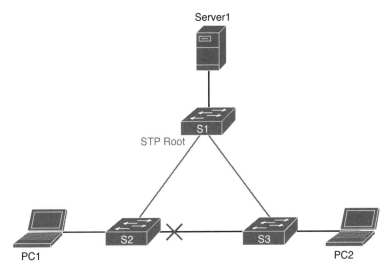

Figure A-16 *Small Network Topology with Spanning Tree Enabled*

In this figure, the links in blue are active links, whereas the red X marks that interface in blocking.

With the same example in Figure A-16, if an Ethernet broadcast would be received from PC1 by S2, S2 would only forward the broadcast to S1. S1 would, in turn, send the broadcast out to S3. S3 would send that broadcast to S2, but because S2 has blocked that interface, it will not forward that packet out. The broadcast storm has been prevented.

Because STP is a Layer 2 protocol (and is enabled by default), STP can lead to odd behaviors when a switch is introduced to the network. It could even lead to the new switch being the root of the network, with odd performance problems and behaviors as a result.

Within the original (and formal IEEE 802.1D standard) STP, the switch would block all traffic for 30 seconds. Because this block would also occur when a PC connects to the network (the switch does not yet know that it is a PC or a switch), it led to connectivity issues and timeouts for obtaining an IP address.

To solve that problem, IEEE introduced Rapid Spanning Tree Protocol (RSTP) as IEEE 802.1w. In this standard the timers were reduced from 30 seconds to three times a hello message, reducing the blocked time to approximately 6 seconds. This resulted in more reliable service to the enterprise with fewer network connectivity problems.

Besides RSTP, Cisco implemented a proprietary optimization, where RSTP could be deployed per VLAN. This protocol was called RPVST. Because RSTP would be run per VLAN on a campus network, the load of the traffic across two distribution or core switches could be shared by having one core be the STP root for a number of VLANs and the other core be the root for the other VLANs. An added benefit of RPVST is that if a link comes up in, for example VLAN 100, only that VLAN would start its STP process and block traffic. However, because RPVST requires more memory and CPU in a switch (a topology per VLAN needs to be maintained), almost all Cisco Catalyst switches have restricted the number of instances to 128. This means that if a campus network has more than 128 VLANs, STP will not function for some VLANs. It is random which VLANs will not work.

Another improvement in STP is called Multiple Spanning Trees Protocol (MST), based on IEEE 802.1s standard. It effectively is a mix between STP and PVSTP, where an instance of STP is configured for a group of VLANs, thus restricting the number of instances. Most Cisco switches support a maximum of 63 MST instances.

In general, STP seems like a very good and solid technology to solve loop problems in the network. However, more modern technologies, such as virtual PortChannel (vPC) and Multichassis EtherChannel (MEC), remove the loops from a network completely, which removes the need for STP. Recommended practice dictates that non-SDA Intent-Based Networks remove STP as a protocol completely to reduce the complexity of the network, as long as there are no loops in that campus network. If there are loops in the network, then use MST as Spanning Tree Protocol.

VTP

VLAN Trunk Protocol (VTP) is probably one of the most underestimated protocols in the campus networks. VTP is a Layer 2 network protocol that can be used to propagate the VLAN creation, modification, and deletion of VLANs across switches. VTP is a Cisco proprietary protocol. The most recent version of the VTP protocol is version 3, and it has a lot of improvements.

The concept of VTP is relatively simple. VTP is based on a client-server approach within a single management domain. Within a single management domain (defined by a domain name), all VLANs are managed on a VTP server. After each change, the VTP server will inform the VTP clients of that change by sending an Ethernet update. All VTP clients within that same domain will receive and process that update. Figure A-17 provides a network that has VTP enabled.

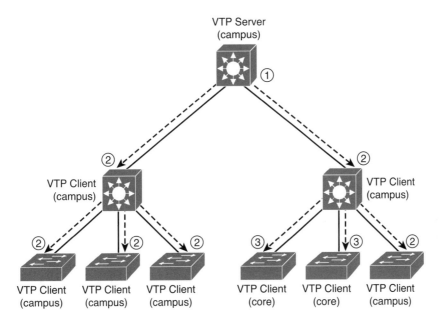

Figure A-17 *Overview of VTP Domain*

The example in Figure A-17 displays that there is a network with a VTP Server for a domain named "campus." As soon as a network operator creates a new VLAN on that switch with the VTP Server role, the switch will generate a VTP update message and broadcast the message to every connected interface (indicated by the number ①).

As soon as a VTP client receives a VTP update message, it performs two validations. The first validation is if the update is meant for its management domain. The second validation is to check the revision number inside the message to see if the update is newer than the latest version known to the VTP client. If both validations are correct, the update message is processed and the change is replicated on the switch. The VTP client will then forward the message to every connected interface (indicated by the number ②).

If both validations fail, the VTP client ignores the messages for its own configuration but will broadcast it to all connected interfaces (indicated by the number ③).

VTP is a powerful protocol that makes the management of VLANs on a large network easy. But the power comes with a cost. VTP is a Layer 2 protocol, and as with any Layer 2 protocol, it is enabled by default. So in case a switch in the network is replaced with a new switch (or one from a lab environment) and that switch has VTP configured as a server, in the same domain, and has a higher revision number than the current VTP server, all VTP clients will use that VLAN database as leading. If that new switch then also has no VLAN configured (write erase does not delete the VTP configuration), all VLANs will be removed from the network.

Because this has happened in the field many times, most enterprises disable VTP to prevent these outages. Although it is a valid reason, the true root cause of such incidents is, of course, that the switch that is placed in the network has not been configured correctly.

With VTP version 3 (the latest version), it is possible to define a primary and secondary switch as VTP server, which prevents these types of problems as well.

For a non-Fabric Intent-Based Network, VTP can be used to deploy VLAN changes via a single change on the distribution switch, which will make the deployment of new intents much easier.

Analytics

Besides technologies used for the configuration of the campus network, several technologies are used to monitor the correct operation of the network. Within an Intent-Based Network, the analytics component is an integral part of how the campus network is operated and managed. The sections that follow describe the technologies (both existing and new) used for the analytics component of an Intent-enabled network.

SNMP

One of the most common protocols used within network management is Simple Network Management Protocol (SNMP). Do not be fooled by the name of the protocol in terms of management. The protocol itself might be simple, but the implementation, configuration, and operation using SNMP can become complex and can have (if misconfigured) a huge impact on the performance of the network.

SNMP is based on the concept that there is a management network, a network management station, and a set of managed devices. Managed devices have SNMP agents installed, and an SNMP manager is running on the network management station. Figure A-18 provides an overview of the concept.

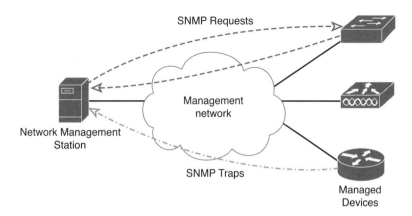

SNMP Requests

Management
network

Network Management
Station

SNMP Traps

Managed
Devices

Figure A-18 *Conceptual Overview of SNMP*

SNMP consists of two different methods of communication:

- **SNMP requests:** Used by the network management station to either request information from a managed device (GetRequest) or to set a value on the device (a
  SetRequest). As an example, the network management station sends a request for
  the CPU load to the managed device (using UDP). The managed device receives the
  request, validates the authenticity of the request, and then sends the response back.
  This is represented in the figure as the blue lines.

- **SNMP traps:** Used by the managed device to inform the network management
  station that something has happened. For example, the managed device detects
  that the CPU of the device is too high; it can send an SNMP trap to the network
  management station to inform that the CPU is high.

Because SNMP is based on UDP (no confirmation), it relies on the resilience of the
network for the trap to be received by the network management station.

As stated, the concept of having a request-response method, where specific information
elements can be requested and the concept of receiving a trap when something is wrong,
is indeed simple. However, the method of how to specify and configure what information
is to be requested is when SNMP becomes complex.

SNMP uses Object Identifiers (OID) to uniquely identify every item that can be
requested via SNMP. That means that there is a unique identifier for the operational
status of every individual interface of a switch, and for every route entry in a router, there
is a unique identifier.

To be flexible and extensible as a network management protocol, the OIDs within SNMP
are grouped in a tree, where each node and element in the tree is identified by a deci-
mal value. The OID 1.3.6.1.2.1.2.2.1.8 translates to the operational status of interface 1.
Management Information Blocks describe (in a specific language) how the OIDs are organized. The same example above would translate to 1(iso).3(org).6(dod).1(internet).2(mgmt).
1(mib-2).2(interface).2(ifTable).1(ifEntry).8(operStatus).

The concept of a tree enables different vendors to define their specific subtree in the same hierarchy. The MIB files are used by the network management station to translate text-based information to the OID to be requested. And this is one of the aspects that makes the configuration of SNMP complex, because every information element that the management station wants to monitor needs to be configured. There are, of course, templates, but the configuration of SNMP requires some manual configuration.

Also, the impact of SNMP on the managed devices can be quite high, because the managed device is for SNMP requests effectively a server. That means that the CPU of the managed device (usually the CPU is very slow compared to switching in optimized ASICs) has to handle these requests, and thus if many requests are sent to the switch, the CPU can easily go to the max.

Although later versions of SNMP support requests in bulk (instead of a single SNMP request per information element), many SNMP management tools still use the single request method. This means that the minimal information for every interface on a stack of four 48-port Cisco Catalyst 3650 switches results in 1152 (6 * 4 * 48) requests. When the management station sends those out in a single burst, it is a serious impact to both the CPU of the switch and the number of connections generated.

The security of SNMP differs from the three versions that are currently available. SNMPv1 is the first version and had no security; everybody could send and receive requests. SNMPv2 introduced the concept of communities, where each community was used both as a pre-shared key for authentication and authorization (the SNMP community would be either read-only [only GetRequests] or read-write [GetRequests and SetRequests]). SNMPv3 is the latest version and includes modern encryption and hashing methods for authentication and authorization. The advantage of SNMPv3 is that it is much more secure but does have a higher impact on the CPU.

In summary, the name Simple Network Management Protocol is a bit misleading. The protocol itself is simple, but the configuration and management are much more complex. Also, the impact of SNMP on the individual devices within a network is quite high, specifically if multiple management stations start to request the same information.

With an Intent-Based Network, the network infrastructure is business critical, which requires monitoring of much more than just the interface status, which results in an even higher impact on the network and network devices. Therefore, it is not recommended to use SNMP for an Intent-Based Network. As explained in Chapter 4, "Cisco Digital Network Architecture," Model-Driven Telemetry is a technology that suits Intent-Based Networking better. Its concept is explained later in the section "Model-Driven Telemetry."

Syslog

Syslog is a technology that originates from the UNIX and mainframe systems environment. Its system is based on having a central (and unified) environment where each process and application could log messages to. The Syslog environment would then distribute the messages to different files, a database, or via the network to a central Syslog server, so that the logging of all workstations is centralized.

Syslog within a network infrastructure operates in the same manner, and commonly uses RFC5454 (The Syslog Protocol) for that. It uses the same Syslog standard, and network devices send their log messages to a central Syslog server. RFC5454 follows the principle that each Syslog message is sent as a single packet to a central Syslog message. Each Syslog message has several fields and descriptors that can be used to provide structured information. The fields follow the Syslog message format that originated from the UNIX environment. Table A-6 provides an overview of all the Syslog fields.

Table A-6   *Overview of Fields in a Syslog Message*

Syslog Field	Description
Facility	The facility originates from the UNIX environment and explains what the originator was (kernel, user, email, clock, ftp, local-usage). Most network devices log using facility level local4.
Severity	A numerical code that describes the severity, ranging from 0 (emergency) to 7 (debugging).
Hostname	The host that sent the Syslog message.
Timestamp	The timestamp of the Syslog message being generated.
Message	The Syslog message itself. For Cisco devices, the Syslog message follows the format %FACILITY-SEVERITY-Mnemonic: Message-text.
	Both the FACILITY and the SEVERITY are often the same as the Facility and Severity of the Syslog protocol message. The Message-Text is the actual text of the Syslog message.
Mnemonic	The mnemonic is the OS-specific identifier of the Syslog message; for example, CONFIG_I within IOS devices informs about a configuration message, and the code 305012 specifies a teardown of a UDP connection on a Cisco ASA firewall.

Within networking, Syslog messages can be compared to the SNMP traps, as they "tell" the Syslog server and network operator what is happening on the network. There are two advantages that Syslog provides over SNMP traps. The first is that there are many more Syslog messages compared to SNMP traps. In comparison, a Catalyst 6500 running IOS 12.2 has approximately 90 SNMP traps but over 6000 different Syslog event messages.

The second advantage is that Syslog provides much more granularity, as the log level, log severity, and message details can be used to create filters and determine which messages need response to.

Several solutions exist that rely on Syslog for monitoring network infrastructures. The most commonly known concept is a Security Incident Event Management (SIEM) system. It collects Syslog information from many sources and uses smart filters and combinations (which you have to define) to detect anomalies in the network.

In general, Syslog is used for two flows within the operation of the network. The first is by looking at the content of the Syslog messages themselves. By looking at the messages, information is provided on what's happening on the network. The Syslog message in Example A-4 is providing information that a MAC address has been moved between two interfaces (which in this case is logical because it is a wireless client that roamed to another AP) and that the user admin changed the running configuration.

Example A-4   *Sample Syslog Messages*

```
Jul 18 2019 14:27:01.673 CEST: %SW_MATM-4-MACFLAP_NOTIF: Host 8cfe.5739.6412 in vlan
  300 is flapping between port Gi0/6 and port Gi0/8
Jul 18 2019 14:29:08.152 CEST: %SYS-5-CONFIG_I: Configured from console by admin on
  vty0 (10.255.5.239)
<166>:Jul 18 14:41:03 CEST: %ASA-session-6-305012: Teardown dynamic UDP translation
  from inside:10.255.5.90/60182 to outside:192.168.178.5/60182 duration 0:02:32
<166>:Jul 18 14:41:03 CEST: %ASA-session-6-305012: Teardown dynamic UDP translation
  from inside:10.255.5.90/61495 to outside:192.168.178.5/61495 duration 0:02:32
```

Another common use case for network operations is to look for variations in the number of log messages produced by the network infrastructure. For example, suppose that the network generates an average of 500 log messages per minute, and at one moment in time the average spiked to 3000 log messages per minute. That spike is effectively the network telling the operator (via log messages) that something is happening on the network.

In summary, SNMP is a widely and commonly deployed technology for monitoring behavior on IT devices, whereas Syslog is specifically used for monitoring what is happening within the network infrastructure. The technology is used by the analytics component within the Intent-Based Network irrelevant of the technology to deploy the intents.

Model-Driven Telemetry

In today's network infrastructures, SNMP is commonly used to get telemetry data (values to determine the operational state and statistics of the network, such as interface statistics). Besides that this method of obtaining telemetry data results in spikes on the CPU, SNMP is limited to only provide telemetry data on the network infrastructure layer. It is not capable of providing telemetry data on how long it takes a user to connect to the network.

To overcome these two problems, Model-Driven Telemetry is used to transport telemetry data from network devices to a network management system. Model-Driven Telemetry uses a subscription-based approach, where the roles of client and server are reversed. The network management system (for example, Cisco DNA Center, as a client) is not hammering the network switch with single telemetry data requests to the network switch (the server); within Model-Driven Telemetry, the network management system requests a subscription to telemetry data from the switch. In return, the switch (as a client) will connect to the network management system (server) and provide data to that subscription. Figure A-19 provides a conceptual flow of this concept.

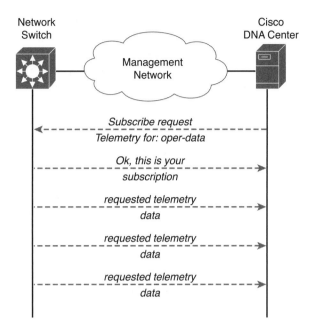

Figure A-19 *Conceptual Flow of Model-Driven Telemetry*

Within Model-Driven Telemetry, Cisco DNA Center (for example) requests a subscription for telemetry data of the network switch. It is not possible to subscribe to all data in a single subscription. In this example, Cisco DNA Center requests for oper-data (like CPU load, memory utilization) and asks for periodic subscription. The network switch validates the request and generates a subscription ID, which will be returned as a response to Cisco DNA Center.

After that initial request, the network switch will periodically push the telemetry data (of that subscription) to the subscriber—in this case, Cisco DNA Center.

This subscription model provides several benefits in comparison to SNMP. The request for telemetry data is only sent once. After that, the switch will send the requested telemetry data periodically (or on a change, which is another subscription option within MDT). Effectively, the switch has become the client, and the switch is not overloaded with many SNMP requests. The data is sent in a bulk stream update to the management station.

MDT uses the subscription model to optimize the flow and reduce the impact and load on the network devices. But another difference is that the data that can be subscribed to is based on open model specifications. Instead of having individual object identifiers for each data element, a model of the telemetry data is defined and used as part of the request. These models are based on YANG data models. YANG is an open data modeling standard that is used by the network industry to allow for a vendor-independent method (and model) for configuring network devices. The YANG models are publicly available on GitHub and are made available per IOS-XE release (as there can be differences between versions).

Model-Driven Telemetry has become available for all switches since Cisco IOS-XE 16.6.1. Newer releases also include support for Cisco routers. Over time, all Cisco devices running IOS-XE will support Model-Driven Telemetry. It is the primary technology used within Cisco Digital Network Architecture to provide data to the analytics component.

NetFlow

NetFlow is a technology developed by Cisco that is used to collect metadata about the traffic flowing through the network. NetFlow's concept is that on strategic entry and exit points in the network (for example, the first Layer 3 hop in the campus network), an exporter is configured. The exporter collects statistics for every connection that flows through that device. The statistics usually consist of source and destination IP information, the time of the connection, and the number of bytes sent and received. Periodically the exporter sends these statistics as flow-records to a collector.

Figure A-20 shows the principle of NetFlow.

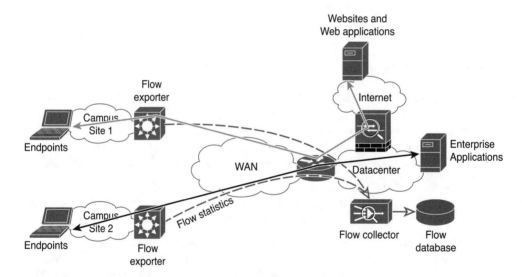

Figure A-20　*Sample Topology with NetFlow*

In Figure A-20, endpoints from different campus locations access applications on the Internet (red flow) and the enterprise applications (green flow). The distribution switch in both campus locations exports flow statistics to the flow collector. Operators connect to the flow collector to see what flows run through the network.

Because NetFlow collects statistics at a higher frequency than SNMP is commonly polled and it collects metadata on the applications and protocols used, NetFlow provides an excellent technology to determine which applications run over the network and how much bandwidth is used for specific applications and links.

Most collectors save the flow information in a database so that the flow information is retained for troubleshooting and forensic analysis (what happened during a specific network outage). Both use cases are an integral part of the analytics component of Cisco Digital Network Architecture, and NetFlow is used as one of the technologies to provide extra information.

Summary

A campus network designed, deployed, and operated based on Intent-Based Networking uses several technologies. The concepts of most technologies have been described in the previous paragraphs. Table A-7 provides an overview of these technologies and which technology is used within each type of deployment for Intent-Based Networking in the campus network.

Table A-7   *A Summary Overview of the Technologies and Their Roles in Intent-Based Campus Networks*

Technology	SDA Fabric	Classic VLAN	Role
Network PnP	✓	✓	PnP is used for LAN Automation and day0 operations.
VRF-Lite	✓	✓	VRF-Lite is used for the logical separation of virtual networks.
IEEE 802.1X	✓	✓	Used to identify and authenticate endpoints connecting to the Intent-enabled network.
RADIUS	✓	✓	RADIUS is used for the authentication and authorization of endpoints between the central policy server and the network access devices.
SGT	✓	✓	Security Group Tags are used for microsegmentation.
Routing protocols	✓	✓	Used to exchange reachability and topology information per virtual network; in case of SDA also used for the underlay network.
VXLAN	✓		Used to isolate and transport virtual networks over the underlay network.
LISP	✓		Used as control protocol within the fabric.
VLAN		✓	Used to logically isolate networks on Layer 2, similar to VXLAN on SDA.

Technology	SDA Fabric	Classic VLAN	Role
STP		✓	Preferably not used at all, but if required, used to prevent Layer 2 loops in the network.
VTP		✓	Used to easily distribute VLAN information across the campus network.
SNMP	✓	✓	Used for basic monitoring of devices not supporting Model-Driven Telemetry.
Syslog	✓	✓	Used for monitoring and analytics within the network.
NetFlow	✓	✓	Used to analyze the flows and application detection in the campus network.
Model-Driven Telemetry	✓	✓	Used by network devices to provide intelligent telemetry data to the analytics component of the Intent-Based Campus Network.

Index

A

ABB (Architecture Building Blocks), 47

access (authorized), example of IBN, 225–226

access layer, 4

access port configuration, 135, 196, 207

access requests, architecture frameworks, 233–235

access switches

configuration, 125–126, 160–161

failures, 4–5

accounting, RADIUS, 293

action plans, 143, 146

action lists, 144

analysis, 144

decision lists, 144

estimated timelines, 144–145

management summaries, 143

Activation process (IBN), 81

ad hoc operations (organizational maturity), 138

ADM (Architecture Development Method), 43

phases of, 43–45

requirements management, 45

Agile software engineering methodology, 33–34

analysis (action plans), 144

analytics, 312

application behavior analytics, 112–113

architecture frameworks, 232

Cisco DNA, 59, 65–66

MDT, 316–318, 320

NetFlow, 318–320

network analytics, 111, 120–121

Ansible, 118–119

application behavior analytics, 112–113

DNAC Assurance, 113–115

NetBrain, 117–118

network function analytics, 111–112

network services availability, 112